Lecture Notes in Artificial Intelligence   4442
Edited by J. G. Carbonell and J. Siekmann

Subseries of Lecture Notes in Computer Science

Luis Antunes   Keiki Takadama (Eds.)

Multi-Agent-Based Simulation VII

International Workshop, MABS 2006
Hakodate, Japan, May 8, 2006
Revised and Invited Papers

 Springer

Series Editors

Jaime G. Carbonell, Carnegie Mellon University, Pittsburgh, PA, USA
Jörg Siekmann, University of Saarland, Saarbrücken, Germany

Volume Editors

Luis Antunes
Universidade de Lisboa
Faculdade de Ciências
Grupo de Estudos em Simulação Social (GUESS)
Campo Grande, 1749-016 Lisboa, Portugal
E-mail: xarax@di.fc.ul.pt

Keiki Takadama
The University of Electro-Communications
Faculty of Electro-Communications
Department of Human Communication
1-5-1, Chofugaoka, Chofu, Tokyo 182-8585, Japan
E-mail: keiki@hc.uec.ac.jp

Library of Congress Control Number: 2007938210

CR Subject Classification (1998): I.2.11, I.2, I.6, C.2.4, J.4, H.4

LNCS Sublibrary: SL 7 – Artificial Intelligence

ISSN   0302-9743
ISBN-10   3-540-76536-0 Springer Berlin Heidelberg New York
ISBN-13   978-3-540-76536-3 Springer Berlin Heidelberg New York

Springer is a part of Springer Science+Business Media

springer.com

© Springer-Verlag Berlin Heidelberg 2007
Printed in Germany

Typesetting: Camera-ready by author, data conversion by Scientific Publishing Services, Chennai, India
Printed on acid-free paper   SPIN: 12186235   06/3180   5 4 3 2 1 0

Preface

This volume groups together the papers accepted for the Seventh International Workshop on Multi-Agent-Based Simulation (MABS 2006), co-located with the Fifth International Joint Conference on Autonomous Agents and Multiagent Systems (AAMAS 2006), which occurred in Hakodate, Japan on May 8, 2006.

MABS 2006 was the seventh workshop of a series that began at ICMAS 1998 (Paris, France), and continued successively with ICMAS 2000 (Boston, USA), AAMAS 2002 (Bologna, Italia), AAMAS 2003 (Melbourne, Australia), AAMAS 2004 (New York, USA) and AAMAS 2005 (Utrecht, The Netherlands). The revised version of the papers of these workshops appeared in Springer's *Lecture Notes in Artificial Intelligence*, in volumes 1534, 1979, 2581, 2927, 3415 and 3891. All information on the MABS Workshop Series can be found at http://www.pcs.usp.br/~mabs.

Multi-agent-based simulation is an inter-disciplinary area which brings together researchers active within the agent-based social simulation (ABSS) community and the multi-agent systems (MAS) community. The scientific focus of MABS lies in the confluence of the ABSS and MAS communities, with a strong empirical/applicational vein, and its emphasis is on (a) exploring agent-based simulation as a principled way of undertaking scientific research in the social sciences and (b) using social theories as an inspiration to new frameworks and developments in multi-agent systems.

To promote this cross-influence, MABS provides a forum for social scientists, agent researchers and developers, and simulation researchers to (a) assess the current state of the art in the modeling and simulation of ABSS and MAS; (b) identify where existing approaches can be successfully applied; (c) learn about new approaches; and (d) explore future research challenges.

MABS 2006 attracted a total of 25 submissions from 11 different countries (Brazil, France, Italy, Japan, Pakistan, Portugal, South Korea, Spain, Sweden, UK, USA). Every paper was reviewed by three anonymous referees, and in the end 12 papers were accepted for long presentation and 3 papers were accepted for short presentation. Every paper was later reviewed again by a Program Committee member for this volume.

We are very grateful to every author who submitted a paper, as well as to all the members of the Program Committee and the additional reviewers for their hard work. The high quality of the papers included in this volume would not be possible without their participation and diligence. We would also like to thank Takao Terano, who gave a very interesting invited talk.

Thanks are also due to Jiming Liu (AAMAS 2006 Workshop Chair), Hideyuki Nakashima and Michael Wellman (AAMAS 2006 General Chairs), and Ei-ichi Osawa (AAMAS 2006 Local Organization Chair). Finally, we would like to thank

Springer staff, especially Alfred Hofmann and Christine Günther for their support of MABS, and their help in the making of this book.

As the social simulation community grows and spreads its multi-disciplinary influence over several scientific areas, the related conferences also get more prominence, autonomy and importance. To illustrate this point, consider the new WCSS (First World Congress on Social Simulation), the recent ESSA (European Association on Social Simulation) conference series, the already established NAACSOS (North American Association for Computational Social and Organization Sciences) conference series, or the PAAA (Pacific Asian Association for Agent-Based Approach in Social Systems Sciences) workshop series. In this new context, we still find that MABS has a place and a relevant role to play, serving as an interface between the community of social simulation and that of computer science, especially multi-agent systems.

April 2007   Luis Antunes
                                                             Keiki Takadama

Organization

Organizing Committee

Luis Antunes (University of Lisbon, Portugal)
Keiki Takadama (The University of Electro-Communcations, Japan)

Program Committee

Frédéric Amblard (University Toulouse 1, France)
Luis Antunes (University of Lisbon, Portugal)
Robert Axtell (The Brookings Institution, USA)
João Balsa (University of Lisbon, Portugal)
François Bousquet (CIRAD/IRRI, Thailand)
José Castro Caldas (ISCTE, Portugal)
Cristiano Castelfranchi (ISTC/CNR, Italy)
Shu-Heng Chen (National Chengchi University, Taiwan)
Sung-Bae Cho (Yonsei University, Korea)
Helder Coelho (University of Lisbon, Portugal)
Rosaria Conte (ISTC/CNR, Italia)
Ernesto Costa (University of Coimbra, Portugal)
Paul Davidsson (Blekinge Institute of Technology, Sweden)
Jim Doran (University of Essex, UK)
Tom Dwyer (UNICAMP, Brazil)
Alexis Drogoul (IRD, France)
Nigel Gilbert (University of Surrey, UK)
Nick Gotts (Macaulay Institute, Scotland, UK)
David Hales (University of Bologna, Italy)
Rainer Hegselmann (University of Bayreuth, Germany)
Wander Jager (University of Groningen, The Netherlands)
Marco Janssen (Arizona State University, USA)
Toshiji Kawagoe (Future University-Hakodate, Japan)
Satoshi Kurihara (Osaka University, Japan)
Juan Pavon Mestras (University Complutense Madrid, Spain)
Scott Moss (Manchester Metropolitan University, UK)
Akira Namatame (National Defense Academy, Japan)
Emma Norling (Manchester Metropolitan University, UK)
Paulo Novais (University of Minho, Portugal)
Jean-Pierre Muller (CIRAD, France)
Mario Paolucci (IP/CNR Rome, Italy)
Juliette Rouchier (Greqam(CNRS), France)
David Sallach (Argonne National Lab and University of Chicago, USA)

Keith Sawyer (Washington University in St. Louis, USA)
Jaime Sichman (University of São Paulo, Brazil)
Carles Sierra (IIIA, Spain)
Liz Sonenberg (University of Melbourne, Australia)
Keiki Takadama (Tokyo Institute of Technology, Japan)
Oswaldo Teran (University of Los Andes, Venezuela)
Takao Terano (University of Tsukuba, Japan)
Jan Treur (Vrije University of Amsterdam, The Netherlands)
Klaus Troitzsch (University of Koblenz, Germany)
Stephen Turner (Nanyang Technological University, Singapore)
Harko Verhagen (Stockholm University, Sweden)

Additional Reviewers

Diana Francisca Adamatti(Brazil)
Anton Bogdanovich (Spain)
Tibor Bosse (The Netherlands)
Eva Bou (Spain)
Annerieke Heuvelink (The Netherlands)

Table of Contents

Learning

Social Dependence

Exploring the Vast Parameter Space
of Multi-Agent Based Simulation

Takao Terano

Department of Computational Intelligence and Systems Sciences,
Tokyo Institute of Technology
4259 Nagatsuda-Cho, Midori-ku, Yokohama 226-8502, Japan
terano@dis.titech.ac.jp

Abstract. This paper addresses the problem regarding the parameter exploration of Multi-Agent Based Simulation for social systems. We focus on the principles of *Inverse Simulation* and *Genetics-Based Validation*. In conventional artificial society models, the simulation is executed straightforwardly: Initially, many micro-level parameters and initial conditions are set, then, the simulation steps are executed, and finally the macro-level results are observed. Unlike this, *Inverse Simulation* executes these steps in the reverse order: set a macro-level objective function, evolve the worlds to fit to the objectives, then observe the micro-level agent characteristics. Another unique point of our approach is that, using Genetic Algorithms with the functionalities of multi-modal and multi-objective function optimization, we are able to validate the sensitivity of the solutions. This means that, from the same initial conditions and the same objective function, we can evolve different results, which we often observe in real world phenomena. This is the principle of *Genetics-Based Validation*.

Keywords: Multi-Agent Based Modeling, Social Systems, Verification and Validation, Parameter Exploration, Genetic Algorithms.

1 Introduction

As Alan Kay stated, *the best way to predict the future is to invent it*. When we use Multi-agent based simulation (MABS) for social systems, we always invent a new world, or a new bird-view-like point, because we are able to design the simulation world as we would like to. Therefore, when we use MABS, we are predicting some future. After several decades of the Allan Kay's statements, we have a new gear for predicting the future: MABS is a new modeling paradigm [1],[2].

MABS focuses from global phenomena to individuals in the model and tries to observe how individuals with individual characteristics or "agents" will behave as a group. The strength of MABS is that it stands between the case studies and mathematical models. It enables us to validate social theories by executing programs, along with description of the subject and strict theoretical development.

In MABS, behaviors and statuses of individual agents are coded into programs by researchers. They also implement information and analytical systems in the

L. Antunes and K. Takadama (Eds.): MABS 2006, LNAI 4442, pp. 1–14, 2007.

environment, so the model itself may be very simple. Even when the number or variety of agents increases, the complexity of simulation descriptions itself will not increase very much [13], [14]. Axelrod [1] has emphasizes that the goal of agent-based modeling is to enrich our understanding of fundamental processes that may appear in a variety of applications. This requires adhering to the *KISS principle*, which stands for the army slogan *"keep it simple, stupid."*

Running an agent-based model is an easy task, however, the analysis is not [7]. Even for a simple simulator with the KISS principle, we must cope with vast parameter space of the model. This paper discusses the problem regarding the parameter exploration of Agent-Based Simulation for social systems.

2 Coping with the Huge Parameter Spaces

There are no Newton's Laws, or the first principles in social systems. This makes MABS approaches both easy and difficult. The easy face is that we are able to build models as we like, on the other hand, the difficult face is that the models are hardly grounded in any rigorous grounding theories. For example, the application of finance engineering is one of good candidates of MABS approaches. They seem to follow the first principles, however, it is not true. The assumptions of finance engineering often come from the principles of statistical physics, one of the first principles of physics. However, the real data and real phenomena sometimes break the assumptions. This means that the assumptions about social phenomena are not based on the first principles.

The real phenomena in our society and social systems are only collections of instances. Therefore, using social simulation techniques, we are able to generate so many instances of simulation results through MABS. This is the very merit of our MABS approach.

However, even simple models with ten step decisions with ten alternatives in every step have 10**10 parameter spaces. This means that it would take over 10,000 days to complete them, if we could search 10 spaces per second. We must compute so many cases. To overcome the problem, one solution of the issue is to follow the *KISS principle*. Simple convincing models are welcome. However, the simpler the model, more explanatory interpretation of the result has to be, in order to avoid easy explanation such as "We did it and we got it." Actually, several extreme explanations were given to the models discussed in Axelrod or Epstein. When the model is simple, the result seems to be obvious, and the harder we try to understand phenomena, the more complex the model becomes against the KISS principle.

To convince the results of MABS, we are required (i) to rigorously validate the models and simulators, (ii) to examine background social and organizational system theories, and (iii) to overcome the vast of parameters of both agent behaviors and models. Also, (iv) we need multiple good results to design and analyze social complex task domains. Therefore, as another solution, we propose a new method, which employs *Generate and Test* techniques in the simulation process. This follows the principles of *Inverse Simulation* and *Genetics-Based Validation*.

3 Principles of Inverse Simulation

In conventional MABS models, the simulation processes are executed straightforwardly: Initially, many micro-level parameters and initial conditions are set, then, the simulation steps are executed, and finally the macro-level results are observed. Unlike in conventional simulation models, in the Inverse simulation, we execute these steps in the reverse order: set a macro-level objective function, evolve the worlds to fit to the objectives, then observe the micro-level agent characteristics. Thus, we solve very large inverse problems. The basic principles are shown in Figure 1. The essential point is that we force to get desired results specified by the macro-level objective functions, then analyze the micro-level structures of the results.

They have thought such brute force approach is infeasible, so far, however, using recent competing genetic algorithms (GAs) [4] has made it possible to get multiple solutions in reasonable times. In our simulators in the following sections, we have employed GAs with tabu-search techniques in Operations Research literatures[5],[6]. The method is able to optimize multi-modal functions [3]. This means that, from the same initial conditions and the same objective function, we can evolve different results, which we often observe in real world phenomena.

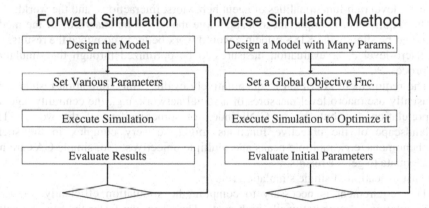

Fig. 1. Basic Cycles of Agent-Based Simulation

The agents, their behaviors, and the world are controlled by many parameters. In our settings, genotypes of GAs are corresponding to initial parameters of agents and the initial world we are considering. Phenotypes of GAs to be evaluated are simulation results, which can be measured macro-level evaluation functions. We will carry out so many simulation cycles to get the results. For example. To get one result, we might need several hundred simulation steps per simulation. To evaluate one generation, we might need several hundred populations in parallel, and to converge the macro-level objective functions, also we need several hundred GA generations. The outline is shown in Figure 2.

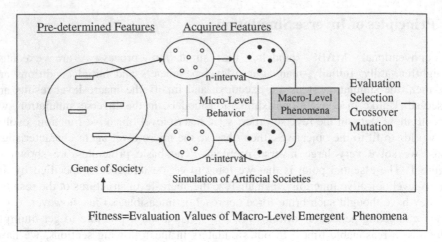

Fig. 2. Inverse Simulation

To apply *Inverse Simulation*, we assume that the MABS models have the following properties:

(i) micro-level rich functionalities of agent behaviors, interactions, and the world;
   The requirement is important to leap simple models to be analyzed. If the model would be simple, the KISS principle would work better to convince the results.

(ii) macro-level clear evaluation measures to be optimized through the simulation processes;
   The requirement is critical to quantitatively evaluate the simulation results. We usually use macro level measures of a social network, e.g., the centrality, agents' population distributions, or GINI index of some welfare of the worlds. The landscape of the objective functions might be very complex in the social phenomena, e.g., multiple peaks and multiple objectives. So, simple GAs are not adequate to get the results.

(iii) Fast execution of single simulation run.
   The requirement is necessary to compute the simulation efficiently. Inverse Simulation is computationally high cost. Therefore, the faster the run, the better the results. We are planning to utilize Grid-based computer systems to apply the technique.

4 Principles of Genetics-Based Validation

Validation is one of the most critical tasks in MABS approach to convince the results. In this section, we address a new statistical validation method: *Genetics-Based Validation* for the solutions of simulation results. This is a kind of sensitivity analyses of parameters in the experimental system we target. The principle is summarized as follows. When *Inverse Simulation* terminates, using GAs for multiple solutions, if there were multiple solutions in the targeted MABS model, then every important parameter of the model would converge. This means that the objective functions have their peaks. However, non-essential parameters would have various distributed values. It is because the variations of non-essential parameters would not contribute to the values of objective functions. If we would have used conventional GAs, because of the effects of genetic drifts, the non-essential parameters would converge. This is a bad situation for our analysis. Competing GAs with the functionalities to cope with the multiple solutions, they keep diversity of the solutions. We are able to utilize the variance of the parameters to determine whether specified parameters are essential for the results of simulations or not.

In Figure 3, we illustrate the situations. we observe some distribution of simulation results. Initially, simulation results are several values in the sense of the objective functions values. In the final steps, the objective function values converge to the same level, however, the distributions of solutions are different according to the essential and/or non-essential dimensions of parameters. Therefore, applying statistical techniques, we are able to uncover the shape of the landscapes of the results measured by the specified objective functions. For example, to apply the principal component analysis technique, we are able to obtain the distributions of solution values, or simulation results, which will reveal both essential and non-essential dimensions of parameters.. We call the method *Genetics-Based Validation.*

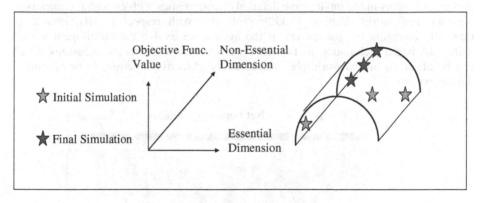

Fig. 3. Principles of Genetics-Based Validation

5   How Inverse Simulation and Genetics-Based Validation Work

We have applied the proposed techniques: *Inverse Simulation* and *Genetics-Based Validation* to various kinds of agent-based simulation models. In this section, we will briefly describe three of them. The first example is a MABS model for social interaction analysis. The second one is a marketing model of competing firms. The last one is concerned with a MABS model for financial decision making. The three models are too complex to understand from the KISS principle, however, we are able to uncover what have happened in the sense of parameter sensitivity analysis.

5.1 Example 1: Social Interaction Analysis [8], [9]

Recently there are so many MABS models from the state-of-the-art literature, they frequently report that simple autonomous agents and artificial worlds are able to evolve global interesting social structures and behaviors.

However, many of the researches seem to report too artificial results, because of the following three reasons:

(I) Although many agent models are developed from the bottom-up, the functions the agents have are so simple that the models can only handle with difficulty to practical social interaction problems.

(II) Although the functions are simple from the viewpoint of simulation experiments, the models have too many parameters that can be tuned and, therefore, it seems as if any good result a model builder desires is already built in.

(III) The results seem to have a weak relationship with emerging phenomena in real-world activities.

Thus, these studies have not yet attained a level necessary to describe the flexibility and practicability of social interactions in real organizations.

To overcome such problems, we have developed a novel multi-agent-based simulation environment TRURL for social interaction analysis.

The basic principles of TRURL can be summarized as follows: To address point (I) above, the agents in the model have detailed characteristics with enough parameters to simulate real world decision making problems; with respect to (II), instead of manually changing the parameters of the agents, we evolve the multi-agent worlds using GA-based techniques; as for (III), we set some socio-metric measures which can be observed in real world phenomena as the objective functions to be optimized during evolution.

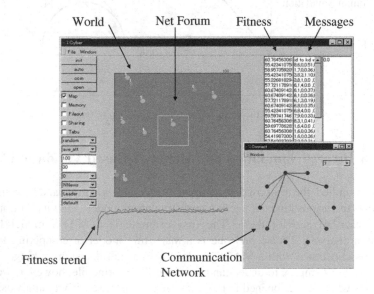

Fig. 4. Execution of TRURL

Using TRURL, therefore, we are able to analyze the nature of social interactions, which are based on such real-world activities as e-mail-oriented organizations and electronic commerce markets. We illustrate the snapshot of TRURL execution in Figure 4.

In TRURL, each agent sends and receives messages according to the received knowledge attribute. The a priori attribute of the agent is described as a gene sequence on the chromosome which represents the society. The characteristics of the agent participating in the TRURL artificial society are represented by the speaking probability, the knowledge transfer rate, the comment attitude, and the like:

$$P_p = (c_p, p_s, p_r, p_a, p_c, n, \alpha, \beta, \gamma, \delta, \mu),$$

where c_p denotes the physical coordinates of the agent, p_s is the speaking probability, p_r is the receiving reliability, p_a is the comment attitude, p_c is the additional remark probability, n is the knowledge width, α is the weight transfer rate, β is the evaluation value transfer rate, γ is the certainty transfer rate, δ is the metabolism, and μ is the mutation rate.

The characteristics of the agent participating in the artificial society TRURL are represented by these parameters. What agents are generated in the society depends on the character of the society. Figure 1 shows the relation between the gene structure and agent generation. The agent has the following a posteriori attributes:

$$P_a = (w, e_s, c, c_c, m).$$

Here w is the weight of the knowledge attribute, e is the evaluation value, c is the certainty, c_c is the reliability coordinate of agent, and m is the behavior energy. When an agent is generated, the a posteriori attribute is initialized as a random variable following the normal distribution. When a communication between agents is performed, the a posteriori attribute is modified. The a posteriori attribute differs from the a priori attribute, being a parameter that changes dynamically according to the interaction between agents.

When an agent is generated, the a posteriori attribute is initialized as a random variable following the normal distribution. When a communication between agents is performed, the a posteriori attribute is modified. The a posteriori attribute differs from the a priori attribute, being a parameter that changes dynamically according to the interaction between agents.

The information transmission process can be considered as a decision-making process based on alignment behavior. In this model, the change of the knowledge attributeparameter when a message is received is defined for each parameter. The weight w, the evaluation value e, and the certainty c are defined as follows:

$$\Delta w_{kd}^i = \sum_{j \in S} \alpha(w_{kd}^j - w_{kd}^i) max(0, c_{kd}^j - c_{kd}^i)$$

$$\Delta e_{kd}^i = \sum_{j \in S} \beta(e_{kd}^j - e_{kd}^i) max(0, c_{kd}^j - c_{kd}^i)$$

$$\Delta c_{kd}^i = \sum_{j \in S} \gamma((1 - 2|e_{kd}^j - e_{kd}^i|) max(0, c_{kd}^j - c_{kd}^i))$$

where, w_{kd}^i, e_{kd}^i, and c_{kd}^i are the weight of the knowledge attribute kd, the evaluation value, and the certainty, respectively. α, β and γ are transfer rates. S represents the set of sending agents of the messages received by $agent_i$ at period t.

The behavior energy m changes in proportion to the change of the information content. At the initial stage of generation, m is specified at random in accordance with the normal distribution. When information is sent, m decreases in accordance with the metabolism δ; when valuable information (with a relatively high certainty) is received from another agent, it is increased; and when no communication occurs, m decreases regularly according to δ.

From the viewpoints of *Inverse Simulation*, In TRURL, the individuals are corresponding to the set of initial agent parameters. The multiple objective functions are corresponding to macro-level measures about social interactions, for example, the GINI indices of social welfare measured by the amount of information the agents have. Through *Genetics-Based Validation*, we are able to observe that free-riders in the information networked society have positive effects to the total welfare of the society. From the simulation studies, for example, we have found the information difference between the information rich and information poor is not increased as much as was expected in the net society, and that although free riders are generated, they do not induce the collapse of norms.

5.2   Example 2: Model of Competing Firms in Marketing [12]

The second example of ABS is to explore 'optimal' marketing strategies on given specific markets. Conventional research in business strategy literature, they state the importance of translating the strategy of a company into action to get the profit. In our study, on the contrary, we will observe agents' action or companies' activity in the artificial society with given conditions and investigate the agents' or companies' strategy. To model this, we must specify both company and customer models.

As the basis of companies' strategy, we use the concepts of the Balanced Scorecard (BSC) to describe the agent functionality. to describe the agent functionality. The origin of BSC by Kaplan and Norton [15] was a performance measurement system of a company. The system was then extended to the one, which organized around four distinct perspectives – financial, customer, internal, and innovation and learning. Innovative companies used BSC not only to clarify and communicate strategy, but also to manage strategy. This means that BSC evolved from an improved measurement system to a core management system [16].

Based on the background, we employ the idea of Treacy and Wirsema [17] about the strategy of a company on the value proposition of customers: (a) operational excellence, (b) customer intimacy, and (c) product leadership. These three criteria determine the company type. However, the criteria are only descriptive ones. They do not explain which types of companies are how characterized in real market places.

We have determined the seven attributes to the value proposition of a company: (1) price, (2) quality, (3) time, and (4) function; (5) services and (6) relationship among customers; and (7) brand image. The company's decision depends on how to distribute these values among the seven attributes.

In order to model customers, they are divided by the two attributes: price and quality of the goods or services. The four clusters are (A) price sensitive and quality sensitive (the lower price and the higher quality the better); (B) price sensitive and quality insensitive; (C) price insensitive and quality sensitive; and (D) prince insensitive and quality insensitive. From survey studies, the attitudes of customers in each category or customers' parameters are determined.

In the simulator, the society contains 40 competing companies. We have tuned up the attributes of a company (1) to (7) as genes of GAs and the attributes of the remaining 39 companies are set to random values and do not change during the simulation. Customers' clusters are determined against the market conditions and remain constant during the simulation.

The simulation is carried out via the following steps:

Step 1: Based on the attribute values, determine the amount of investment to each division

Step 2: Determine the sales goal based on the previous market demand and sales

Step 3: Calculate the logistic and material cost per good based on the amount of the products.

Step 4: Calculate the cash expenditure and determine the excess to borrow.

Step 5: Calculate the market demand in each cluster of customers.

Step 6: Calculate sales amount as the minimum values of sales stocks and market demands.

Step 7: Generate the corresponding balance sheet to be evaluated.

Step 8: If the current term is 10 then stop, else increase the step.

Figure 5 shows the architecture.

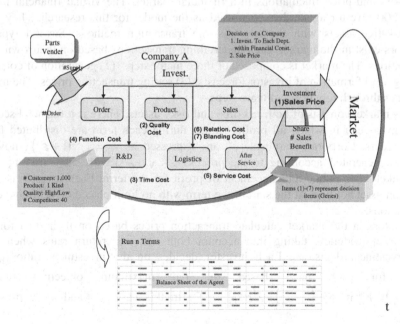

Fig. 5. Architecture of the Market Simulator

When the simulation reaches term 10, the four objective values are evaluated by the BSC information: Benefit, Market Share, Cash flow, and Borrowing. This means that the target society is evaluated by independent four objective functions: Max_benefit, Max_market-share, Max_cash-flow, and Min_borrowing.

From the viewpoints of *Inverse Simulation*, In the marketing simulator, the individuals are corresponding to the set of initial parameters of value propositions of a company. The multiple objective functions are corresponding to measures of a company about financial benefits, market share, cash flows, and borrowings. From *Genetics-Based Validation*, we are able to observe that the changes of markets, e.g., the ratio of kinds of customers will cause the changes of the strategies.

From the simulation studies, we have observed that 1) the price and service are important for benefit and cash flow maximize and strategies; 2) about the share maximization, there are few dominate strategies; and 2) on the other hand, price and time will affect for borrowing strategy.

About the other two markets, the variances of genes show the similar tendency. About the share of the market, the TV set market has the smallest effect about the cost. About the radio cassettes market, time is important factor. About the electric shaver market, function is critical. The results partly coincide with the discussion of some of marketing research results: the operational excellence strategy is the dominated one in the simulation.

5.3   Example 3: Investors in Behavioral Finance [10], [11]

The Third example is to investigate the risks of financial markets. We have developed a simulator to clarify microscopic and macroscopic links between investor behaviors and price fluctuations in a financial market. The virtual financial market with 1000 investor agents has been used as the model for this research. They share and risk-free assets with the two possible transaction methods. Several types of investors exist in the market, each undertaking transactions based on their own stock calculations. The market is composed of three major steps, (1) generation of corporate earnings, (2) formation of investor forecasts, (3) setting transaction prices. The market advances through repetition of these steps.

This market consists of both risk-free and risky assets. There is a financial security (as risky assets) in which all profits gained during each term are distributed to the shareholders. Corporate earnings (y_t) are expressed as $y_t = y_{t-1}(1+\varepsilon_t)$, however they are generated according to the process $\varepsilon_t \sim N(0, \sigma_y^2)$ with share trading being undertaken after public announcement of profit for the term. Each investor is given common asset holdings at the start of the term with no limit placed on debit and credit transactions.

Investors in the market calculate transaction prices based on their own forecast for market tendency, taking into account both risk and return rates when making investment decisions. Each investor decides on the investment ratio (w_t^i) of stock for each term based on the maximum objective function of $f(w_t^i) = r_{t+1}^{int,i} w_t^i + r_f(1 - w_t^i) - \lambda(\sigma_{t-1}^{s,i})^2(w_t^i)^2$. In this case, $r_{t+1}^{int,i}$ and $\sigma_{t-1}^{s,i}$ express the expected rate of return and risk for stock as estimated by each investor i. r_f represents the risk-free rate. w_t^i is the stock investment ratio of investor i for term t [2][5].

Expected rate of return for shares $\left(r_{t+1}^{int,i}\right)$ is calculated as

$$r_{t+1}^{int,i} = \left(1 \cdot c^{-1}\left(\sigma_{t-1}^{s,i}\right)^{-2}\right)\Big/\left(1 \cdot c^{-1}\left(\sigma_{t-1}^{s,i}\right)^{-2} + 1 \cdot \left(\sigma_{t-1}^{s,i}\right)^{-2}\right)r_{t+1}^{f,i} + \left(1 \cdot \left(\sigma_{t-1}^{s,i}\right)^{-2}\right)\Big/\left(1 \cdot c^{-1}\left(\sigma_{t-1}^{s,i}\right)^{-2} + 1 \cdot \left(\sigma_{t-1}^{s,i}\right)^{-2}\right)r_t^{im} .$$

Here, $r_{t+1}^{f,i}, r_t^{im}$ express the expected rate of return, calculated respectively from short-term expected rate of return, and risk and gross current price ratio of stock etc[2][5].

Short-term expected rate of return $\left(r_t^{f,i}\right)$ is obtained by $r_{t+1}^{f,i} = \left(\left(P_{t+1}^{f,i} + y_{t+1}^{f,i}\right)\middle/P_t - 1\right)\left(1 + \eta_t^i\right)$, $\left(P_{t+1}^{f,i}, y_{t+1}^{f,i}\right)$ being the equity price and profit forecast for term t+1 as estimated by the investor. Short-term expected rate of return includes the error term $\left(\eta_t^i \sim N\left(0, \sigma_n^2\right)\right)$ reflecting that even investors of the same forecast model vary slightly in their detailed outlook.

Expected rate of return for stock $\left(r_t^{im}\right)$ as obtained from stock risk etc. is calculated from stock risk $\left(\sigma_{t-1}^{s,i}\right)$, benchmark equity stake $\left(W_{t-1}\right)$, investors' degree of risk avoidance (λ), and risk-free rate $\left(r_f\right)$ in the equation $r_t^{im} = 2\lambda\left(\sigma_{t-1}^s\right)^2 W_{t-1} + r_f$.

This analysis looks at (1) forecasting based on fundamental values, (2) forecasting based on trends (4 terms), and (3) forecasting based on past averages (4 terms).

The fundamental value of shares is estimated using the dividend discount model. Fundamentalists estimate the forecast stock price $\left(P_{t+1}^{f,i}\right)$ and forecast profit $\left(y_{t+1}^{f,i}\right)$ from profit for the term $\left(y_t\right)$ and discount rate of stock (δ) respectively as $P_{t+1}^{f,i} = y_t/\delta$, $y_{t+1}^{f,i} = y_t$.

Forecasting based on trends involves forecasting next term equity prices and profit through extrapolation of the most recent stock value fluctuation trends. This analysis looks at the 4 terms of 1 day, 5 days, 10 days, and 20 days for trend measurements. Forecasting based on past averages involves estimating next term equity prices and profit based on the most recent average stock value. Average value was measured for the 4 terms of 1 day, 5 days, 10 days, and 20 days.

Stock risk is measured as $\sigma_{t-1}^{s,i} = s_i\sigma_{t-1}^h$. In this case, σ_{t-1}^h is an index that represents stock volatility calculated from price fluctuation of the most recent 100 steps, and s_i the degree of overconfidence. The presence of a strong degree of overconfidence can be concluded when the value of s_i is less than 1, as estimated forecast error is shown as lower than its actual value. Transaction prices are set as the price where stock supply and demand converge $\left(\sum_{i=1}^{M}\left(F_t^i w_t^i\right)\middle/P_t = N\right)$.

The architecture is illustrated in Figure 6.

The Inverse Simulation Analysis consists of the following 3 steps. (1) Carry out 100 times a simulation with an investment period of 100 terms. (2) Calculate the index of deviation between transaction prices and the fundamental value for each simulation. (3) Set the calculated index as the adaptive value and select 100 simulation conditions (investors' forecasts, confidence). This analysis is undertaken through repetition of these 3 steps. The index (q) of deviation between transaction prices and the fundamental value expresses the deviation ratio with the fundamental value and is specifically calculated as $q = E[x]^2 + Var[x]$. However, P_t^0 represents the fundamental value $x_t = \left(P_t - P_t^0\right)\middle/P_t^0$ for term t.

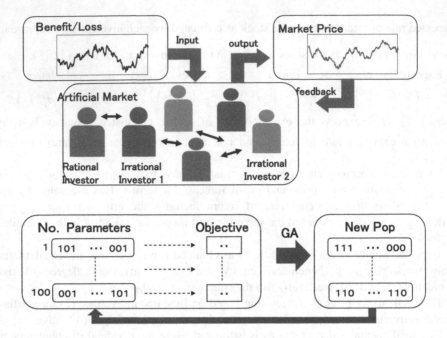

Fig. 6. Architecture of the Financial Market Simulator

From the simulation study of the agent-based virtual market, we have found that (1) overconfident investors emerge in a bottom-up fashion in the market, and (2) these overconfident investors have the ability to contribute to the market, in which the trading prices are coincide with theoretical fundamental values.

Traditional finance argues that market survival is possible for those investors able to swiftly and accurately estimate both the risk and rate of return on stock, achieving market efficiency. However, analysis results obtained here regarding the influence irrational investors have on prices suggests a different situation, pointing to the difficulty of market modeling which takes real conditions into account.

6 Concluding Remarks

This paper addresses the problem regarding the parameter exploration of Agent-Based Simulation for social systems. In this paper, in order to enhance the power of MABS models, we have discussed the critical issues of validations, background theories, and vast parameter spaces. Then we have explained the principles of *Inverse Simulation* and *Genetics-Based Validation*. After the proposal, to convince the effectiveness of the proposed methods, based on our previous and on-going research projects, we have demonstrated the applications of the principles to MABS models: Social Interaction analysis, Marketing strategies, and Financial decision making.

Future work includes the refinement of the principles to apply the ones to much more complex task domains: (1) Determination of effective objective functions or macro-level evaluation method of the simulation results; (2) Design of micro level agent functionalities including the concepts of distributed artificial intelligence and machine learning; (3) New competing genetic algorithms for the purpose, (4) Development of very large scale simulation environments including grid computing, and (5) Development of validation methods based on the concepts of estimation of distribution algorithms in genetic algorithm literatures.

Acknowledgments. The referred researches are joint work of our members: Prof. Setsuya Kurahashi, University of Tsukuba, Mr. Ken-ichi Naitoh, Tokyo Institute of Technology, and Dr. Hiroshi Takahashi, Okayama University.   The research is supported in part by JSPS Scientific Research Grant No. 18650030.

References

1. Axelrod, R.: The Complexity of Cooperation: Agent-Based Models of Competition and Collaboration. Princeton University Press, Princeton (1997)
2. Axtell, R.: Why Agents? On the Varied Motivation for Agent Computing in the Social Sciences. Brookings Institution CSED Technical Report No. 17 (November 2000)
3. Coello, C.A., Van Veldhuizen, D.A., Lamont, G.B.: Evolutionary Algorithms for Solving Multi-Objective Problems. Kluwer Academic Publishers, New York (2002)
4. Goldberg, D.E.: The Design of Innovation, Lessons from and for Competent Genetic Algorithms. Kluwer Academic Publishers, Boston (2002)
5. Yuji, K., Kurahashi, S., Terano, T.: We Need Multiple Solutions for Electric Equipments Configuration in a Power Plant - Applying Bayesian Optimization Algorithm with Tabu Search –. In: Proc. 2002 IEEE World Congress on Computational Intelligence, pp. 1402–1407 (2002)
6. Kurahashi, S., Terano, T.: A Genetic Algorithm with Tabu Search for Multimodal and Multiobjective Function Optimization. In: Proc. the Genetic and Evolutionary Computation Conference (GECCO-2000), pp. 291–298 (2000)
7. Richiardi, M., Leombruni, R., Saam, N., Sonnessa, M.: A Common Protocol for Agent-Based Social Simulation. Journal of Artificial Societies and Social Simulation 9(1) (2006), http://jasss.soc.surrey.ac.uk/
8. Terano, T., Kurahashi, S., Minami, U.: TRURL: Artificial World for Social Interaction Studies. In: Proc. 6th Int. Conf. on Artificial Life (ALIFE VI), pp. 326–335 (1998)
9. Kurahashi, S., Terano, T.: Analyzing Norm Emergence in Communal Sharing via Agent-Based Simulation. Systems and Computers in Japan 36(6) (2005) (Translated from Denshi Joho Tsushin Gakkai Ronbunshi, Vol. J84-D-I, No. 8, August 2001, pp. 1160.1168)
10. Takahashi, H., Terano, T.: Agent-Based Approach to Investors' Behavior and Asset Price Fluctuation in Financial Markets. Journal of Artificial Societies and Social Simulation 6(3) (2003)
11. Takahashi, H., Terano, T.: Exploring Risks of Financial Markets through Agent-Based Modeling. In: Proc. SICE-ICASS Joint Conference 2006 (to appear)
12. Terano, T., Naitoh, K.: Agent-Based Modeling for Competing Firms: From Balanced-Scorecards to Multi-Objective Strategies. In: Proceedings of the 37th Annual Hawaii International Conference on System Sciences 2004 (HICCS 2004), pp.1–8 (January 5-8, 2004)
13. Terano, T., Deguchi, H., Takadama, K. (eds.): Meeting the Challenge of Social Problems via Agent-Based Simulation. Springer, Japan (2003)

14. Terano, T., Kita, H., Kaneda, T., Arai, K., Deguchi, H.: Agent-Based Simulation – From Modeling Methodologies to Real World Applications. Springer, Japan (2005)
15. Kaplan, R.S., Norton, D.P.: The Balanced Scorecard - Translating Strategy into Action -. Harvard Business School Press, Massachusetts (1996)
16. Kaplan, R.S., Norton, D.P.: The Strategy Focused Organization: How Balanced Companies Thrive in the New Business Environment. Harvard Business School Press, Massachusetts (2001)
17. Treacy, M., Wiersema, F.: The Discipline of Market Leaders: Choose Your Customers, Narrow Your Focus, Dominate Your Market. Addison-Wesley, Readings, Massachusetts (1997)

Applications of Agent Based Simulation

Paul Davidsson, Johan Holmgren, Hans Kyhlbäck, Dawit Mengistu,
and Marie Persson

School of Engineering, Blekinge Institute of Technology
Soft Center, 372 25 Ronneby, Sweden

Abstract. This paper provides a survey and analysis of applications of Agent Based Simulation (ABS). A framework for describing and assessing the applications is presented and systematically applied. A general conclusion from the study is that even if ABS seems a promising approach to many problems involving simulation of complex systems of interacting entities, it seems as the full potential of the agent concept and previous research and development within ABS often is not utilized. We illustrate this by providing some concrete examples. Another conclusion is that important information of the applications, in particular concerning the implementation of the simulator, was missing in many papers. As an attempt to encourage improvements we provide some guidelines for writing ABS application papers.

1 Introduction

The research area of Agent Based Simulation (ABS) continues to produce techniques, tools, and methods. In addition, a large number of *applications* of ABS have been developed. By ABS application we here mean actual computer simulations based on agent-based modelling of a real (or imagined) system in order to solve a concrete problem. The aim of this paper is to present a consistent view of ABS applications (as they are described in the papers) and to identify trends, similarities and differences, as well as issues that may need further investigation.

As several hundreds of ABS applications have been reported in different publications, we had to make a sample of these. After having performed a preliminary search for papers describing ABS applications that resulted in about 50 papers, we identified one publication that was dominating. About 30% of the papers were published in the post-proceedings of the MABS workshop series [1, 2, 3, 4, 5] whereas the next most frequent publications covered only 10%. We then chose to focus on the MABS publication series and found 28 papers containing ABS applications (out of 73). Even if we cannot guarantee that this is an unbiased sample, we think that selecting all the applications reported in a particular publication series with a general ABS focus (rather than specializing in particular domains etc.), is at least an attempt to achieve this.

In the next section, we present the framework that will be used to classify and assess the applications. This is followed by a systematic survey of the sampled papers. Finally, we analyze our findings and present some conclusions.

L. Antunes and K. Takadama (Eds.): MABS 2006, LNAI 4442, pp. 15–27, 2007.
© Springer-Verlag Berlin Heidelberg 2007

2 Evaluation Framework

An ABS application models and simulates some real system that consists of a set of entities. The ABS itself can be seen as a multi-agent system composed of a set of (software) agents. That is, there is a correspondance between the real system and the multi-agent system as well as between the (real) entities and the agents. We will use the terms "system" and "entity" when referring to reality and "multi-agent system" and "agent" when referring to simulation models. For each paper we describe different aspects of the problem studied, the modeling approach taken to solve it, the implementation of the simulator, and how the results are assessed.

2.1 Problem Description

Each problem description includes the domain studied, the intended end-user, and the purpose of the ABS application.

Domain: The domain of an application refers to the type of system being simulated. We identified the following domains after analyzing the sampled papers:

1) An *animal society* consists of a number of interacting animals, such as an ant colony or a colony of birds. The purpose of a simulation could be to better understand the individual behaviors that cause emergent phenomena, e.g., the behavior of flocks of birds.

2) A *physiological system* consists of functional organs integrated and co-operatively related in living organisms, e.g., subsystems of the human body . The purpose could be to verify theories, e.g., the regulation of the glucose-insulin metabolism inside the human body.

3) A *social system* consists of a set of human individuals with individual goals, i.e., the goal of different individuals may be conflicting. An example could be to study how social structures like segregation evolve.

4) An *organization* is here defined as a structure of persons related to each other in purposefully accomplishing work or some other kind of activity, i.e., the persons of the organization have common goals. The aim of a simulation could be to evaluate different approaches to scheduling work tasks with the purpose of speeding up the completion of business processes.

5) An *economic system* is an organized structure in which actors (individuals, groups, or enterprises) are trading goods or services on a market. The applications which we consider under this domain may be used to analyze the interactions and activities of entities in the system to help understand how the market or economy evolves over time and how the participants of the system react to the changing economic policies of the environment where the system is operating.

6) In an *ecological system* animals and/or plants are living and developing together in a relationship to each other and in dependence of the environment. The purpose could be to estimate the effects of a plant disease incursion in an agricultural region.

7) A *physical system* is a collection of passive entities following only physical laws. For example, a pile of sand and the purpose of the simulation may be to calculate

the static equilibrium of a pile considering forces between beads and properties within the pile considered as a unit.

8) A *robotic system* consists of one or more electro-mechanical entities having sensory, decision, tactile and rotary capabilities. An example is the use of a set of robots in patrolling tasks. The purpose of the simulation could be to study the effectiveness of a given patrolling strategy.

9) *Transportation & traffic systems* concern the movement of people, goods or information in a transportation infrastructure such as a road network or a telecommunication network. A typical example is a set of interacting drivers in a road network. The purpose of a simulation could be to create realistic models of human drivers to be used in a driving simulator.

End-users: The end-users of an ABS application are the intended users of the simulator. We distinguish here between four types of end-users: *scientists*, who use the ABS in the research process to gain new knowledge, *policy makers*, who use ABS for making strategic decisions, *managers* (of a systems), who use ABS to make operational decisions, and *other professionals*, such as architects, who use ABS in their daily work.

Purpose: The purpose of the studied ABS applications is classified according to *prediction, verification, training* and *analysis*. We refer to prediction as making prognoses concerning future states. Verification concerns the purposes of determining whether a theory, model, hypothesis, or software is correct. Analysis refers to the purpose of gaining deeper knowledge and understanding of a certain domain, i.e., there is no specific theory, model etc to be verified but we want to study different phenomena, which may however lead to theory refinement. Finally, training is for the purpose of improving a person's skills in a certain domain.

2.2 Modeling Approach

The modeling aspects are captured by the eight aspects described below.

Simulated Entities: They are the entities distinguished as the key constituents of the studied systems and modeled as agents. Four different categories of entities are identified: *Living thing* - humans or animals, *Physical entity* - artifacts, like a machine or a robot, or natural objects, *Software process* - executing program code, or *Organization* - an enterprise, a group of persons, and other entities composed by a set of individuals.

Number of Agent Types: Depending on the nature of the studied application, the investigators have used one or more different agent types to model the distinct entities of the domain.

Communication: The entities can have some or no interaction with one another. The interactions take place in the form of inter-agent communication, i.e., messaging. Here, we defined two values to indicate whether communication between agents exists or not.

Spatial Explicitness refers to the assumption of a location in the physical space for the simulated entities. This can be expressed either as absolute distance or relative positions between entities.

Mobility refers to the ability of an entity to change position in the physical space. Although the real world entities may be spatially situated or moving from place to place, this fact need not be considered in the simulation if its inclusion or omission does not affect the outcome of the study.

Adaptivity is the ability of the entities to learn and improve with experience that they may acquire through their lifetime. Two values are defined to indicate whether the simulated entities are adaptive or not.

The structure of MAS refers to the arrangement of agents and their interaction in the modeled system to carry out their objectives. This arrangement could be in one of the following three forms: peer-to-peer, hierarchical, or recursive. In a peer-to-peer arrangement, individual entities of the modeled system are potentially interacting with all other entities. In a hierarchical structure, agents are arranged in a tree-like structure where there is a central entity that interacts with a number of other entities which are located one level down in the hierarchy. Whereas, in a recursive structure, entities are arranged in groups, where the organization of each group could be in either of the forms above, and these groups are interacting among each other to accomplish their tasks. The three types of MAS structure are illustrated in Fig 1.

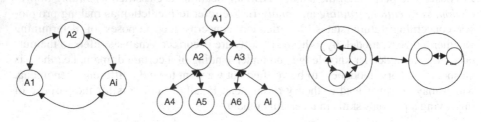

Fig. 1. Peer-to-peer, hierarchical, and recursive organization of a MAS

Dynamic: If the modeled entities are able to come into existence at different instances of time during a simulation, we regard them as *dynamic*.

2.3 Implementation Approach

The implementation approach used is described in terms of the following aspects:

Platform used: The software platform is the development environment, tool or language with which the ABS application is developed. The platforms provide support to different degrees for the developers so that they need not worry about every implementation detail.

Simulation size describes the number of agents participating in the implementation of the ABS application. If the number is different between simulations or is changing dynamically during a simulation, we will use the largest number.

Scale: The size of data used in the actual simulations has been divided into *limited/partial* or *full-scale* data. The full-scale data represents data for a whole system, while the limited/partial data only covers parts of the system.

Input data: The data used in the experiment can either be *real data*, i.e. taken from existing systems in the real world, or data that is not real, i.e. *artificial*, synthetic or generated.

Distributed: ABS applications, depending on the size and sometimes the nature of the application, may require different execution environments: a single computer, if the number is small or several computers in a distributed environment, if the number of agents is large.

Mobile agents: Agents executing in a distributed environment can be described by their mobility, as static or mobile. Static agents run on a singular computer during their lifetime. Mobile agents, on the other hand, are able to migrate between computers in a network environment.

2.4 Results

The classification of the result of the approaches will be in terms of maturity of the research, comparison to other approaches and the validation performed.

Maturity: ABS applications can have varying degree of maturity. In our framework the lowest degree of maturity is *conceptual proposal*. Here the idea or the principles of a proposed application is described, but there is no implemented simulator. The next level in the classification is *laboratory experiments* where the application has been tested in a laboratory environment. The final level, *deployed system*, indicates that the ABS system actually is or has been used by the intended end-users, e.g., traffic managers that use a simulator for deciding how to redirect the traffic when an accident has occurred. If the authors of the paper belong to the intended end-users (researchers), we classify the application as deployed if the authors draw actual conclusions from the simulation results regarding the system that is simulated (rather than just stating that ABS seems appropriate).

Evaluation comparison: If a new approach is developed to solve a problem which has been solved previously using other approaches, the new approach should be compared to existing approaches. That is, answer the question whether ABS actually is an appropriate approach to solve the problem. Such an evaluation could be either qualitative, by comparing the characteristics of the approaches, or quantitative, by different types of experiments.

Validation: In order to confirm that an ABS correctly models the real system it needs to be validated. This can be performed in different ways, *qualitatively*, e.g., by letting domain experts examine the simulation model, or *quantitatively*, e.g., by comparing the output produced by the simulator with actual measurements on the real system.

3 Results

In table 1 the framework is summarized. Table 2 shows how the papers were classified according to the framework. If a paper does not explicitly state to which category the simulator belongs but there are good reasons to believe that it belongs to a particular category, it is marked by an asterisk (*). If we have not managed to make an educated guess, it is marked by "-".

Table 1. Summary of the framework

	Aspect	Categories
Problem description	Domain	1. Animal societies 2. Physiological systems 3. Social systems 4. Organizations 5. Economic systems 6. Ecological systems 7. Physical systems 8. Robotic systems 9. Transport/traffic systems
	End-user	1. Scientists 2. Policy makers 3. Managers 4. Other professionals
	Purpose	1. Prediction 2. Verification 3. Analysis 4. Training
Modeling approach	Simulated entity	1. Living 2. Physical artefact 3. Software process 4. Organisation
	Agent types	1 - 1.000
	Communication	1. no 2. yes
	Spatial explicitness	1. no 2. yes
	Mobility	1. no 2. yes
	Adaptivity	1. no 2. yes
	Structure (of MAS)	1. Peer-to-peer 2. Hierachical 3. Recursive
	Dynamic	1. no 2. yes
Implementation approach	Platform used	NetLogo, RePast, Swarm, JADE, C++, etc.
	Simulation size	1 - 10.000.000
	Scale	1. Limited/partial 2. Full-scale
	Input data	1. Artificial data 2. Real data
	Distributed	1. no 2. yes
	Mobile agents	1. no 2. yes
Results	Maturity	1. Conceptual proposal 2. Laboratory experiment 3. Deployed
	Evaluation	1. None 2. Qualitative 3. Quantitative
	Validation	1. None 2. Qualitative 3. Quantitative

Table 2. The classification of the studied papers

Paper	Problem			Modeling								Implementation						Results		
	Domain	End-user	Purpose	Sim. Entity	N.o. types	Commun.	Spatial	Mobile	Adaptive	MAS str.	Dynamic	Platform	Size	Scale	Input data	Distributed	Mobile	Maturity	Evaluation	Validation
[6]	4	3	1	3	2	2	1	1	1	2*	1	C++	10	1	1	1*	1*	2	1	1
[7]	4	3,4	3	1	-	2	2	-	2	-	-	-	-	-	-	-	-	-	1	1	1
[8]	4	1,2	1,3	1	4	1	1	1	1*	1*	1	-	-	1	2	1*	1*	3	1	3*
[9]	4	1,2	3	1,4	2	1	1	1	1	2*	1	RePast	60	1	1	1*	1*	3	1	1
[10]	9	1,2	1	2	-	1	2	2	1	-	1	-	120	2	1	-	-	3	1	1
[11]	3	1	3	1	1	1	2	1	1	1	1	-	100	1	1	1*	1*	3	1	2*
[12]	3,9	1	2	1,2	3	2	2	2	1	1	2	-	12000	2	2	2*	2*	2	1	1
[13]	4	1,4	3	1	2	2	2	2	2	1	2	WEA	25*	2	2	2*	2*	2	1	3
[14]	9	3	2	1	1	1	2	2	1*	1	1*	-	100*	1	1	1*	1*	2	2	3
[15]	3,6	1	3	1	3	1*	2	2	2*	1	2	Swarm	540	1	1	1*	1*	3	1	1
[16]	5,9	2	3	1	6	2	1	1	1	2	1	Jade	7	1	2	1*	1*	2	1	1
[17]	7	1	3	2	1	2	2	1	1	1	1*	-	10^6	1	1	1*	1*	2	2,3	2
[18]	5	1	2,3	1,4	3	2	1	1	1*	2	2	-	102	1	1	1*	1*	3	1	2
[19]	3	1,4	2	1	1	1	2	2	1*	1	2	NetLogo	200	1	1	1*	1*	2	2	1
[20]	1	1	3	1	2	1*	2	2	1	1	1	ObjectPascal	8	1	1	1	1	3*	1	3
[21]	3	1	2	1	1	1*	2	2	1	1	1	-	250	1	1	1*	1*	3*	1	1
[22]	2	1	2	2	3	2	1	1	2	3	1	Java	4	2	1*	2*	1*	3	1	3
[23]	3	1	3	1	3	2	1	1	1	1	1	-	9	1	1	1*	1*	2	1	1
[24]	3	1	3	1	1	2	2	2	1	1	2	Sugarscape	700	1	1	1*	1*	3*	1	1
[25]	3,6	2	3	1	3	2	2	2	1	1	1	Cormas	-	1	2	1*	1*	2	1	3
[26]	3	1,2	3	1,3	3	2*	1	1	1	1	2	VisualBasic	10000	1	1	1	1	2	3	1
[27]	4,7	3	3	1,2	5	2	2	2	2	1	1	C++	1	1	1	1	1	2	1	1
[28]	3	1	2,3	1	2	1	1	1	2	1	1	NetLogo	500	1	1	1*	1*	2	2	1
[29]	4	2	3	1,2	3	2	2	2	2	1	1	RePast	61	1	2	1*	1*	3	2	1
[30]	8	1	1,2	2	1	2	2	2	1	1	1	C++	25	1	1	1*	1*	3*	1	1
[31]	5	1	3	1	7	2	1	1	2	2	1	DECAF	3	1	1	1*	1*	2	1	1
[32]	3	2	3	1	1*	2	2	1	2*	1	1	-	-	1	1	1*	1	3*	2	2
[33]	5	1	3	1	1	2	1	1	1	1	1	-	24*	2	1	1*	1*	2	3	1

4   Analysis

4.1   Problem Description

The results indicate that ABS is often used to study systems involving interacting human decision makers, e.g., in social, organizational, economic, traffic and transport systems (see Fig. 2). This is not surprising given the fact that qualities like autonomy, communication, planning, etc., often are presented as characteristic of software agents (as well as of human beings). However, as (some of) these qualities are present also in other living entities, it is interesting to note that there was only one paper on simulating *animal societies* and just two involving *ecological systems*. Very few papers are found on simulating technical systems, such as *ICT systems*, i.e., integrated systems of computers, communication technology, software, data, and the people who manage and use them, *critical infrastructures, power systems etc.*. The aim of such models might be to study and have a deeper understanding of the existing and emerging functionalities of the system and analyze the impact of parameter changes. (The only paper on simulating technical systems concerned robotic systems.)

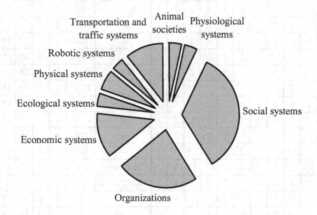

Fig. 2. The distribution of the type of domains simulated

In more than half of the applications, researchers were the intended end-user. As can be seen in Fig 3., the most common purpose of the applications included in the study was analysis. However, no paper reported the use of ABS for training purposes indicating that this may be an underdeveloped area.

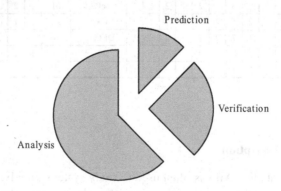

Fig. 3. The distribution of purpose

4.2 Modeling Approach

The simulated entities are mostly living things, indicating that ABS is believed to be better suited to model the complexity of human (and animal) behaviour compared to other techniques. However, it should be noted that in some applications there were entities not modeled and simulated and implemented as agents. Hybrid systems of this kind are motivated by the fact that some entities are passive and are not making any decisions, especially in socio-technical systems. The model design choices for some of the aspects seem to be consequences of the characteristics of the systems simulated. After all, the aim is to mirror the real system. These aspects include number of agent types, only about 15% of the applications had more than three different agent types, spatial explicitness (60% do use it), mobility of entities (50%), communication between entities (64%), and the structure of the MAS where a vast majority used a peer-to-peer structure (77%). However, as illustrated in Fig. 4, there are some modelling aspects where the strengths of the agent approach do not seem to have been explored to its full potential. For instance, only 9 of the 28 papers make use of adaptivity, and just 7 out of the 27 implemented systems seem to use dynamic simulations.

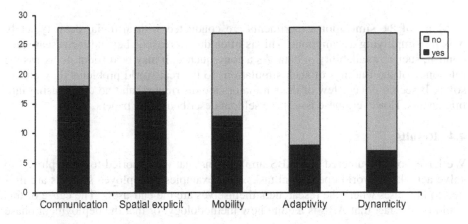

Fig. 4. The distribution of modeling aspects

4.3 Implementation Approach

Nearly half of the papers do not state which software were used to develop the ABS. In particular, it is interesting to note that the two papers with the largest number of agents do not state this. Of the agent platforms and simulation tools available, none is dominantly used. In fact, many of the simulations were implemented with C++ or programs developed from scratch. A possible reason for this may be that many ABS tools and platforms make limiting assumptions regarding the way that entities are modeled. The number of agents in the simulation experiments is typically quite small (see Fig. 5). In 50% of the papers the number of agents were 61 or less. The fact that most simulation experiments were limited covering only a part of the simulated system, may be an explanation for this. The reasons for this are seldom discussed in the papers but are probably lack of computing hardware, software (such as proper agent simulation platforms), or the time available to perform the experiments. Moreover, there may be a "trade-off" between the complexity of the agents and the number of agents in the experiments, i.e., that large sized simulations use relatively simple agents whereas smaller simulations use more complex agents. However, further analysis is necessary before any conclusions can be drawn.

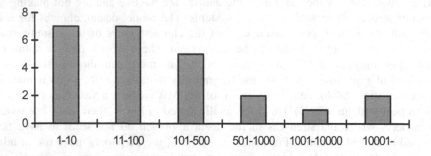

Fig. 5. The frequency of different simulation sizes (number of agents)

Many of the simulation experiments are conducted with artificial data, typically making simplifying assumptions. This is often due to reasons beyond the researchers' control, such as availability of data. As a consequence, it may be difficult to assess the relevance of the findings of such simulations to the real world problems they aim to solve. It seems as very few of the simulators are distributed, and no one is using mobile agents. However, these issues are seldom described in the papers.

4.4 Results

We have not encountered any ABS applications that are reported to be deployed to solve actual real world operational tasks. The examples of deployed systems are limited to the cases where the researchers themselves are the end-users. The cause of this could be the fact that ABS is a quite new methodology, or that the deployment phase

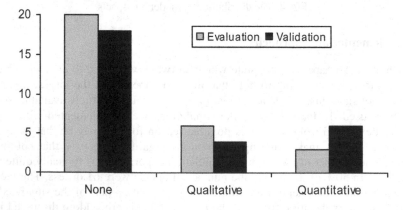

Fig. 6. The frequency of different types and evaluation

often is not described in scientific publications. As illustrated in Fig. 6, less than half of the simulations are actually reported to be validated. This is particularly striking as it is in most cases the complex behaviors of humans that are being simulated. Also, comparisons to other approaches are very rare.

4.5 Limitations of the Study

Although the conclusions drawn from our study are valid for the work published in the MABS proceedings, a larger sample is probably needed to verify that they hold for the whole ABS area. There were a number of interesting aspects that we were not able to include in our study. For example, regarding the problem description, the *size* of the actual problem, i.e., the system being simulated would be interesting to know. Typically, only a partial simulation is made, i.e., the number of entities in the real system is much larger than the number of agents in the simulation. However, in most papers the size of the real system is not described and often it was very difficult for us to estimate the size. Another interesting aspect not included in this study is the modeling of entities. The representation of the behavior and state of the real world entities should be sufficiently sophisticated to capture the aspects relevant for the problem studied. We initially categorized the ways of modeling the entities in the following categories: Mathematical models; Cellular automata; Rule-based (a set of explicit rules describe the behavior of the agent); Deliberative (the behavior is determined by some kind of reasoning such as planning). Unfortunately, there were often not enough information in the papers concerning this aspect. Related to this is the distinction between proactive versus reactive modeling of entities, which also was very difficult to extract from the papers due to lack of information. Regarding the implementation, we wanted to investigate how the agent models were implemented in the simulation software. We found examples ranging from simple feature vectors (as used in traditional dynamic micro simulation) to sophisticated software entities corresponding to separate threads or processes. However, also in this case important information was often left out from the presentation.

5 Conclusions

The applications reviewed in this study suggest that ABS seems a promising approach to many problems involving simulating complex systems of interacting entities. However, it seems as the full potential of the agent concept often is not utilized, for instance, with respect to adaptivity and dynamicity. Also, existing ABS tools and platforms are seldom used and instead the simulation software is developed from scratch using an ordinary programming language. There may be many reasons for this, e.g., that they are difficult to use and adopt to the problem studied, or that the awareness of the existence of these tools and platforms is limited.

Something that made this study difficult was that important information, especially concerning the implementation of the simulator, was missing in many papers. This makes it harder to reproduce the experiments and to build upon the results in further advancing the state-of-the-art of ABS. A positive effect of our study would be if researchers became more explicit and clear about how they have dealt with the different aspects that we have used in the analysis. Therefore, we suggest the following checklist for ABS application papers:

1. Clearly describe the purpose of the application and the intended end-users.
2. Indicate the typical size of the system (that is simulated) in terms of entities corresponding to agents.
3. For each agent type in the simulation model, describe
   a. what kind of entities it is simulating,
   b. how they are modelled (mathematical, rule-based, deliberative, etc.),
   c. whether they are proactive or not,
   d. whether they are communicating with other agents or not,
   e. whether they are given a spatial position, and if so, whether they are mobile
   f. whether they are capable of learning or not.
4. Describe the structure of the collection of agents, and state whether this collection is static or agents can be added/removed during a simulation.
5. State which simulation (or agent) platform was used, or in the case the simulator was implemented from scratch, what programming language was used.
6. State the size of the simulation in terms of number of agents.
7. Describe how the agents were implemented; feature vectors, mobile agents, or something in-between.
8. State whether the simulator actually has been used by the intended end-users, or just in laboratory experiments. In the latter case indicate whether artificial or real data was used.
9. Describe how the simulator has been validated.
10. Describe if and how the suggested approach has been compared to other approaches.

Future work includes extending the study using a larger sample, e.g., include other relevant workshops and conferences, such as Agent-Based Simulation, and journals such as JASSS, in order to reduce any bias. Another interesting study would be to make a comparative study with more traditional simulation techniques including aspects such as size, validation, etc.

References

1. Moss, S., Davidsson, P. (eds.): MABS 2000. LNCS (LNAI), vol. 1979. Springer, Heidelberg (2001)
2. Sichman, J.S., Bousquet, F., Davidsson, P. (eds.): MABS 2002. LNCS (LNAI), vol. 2581. Springer, Heidelberg (2003)
3. Hales, D., et al.: MABS 2003. LNCS (LNAI), vol. 2927. Springer, Heidelberg (2003)
4. Davidsson, P., Logan, B., Takadama, K. (eds.): MABS 2004. LNCS (LNAI), vol. 3415. Springer, Heidelberg (2005)
5. Sichman, J.S., Antunes, L. (eds.): MABS 2005. LNCS (LNAI), vol. 3891. Springer, Heidelberg (2006)
6. Kafeza, E., Karlapalem, K.: Speeding Up CapBasED-AMS Activities through Multi-Agent Scheduling, in [1]

7. Wickenberg, T., Davidsson, P.: On Multi Agent Based Simulation of Software Development Processes, in[2]
8. Rouchier, J., Thoyer, S.: Modelling a European Decision Making Process with Heterogeneous Public Opinion and Lobbying: The Case of the Authorization Procedure for Placing Genetically Modified Organisms on the Market, in [3]
9. Robertson, D.A.: The Strategy Hypercube: Exploring Strategy Space Using Agent-Based Models, in [3]
10. Noda, I., Ohta, M., Shinoda, K., Kumada, Y., Nakashima, H.: Evaluation of Usability of Dial-a-Ride Systems by Social Simulation, in [3]
11. Sosa, R., Gero, J.S.: Social change: exploring design influence, in [3]
12. Miyashita, K., Agent-based, S.A.P.: Simulator for Amusement Park - Toward Eluding Social Congestions through Ubiquitous Scheduling, in [4]
13. Shah, A.P., Pritchett, A.R.: Work Environment Analysis: Environment Centric Multi-Agent Simulation for Design of Socio-technical Systems, in [4]
14. S. El hadouaj, A. Drogoul, S. Espié, How to Combine Reactive and Anticipation: The Case of Conflicts Resolution in a Simulated Road Traffic, in [1]
15. Premo, L.S.: Patchiness and Prosociality: An Agent-Based model of Plio/Pleistocene Hominid Food Sharing, in [4]
16. Bergkvist, M., Davidsson, P., Persson, J.A., Ramstedt, L., Hybrid, A.: Micro-Simulator for Determining the Effects of Governmental Control Policies on Transport Chains, in [4]
17. Breton, L., Zucker, J.-D., Clément, E., Multi-Agent, A.: Based Simulation of Sand Piles in a Static Equilibrium, in [1]
18. Takahashi, I., Okada, I.: Monetary Policy and Banks' Loan Supply Rules to Harness Asset Bubbles and Crashes, in [3]
19. Henein, C.M., White, T.: Agent Based Modelling of Forces in Crowds, in [4]
20. Hemelrijk, C.K.: Sexual Attraction and Inter-sexual Dominance among Virtual Agents, in [1]
21. Pedone, R., Conte, R.: The Simmel Effect: Imitation and Avoidance in Social Hierarchies, in [1]
22. Amigoni, F., Gatti, N.: On the Simulation for Physiological Processes, in [2]
23. Rodrigues, M.R., da Rocha, A.C.: Costa, Using Qualitative Exchange Values to Improve the Modelling of Social Interaction, in [3]
24. Tomita, S., Namatame, A.: Bilateral Tradings with and without Strategic Thinking, in [3]
25. Elliston, L., Hinde, R., Yainshet, A.: Plant Disease Incursion Management, in [4]
26. Winoto, P., Simulation, A.: of the Market for Offenses in Mulitagent Systems: Is Zero Crime Rates Attainable?, in [2]
27. Sahli, N., Moulin, B.: Agent-based Geo-simulation to Support Human Planning and Spatial Cognition, in [5]
28. Antunes, L., Balsa, J., Urbano, P., Moniz, L., Palma, C.R.: Tax Compliance in a Simulated Heterogeneous Multi-agent Society, in [5]
29. Furtado, V., Melo, A., Belchior, M.: Analyzing Police Patrol Routes by Simulating the Physical Reorganization of Agents, in [5]
30. Machado, A., Ramalho, G., Zucker, J.-D., Drogoul, A.: Multi-Agent Patrolling: an Empirical Analysis of Alternative Architectures, in [2]
31. McGeary, F., Decker, K.: Modeling a Virtual Food Court Using DECAF, in [1]
32. Downing, T., Moss, S., Pahl-Worstl, C.: Integrated Assessment: Prospects for Understanding Climate Policy Using Participatory Agent-Based Social Simulation, in [1]
33. Ebenhöh, E.: Modeling Non-linear Common-pool Resource Experiments with Boundedly Rational Agents, in [5]

Analyzing Dynamics of Peer-to-Peer Communication - From Questionnaire Surveys to Agent-Based Simulation

Shinako Matsuyama[1,2] and Takao Terano[1]

[1] Dept. Computational Intelligence and Systems Sciences, Tokyo Institute of Technology
4259 Nagatsuda-cho, Midori-ku,
Yokohama 226-8502 Japan
terano@dis.titech.ac.jp
[2] Sony Corporation
6-7-35 Kitashinagawa Shinagawa-ku,
Tokyo 141-0001 Japan
Shinako.Matsuyama@jp.sony.com

Abstract. This paper discusses dynamic properties of peer-to-peer communication networks, which emerge from information exchanges among people. First, we gather activity data of communication among people through questionnaires in order to categorize both information (contents) and people, then we develop agent-based simulation models to examine implicit mechanisms behind the dynamics. The agent-based models enable us to discover the quality of information exchanged and the preferences of specific communication groups. The simulation results have suggested that 1) peer-to-peer communication networks have scale-free and small world properties, 2) the characteristics of contents and users are observed in word-of-mouth communications, and 3) the combination of real survey data and agent-based simulation is effective.

Keywords: Agent-Based Simulation, peer-to-peer communication, network analysis.

1 Introduction

This paper addresses models of dynamic peer-to-peer communications through agent-based simulation and artificial social networks. The work is motivated by recent expanding use of personal information devices which have increased the content exchanges among people and have increased the number of interesting opportunities for communication. Additionally, a lot of SNS (Social Networking Site/Service) have appeared on the Internet. Also, Consumer Generated Media (CGM) has become popular allowing information exchanges at the consumer's initiative. Service providers have an increased interest in issues related to peer-to-peer communications.

The main goals of our research are summarized as follows: (i) to analyze the communications platforms from the bottom, and (ii) to propose a novel method and technique for these analyses, which will be used as market decision tools by service providers.

L. Antunes and K. Takadama (Eds.): MABS 2006, LNAI 4442, pp. 28–40, 2007.

Our research follows three steps: (i) Data collection: We have used questionnaire surveys on the communications among people; (ii) Communication model development: Using the data, we have categorized both information (contents) and people involved in the peer-to-peer communications, and (iii) Agent based simulation: We have carried out agent-based simulations to analyze the implicit mechanisms behind the dynamics.

The main contributions of this paper are summarized in the following three points: (i) we propose an agent-based simulation system which enables dynamic peer-to-peer communication analysis, (ii) we evaluate the degree distribution of communication partners and the network density of communications, which will characterize the network features for various analyses, and (iii) we show that agent-based models enable us to discover the quality of information exchanged and the preferences of specific communication groups.

2   Related Work and Research Objectives

Information delivery between people known as "word-of-mouth" (WOM) is considered as one of the promising gears for marketing promotions (see [1],[2], for example). It is well recognized that analyses of the information-spreading mechanisms reveal valuable information to service providers.

On the other hand, there are a large number of results regarding social networks (see [3], [4], for example). Particularly, network structure analyses such as scale-free and small-world phenomena ([5], [6], [7]) have recently become one of the hot topics in the literature.

The human communication analysis includes the following two issues: (i) most network structures in our society have a very dynamical nature and, thus, it is not enough to know just the static statuses at certain past time instances, and (ii) a number of different features have such strong impacts that, for example, it is not enough to know only the popular contents (products, services) or to identify only the users with heavy access records.

For dynamic analysis, agent-based simulation (ABS) is a very useful approach, because: (a) ABS is good at analyzing macro phenomena by setting micro level characteristics to each entity, and yielding the factors which determine the resultant network, and (b) ABS repeatedly examines different scenarios of interest. ABS has already been employed for the related analysis ([8], [9]); it has also been employed for marketing and human-centered systems ([10]).

We have extended our previous work ([11]) so that we utilize real-world survey data to improve the simulation model. The rest part of the paper is organized as follows. The developed agent-based simulation system is specified in Section 3 and 4. In Section 3, we define first the classes of contents and persons according to the results of the questionnaire survey, and then we built a model of human communications employing the results of the survey and other data from online-sites, as well as the existing theory for network growth. Section 4 describes the agent-based simulation we have developed based on the model established in Section 3. The considered experimental setting and the simulation results on evaluation of the degree distribution and the network density distribution are given in Section 5. Finally the main conclusions and directions for future work are given in Section 6.

3 Model Description

This section provides a basic simulation model and data collection for model generation.

3.1 Basic Concepts of the Artificial World

The basic assignment is as follows: (i) Each "node" in the network is a person and a "network edge" corresponds to a connection between two persons; and (ii) we assigned each person to an agent for information delivery via peer-to-peer communication.

In peer-to-peer communication, each agent makes edges by choosing the information to be sent to /received from another agent or partner. To choose the partner, node attributes such as preference similarities and the advantages of having a node with an edge are used. Therefore, the underlying model of peer-to-peer communication is considered to be a part of an extended Barabasi and Albert (BA) model ([12]).

However, the mutual links between people do not grow infinitely since they converge to a specific value. As part of the dynamic process a node may make new favorite edges while the other edges disappear with time. This mechanism corresponds to the deactivation model described in [13],[14]. Therefore, the peer-to-peer communication networks considered in this paper follow a model that combines the extended BA model and the deactivation model.

The selection of a communication partner (agent decision making rule) depends on both of the following two properties: (i) the persons to communicate, and (ii) the information (contents) to be sent and/or received. Accordingly, we categorize the people and the contents as follows:

- By clustering the contents along the characteristics implied by their distribution within the considered system; and
- By clustering the persons according to the contents in their possession and according to the volume of transactions they are involved in, i.e. amount of the related communications assuming a constant rate.

To define the agent decision making rules, we have used the above clusters of the contents and persons. As for the deactivation criterion, the limit of the transaction volume related to each person is employed.

3.2 Data Collection for Model Generation

3.2.1 Clustering the Contents and Persons
In order to identify the clusters of contents and persons, we have carried out the following questionnaire surveys:

The questionnaires were designed to gather information on daily communications of the following two groups of subjects with 78 persons in total: (i) Group1: 30 business people ranging in age from 20 to 50 (male: 60%, female: 40%), and (ii) Group2: 48 students around 20 years old (male: 30%, female: 70%).

The questionnaire required the subjects to:

- select the contents which they usually share with others from 30 listed content categories; if the preferred category is not listed among the 30 given, it could be added in the space provided;
- designate the number of partners they communicate with (for example, between just 1, or 2 to 3, or 4 to 5, or 6 to 7, and so on);
- choose the frequency of communication (for example, once a day, 2 to 3 times a week, 2 to 3 times a month, once a month, or once every 2 to 3 months);
- rate on a 1 to 5 points scale (5: very good to 1: very bad) the information they send/receive[1].

The collected data was processed as follows.

On a hierarchical clustering with group average method, the contents were categorized to a two dimensional plot where the axes correspond to transaction volume for 30 days and the number of people who share the content category, respectively. Figure 1 displays the result of the clustering when 5 clusters per group are allowed. C1 to C8 serve as labels of the clustered items: music, movies, and so on being the typical topics that belong to the cluster. The number inside the parentheses is the ratio of the contents corresponding to the cluster. For example in Group2, music and movies are shared by a wide range of people and communicated on frequently, while stocks and child-care are shared by few people and communicated on rarely.

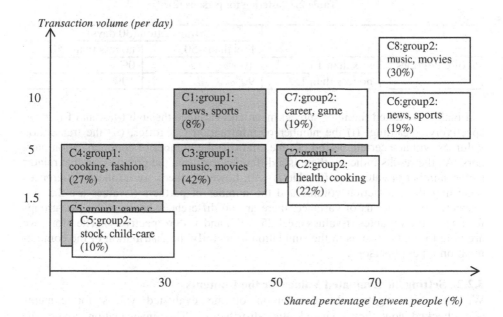

Fig. 1. Diagram of clustering the contents categories

---

[1] "Good information" depends on the subjects' preferences. For example, "The restaurant was great", "I like this movie", and so on. "Bad information" has an opposite meaning.

Next, we categorized the subjects (persons) into 5 clusters based on contents categories related to them. Table 1 summarizes the clustering. For example, cluster 1 corresponds to the persons, who share contents from clusters C1 and C2. The column "distribution" shows the percentage of examinees in each cluster.

Table 1. Clustering for persons (1)

cluster	group 1						group 2					
	categories *					distribution	categories *					distribution
	C2	C1	C3	C4	C5		C8	C6	C7	C2	C5	
1	1	1	0	0	0	48%	1	1	0	0	0	21%
2	1	1	0.5	0	0	14%	1	1	0.5	0	0	30%
3	0.5	1	1	0.5	0	17%	1	1	0.5	0.5	0	14%
4	1	1	1	1	0	14%	1	1	1	1	0	21%
5	1	1	1	1	1	7%	1	1	1	1	1	14%

* 0 : less than 50% of contents in the category are shared by persons in the cluster
  0.5 : about 50% of contents in the category are shared by persons in the cluster
  1: more than 50% of contents in the category are shared by persons in the cluster

We have divided the subjects according to their transaction volumes over the 30 days. The correlation between the number of the content categories and transaction volume is high (over 0.7). Accordingly, we relate the transaction volume based on the number of the content categories at each cluster, and Table 2 shows the result.

Table 2. Clustering for persons (2)

		transaction (30 days)	
		less than 150	no less than 150
# of categories	less than 15	100%	0%
	no less than 15	90%	10%

Finally, we tested the inter-subject mean and variance through t-test and f-test, respectively, regarding: (i) the number of information categories, (ii) the transaction volumes within a certain period of time, and (iii) the number of communication partners. As the results indicate, there is a difference between the group mean that relates to the number of categories (t value is 4.0); however, there are no mean differences regarding the transaction volume and the number of partners (t-values are 2.5, 1.6 respectively). In terms of variance, there are no differences between the two groups for any of the variables (f-values are 1.25, 1.03, and 1.38 respectively). Therefore, we are able to use the results in the simulation to identify the distribution of the communication types of persons.

3.2.2 Setting the Evaluated Values for the Contents
We have investigated the distribution of the evaluated values for contents and checked how they changed after distribution. This investigation covers the following points: i) distribution of the evaluation of arbitrary information (contents), ii) the level of evaluated value for the content to be sent (which level of contents regarding the evaluated value is sent to others and which one is not), iii) the difference

between the evaluated value by the sender and the one by the receiver. To estimate
i) distribution, we have obtained the data from two online sites; restaurants sites [2](The
number of restaurants is 3450, the number of comments for them with a 5-point scale
(1 to 5) evaluated value is 78139) and movies sites[3] (The number of movies is 2016,
the number of comments is 4138). Then we measured the mean value of the 5-point
scale evaluated value for restaurant data and movies data. To obtain the ii) the level of
the evaluated value, we have used the results of the questionnaires to group1 and
group2 described in 3.2.1. Finally for iii) difference of evaluated value, we have performed the following experiment with 30 subjects:

- picking up 10 contents from the online sites in i), and letting the subjects select one
  from them;
- allowing the subjects to use the 5-point scale (1 to 5) for the selected content;
- allowing them to send the content to another person and asking the latter for evaluation in the same manner.

The number of contents is 18, the number of evaluated value obtained is 60, and
the number of pairs (sender & receiver) is 18. We measured the distribution for the
pairs of evaluated value by senders and receivers.

Figure2 shows the distribution of the evaluated value for the contents (average of
each content and average of all content). Evaluation 3 and 4 cover 80% of all, and
value 4 shares the top.

Table 3 summarizes the distribution of the evaluated value for two subject groups.
The results clearly indicate that value 3 covers 50%, and higher values (4 and 5) cover

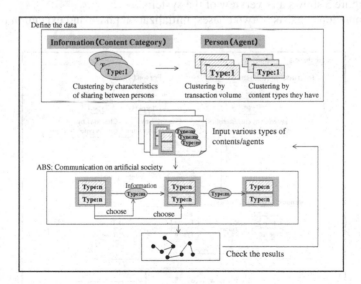

Fig. 2. Distribution of evaluated values

---

[2] http://gourmet.livedoor.com/, 2005/8/25
[3] http://community.movie.livedoor.com/, 2005/8/25

40%. Table 4 shows the difference between two evaluated values ("experiment sender/receiver pair" in the table) made by the senders and receivers. To compare the difference between two evaluated values, we have also calculated the difference for the randomly chosen pairs ("random pair"). Differences in the data between senders' and receivers' are slightly smaller than the ones between random pairs, and over 80% of them is one or less.

Table 3. Distribution of the evaluated value

	group1	group2
5(very good)	10%	15%
4	30%	26%
3	50%	57%
2	5%	1%
1(very bad)	5%	1%

Table 4. Difference for the evaluated value

Difference	Distribution	
	Experiment sender/receiver pair	Random pair
+/− 0	39%	27%
+/− 1	44%	50%
+/− 2	17%	23%

4 Simulation System Implementation

This section describes the simulation system we have developed. We define the information as contents and people as agents. After setting the characteristics of the agents/contents described in section 3, the simulation analyzes the features of the network that accumulate through communication between agents for a certain period of time. Figure 3 shows an overview of the system.

The simulation consists of two phases: initialization phase and execution phase.

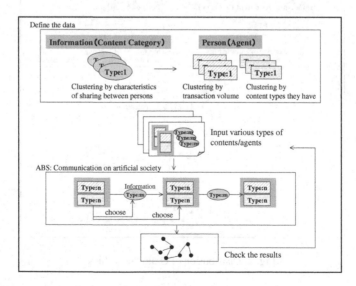

Fig. 3. System overview

4.1 Initialization Phase

At the initialization phase, the cluster type and number of the contents (information) are set based on the categorization, which is based on the clustering process devised in Section 3.2.1. Each content item has an evaluated value based on the measure in i) Section 3.2.2. In detail, 70% to 80% of all the content has an evaluated value 3 or 4 and the rest of the content has a value of 1, 2 or 5. In the same way, the cluster type and number of the agents are assigned. Then, all agents are given some content based on their described characteristics (Table 1), and are assigned a content sending/receiving frequency based on Table 2.

4.2 Execution Phase

At the execution phase, each agent communicates with others based on their characteristics and the characteristics of the content they have. Communication includes contents sending and receiving. There are two types of receiving: receiving directly from the partner or through a third person introduced by the partner. Figure 4 illustrates the simulation flow.

```
Agent action for certain period (for example 1 day)
begin
for all Aᵢ ∈Agents in generated order
    if Aᵢ should send/receive contents (send/receive timing)
       Aᵢ chooses a content to be sent/received (Ck)
       for all Aⱼ ∈Agents in generated order i≠i
          if Aᵢ should send/receive Ck to/from Aj
             • Aᵢ sends Ck to Aᵢ or receives Ck from Aj
             • set an evaluation value to Ck
               (in the case of receive)
          end if
    (snip)
```

Fig. 4. Basic Algorithm of the Simulation flow

Determination of how content is sent and received between agents is defined as an agent decision-making rule. This determination consists of two indicators: an indicator for the contents to be sent/ received and one for communication between agents.

Measures for the contents

Table 5 shows the measures for sending/receiving the contents C_k between Agent A_i and A_j. Table 6 shows an overview of the functions.

Each agent chooses a content category from his content list and decides whether the content should be sent or received by using the above criteria. In the case of receiving, if there is no appropriate content category in their content list, a content category is chosen from all content categories.

Table 5. Measures for choosing contents

Action	Decision whether A_i chooses C_k or not
Send	*HasInterest(A_i, G_k) AND SendRecvTiming(C_k) AND IfSendEval(A_i, C_k)*
Receive	*Condition1 : HasInterest(A_i, G_k) AND* *SendRecvTiming(C_k) AND IfSendEval(A_i, C_k)* *OR* *Condition2 : SendRecvTiming(C_k) AND IfSendEval(A_i, C_k)*

Notation: A_i, A_j:Agent, C_k: Information(content), G_k: content category of C_k

Table 6. Functions summaries

SendRecvTiming(A_i) [Whether A_i should send/receive contents at that point or not]	
Return	True...current time-preceding send/receive time is greater than send/receive interval
	False...other

SendRecvTiming(C_k)[Whether C_k should be sent/received at that point or not]	
Return	True...current time-preceding send/receive time is greater than send/receive interval
	False...other

CommuAmount(A_i, A_j)[Transaction amount between A_i and A_j]	
Return	True...transaction volume between A_i and A_j exceeds the average of all transaction volume of A_i
	False...other

HasInterest(A_i, G_k) [Whether A_i is interested in G_k or not]	
Return	True ... A_i has sent/received the contents which belong to G_k
	False ... other

IsSpecialist(A_i, G_k)[Authority level of A_i for G_k]	
Return	True... Transaction volume of A_i regarding contents in G_k is greater than the average of whole transaction volume of G_k
	False...other

HasSimilarity(A_i, A_j, G_k)[Evaluation similarity for G_k between A_i and A_j]	
Return	True... Difference of the evaluated value by A_i and A_j regarding contents in G_k is smaller than 2
	False... other

IfSendEval(A_i, C_k)[If C_k has an evaluated value which should be sent]	
Return	True... C_k should be sent/received by its evaluated value by A_i (the probability in Table 3 is used for the evaluated value)
	False...other

Notation: A_i, A_j:Agent, C_k:Information(content), G_k:content category of C_k

Table 7. Criteria for partner

Action	Decision whether A_i send/receive C_k to/from A_j or not
Send	*Condition1 : SendRecvTiming(A_i) AND* *(HasInterest(A_j, G_k) OR HasSimilarity(A_i, A_j, G_k))* *OR* *Condition2:SendRecvTiming(A_i) AND CommuAmount(A_i, A_j)*

Receive	*Condition1 : SendRecvTiming(A_j) AND HasInterest(A_j, G_k)*
	         OR HasSimilarity(A_i, A_j, G_k)) AND CommuAmount(A_i, A_j)
	 OR
	 Condition2 : SendRecvTiming(A_j) AND IsSpecialist(A_j, G_k)
	 OR
	 Condition3 : From all agents who communicated with A_j ,find the partner
	       with the above condition

Notation: A_i, A_j:Agent, C_k:Information(content), G_k:content category of C_k

Selection of partner agent
Table 7 shows the criteria indicating whether or not Agent A_i sends/receives the content C_k to/from Agent A_j.

Set the evaluated value
When agents receive contents from categories   in their contents list, they set the evaluated value, which has a difference of 0, -1, or 1, from the original evaluated value. If the content category is not in the given agent's contents list, the random value function described in Section 3.2.2 is used to calculate a new evaluated value.

5 Experiment

5.1 Experimental Set Up

We performed three experiments: a) first, with environments similar to the two examinee groups, b) second, with the same environments but with a larger number of people (agents), and c) third, different environments with monotypic agents, that is, we changed the parameters of the simulation (contents type and agents type). In each scenario, different types of agents were created and we compared the results of communication network. In c), all agents were in the same cluster (cluster 5). We observed the distributions of the number of edges as well as the network density.

5.2 Results

Degree distribution
Figure 5 to Figure 7 illustrate the distribution of edges. In Figure 5, graph a) is drawn on a log scale. However, to check the difference between graph b) and c), Figure 6 and Figure 7 are drawn from real data, not on a log scale.

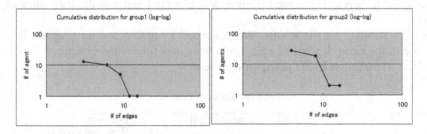

Fig. 5. a) Degree distribution for experimental subject group

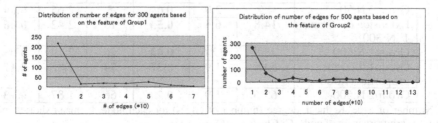

Fig. 6. b) Degree distribution for expanded experimental subject group

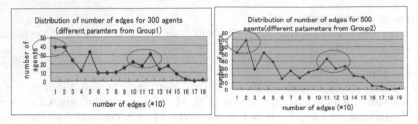

Fig. 7. c) degree distribution for different attribute group

We performed the experiment 10 times. We checked the differences between arbitrary pairs of groups by t-test, f-test. The compared value in t-test is the coefficient of determination for function approximation; $y=\alpha x^{-\beta}(1.5\leq\beta\leq2.0)$ where x is number of edges and y is number of nodes. There is no difference between the two groups (T value is 0.07, F value is 1.105).

Density
To check the density of the network, we calculated the shortest path L and clustering coefficient C. L and C are defined in [6] and they are measurements for the small-world property. They are calculated as follows:

$$L = \frac{1}{\frac{1}{2}n(n+1)}\sum_{i\geq j}d_{ij} \tag{1}$$

$$C_i = \frac{number\ of\ triangles\ connected\ to\ node\ i}{number\ of\ triples\ centered\ on\ node\ i}, \quad C=\frac{1}{n}\sum_i C_i \tag{2}$$

where d_{ij} is the geodesic distance from node i to node j and n is the total number of nodes.

Table 8 summarizes the results. We generated k-regular random graphs whose k are close to the mean degrees of each graph from experiment and compared the L and C of them to the graph from the experiment results.

Table 8. Network density

		Experiment Graph			k-Regular Random Graph		
		K	L	C	K	L	C
a)	Group1 N:30	4.6	4.2	**0.57**	5	2.23	**0.13**
	Group2 N:50	4.5	2.9	0.64	5	2.65	**0.09**
b)	Extension of Group 1 N:300	14.8	6.8	**0.53**	15	2.42	**0.06**
	Group2 N:500	25.8	12.6	**0.44**	26	2.19	**0.05**
c)	Group1different properties N:300	53.6	1.9	**0.37**	54	1.82	**0.17**
	Group2 N:500	65.6	1.9	**0.28**	66	1.87	**0.13**

N: Number of node, K: mean degree (number of edges) for each node, L: mean shortest path between arbitrary pairs of node, C: Clustering Coefficient

5.3 Discussion

Degree distribution

- In a) and b), the networks can best be described as scale-free, rather than being classified as related to random graphs. From the results, it is evident that a few people communicate with many others and that almost all of them communicate with a few people.
- To check the high degree edges, there are high correlations between transaction volume per day and the number of content categories (the correlations are 0.68 and 0.80 respectively).
- In c) the total number of edges increased for the group in which all members have content categories belonging to the same cluster. This means the communication here is more active than in the environments in a) and b). However, it was polarized between the high-degree group and the low degree group. The results also reveal that communication in the group including the same type of people is not uniform and that it is divided into two groups: an active communication group and inactive communication group.

Density

In [6], a small-world network is defined as the following: L is almost similar to the one in k-regular random graph (k is the mean degree of the network) but C is much bigger than the one in k-regular random graph. In our experiments, a) and b) meet the conditions. Accordingly, it is clear that they have small-world properties.

Although c) has a lower density than a),b), it has a higher one than k-regular random graph.

These are explained by the fact that people often make groups with those they frequently communicate with.

6 Conclusion

This paper has analyzed peer-to-peer information delivery among people. For this purpose, we developed an agent-based simulation (ABS) system for different network types and dynamics. To set ABS system parameters, we utilized questionnaire survey data.

We have obtained two main results: (1) the simulated network with the real-world parameters has scale-free and small-world properties, while the one with the different parameters (with monotypic agents) does not; and (2) we identified the characteristics of contents and users to obtain the desired network properties: From the marketing point of view, (a) focus on the small number of high-degree users assuming that they have a strong influence, and (b) send different information to each person in the high-density network in order to spread information as widely as possible.

The approach has suggested that through the ABS, we are able to analyze the communication network in various circumstances with a dynamic environment.

We should, however, consider carefully the parameters to ABS and the definition of agent behaviors. In this paper, we have used data from the questionnaire survey, but the data is a small portion of real-world data, and it is very difficult to collect exact data which represents the real-world. Accordingly, we also need to compare the results on real-world data from e-mails, blogs etc.

Future work in this area includes (1) to develop methods for marketing purposes, particularly for finding high-grade users from the set of low-degree ones; (2) to examine network structures which will enhance communications; and (3) to compare simulation results to real-world data (e-mails, blogs).

References

1. Rosen, E.: The Anatomy of Buzz: How to Create Word of Mouth Marketing. Doubleday (2002)
2. Kokokusha: Survey for the word of mouth (In Japanese) (2005), http://www.kokokusha.co.jp/service/kuchikomi.html
3. Ebel, H., et al.: Dynamics of Social Networks. Complexity 8(2), 24–27 (2003)
4. Scott, J.: Social Network Analysis. Sage Publications, Thousand Oaks (2000)
5. Barabasi, A-L.: Linked: The New Science of Networks. Perseus Books Group (2002)
6. Watts, D.J.: Small Worlds: The Dynamics of Networks Between Order and Randomness (Princeton Studies in Complexity). Princeton Univ. Pr., Princeton (2004)
7. Newman, M.E.J.: The Structure and Function of Complex Networks. SIAM REVIEW 2003 Society for Industrial and Applied Mathematics 45(2), 167–256 (2003)
8. Terano, T., Deguchi, H., Takadama, K.: Meeting the Challenge of Social Problems via Agent-Based Simulation. Springer, Japan (2003)
9. Gilbert, N.: Agent-based social simulation: dealing with complexity. The Complex Systems Network of Excellence (2004)
10. Bonabeau, E.: Agent-based modeling: Methods and techniques for simulating human systems. PNAS 99(suppl 3), 7280–7287 (2002)
11. Matsuyama, S., Kunigami, M., Terano, T.: Multi-Agent Modeling of Peer to Peer Communication with Scale-Free and Small-World Properties. In: Khosla, R., Howlett, R.J., Jain, L.C. (eds.) KES 2005. LNCS (LNAI), vol. 3684, pp. 772–778. Springer, Heidelberg (2005)
12. Barabasi, A.L., Albert, R., Jeong, H.: Mean-field theory for scale-free random networks. Physica A 272, 173–187 (1999)
13. Dorogovtsev, S.N., Mendes, J.F.F.: Scaling behaviour of developing and decaying networks. Europhys. Lett. 52, 33–39 (2000)
14. Holme, P.: Edge overload breakdown in evolving networks. Phys. Rev. E 66 art. no.036119 (2002)

Modeling Human Education Data: From Equation-Based Modeling to Agent-Based Modeling

Yuqing Tang[1], Simon Parsons[1,2], and Elizabeth Sklar[1,2]

[1] Department of Computer Science
Graduate Center, City University of New York
365, 5th Avenue, New York, NY 10016, USA
ytang@gc.cuny.edu

[2] Department of Computer & Information Science
Brooklyn College, City University of New York
2900 Bedford Avenue, Brooklyn, NY 11210, USA
{parsons,sklar}@sci.brooklyn.cuny.edu

Abstract. Agent-based simulation is increasingly used to analyze the performance of complex systems. In this paper we describe results of our work on one specific agent-based model, showing how it can be validated against the equation-based model from which it was derived, and demonstrating the extent to which it can be used to derive additional results over and above those that the equation-based model can provide.

The agent-based model that we build deals with *human capital*, the number of years of formal schooling that an individual chooses to undertake. For verification, we show that our agent-based model makes similar predictions about the growth in inequality — that is the growth of the variance in human capital across the population — as th equation-based model from which it is derived. In addition, we show that our model can make predictions about the change in human capital from generation to generation that are beyond the equation-based model.

1 Introduction

We have been examining various sets of data related to human education. Typically, this data is collected in one of two ways: (1) very large, aggregate data sets over entire populations (like whole cities, school districts, states or provinces) or (2) very small, localized experimental samples. In both cases, the data is usually analyzed using standard statistical methods. Often, the most highly publicized statistics are the simplest, for example the mean and standard deviation of standardized test scores. These values are frequently the ones used to make policy decisions. Occasionally, analysis is performed that examines how multiple factors influence each other, such as the relationship between student-teacher ratios and test scores, dollars per student and test scores, or class size and test scores. In this example, it is difficult to analyze and understand the relationships between these four factors (student-teacher ratios, test scores, dollars per student and

L. Antunes and K. Takadama (Eds.): MABS 2006, LNAI 4442, pp. 41–56, 2007.

class size) using standard statistical techniques; and as the set of factors increases in number and complexity, the analysis becomes even more complicated. Additionally, the statistical methods do not provide a means for examining students who fall more than one standard deviation outside the mean (either above or below). For example, maybe students who perform above the mean benefit from higher student-teacher ratios and smaller class sizes, while students who perform below the mean prefer lower student-teacher ratios but also smaller class sizes. Further, the statistical methods do not provide a means for modeling the interactions between students. For example, some students may learn better in a homogeneous classroom, where all their classmates are of similar ability, while others might do better in a classroom where they can learn from social peers whose ability differs from theirs by more than a standard deviation. Our aim is to develop models that can make use of these subtle interactions, and use them to analyze the effects of education policy [11,12]. We are using agent-based modeling to do this.

Agent-based modeling can help bridge the gap between macro and micro data sets, using both interpolation and extrapolation techniques to combine information and produce comprehensive, interactive and flexible environments for experimentation. Agent-based modeling is particularly appropriate [9] for systems in which there are many different loci of control [16], something that is a particular feature of the kinds of system that we are interested in modeling. In this paper, we describe results of our work on one specific agent-based model, showing how it can be validated against the more traditional model from which it was derived, and highlighting the extent to which it can be used to derive additional results over and above those that the traditional model can provide.

2   Agent-Based Modeling

Agent-based modeling contrasts with traditional approaches to simulation, which are typically built up from sets of interrelated differential equations. Such traditional models, commonly called *equation-based models* (EBMs), have been widely applied and generate useful predictions about the behavior of populations. So why use agent-based models? There seem to be four main answers [2]: (i) agent-based models are a natural way to describe systems comprised of interacting entities; (ii) agent-based models are flexible; (iii) agent-based models capture emergent phenomena; and (iv) agent-based models provide access to a greater level of useful detail. In particular, modeling interactions between entities can be much easier in agent-based systems than in EBMs, even when one is comfortable with the concepts of partial differential equations.

This naturalness and ease of modeling helps to make agent-based models more flexible than EBMs. As Bonabeau argues [2], agent models are typically simple, and so are easy to understand and thus to change. It is usually easy to increase the size of a simulation, adding new agents to see if interesting effects are swamped by agent numbers, or taking agents away if interesting detail is obscured. It is also possible to look at the results of simulations at different

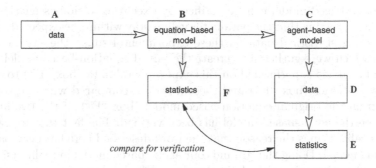

Fig. 1. Deriving an agent-based model from an equation-based model and then verifying it

levels of detail—at the level of a single agent, at the level of some specific group of agents, or at the level of all agents together. All these things are harder to manage in EBMs.

In addition to their inherent naturalness and flexibility, agent-based simulations allow one to identify *emergent phenomena.* Emergent phenomena result from the actions and interactions of individual agents, but are not directly controlled by the individuals. Indeed, they have an existence that is partly independent of those individuals—the classic example of an emergent phenomenon is a traffic jam, which, while caused by the actions of drivers moving in one direction, may travel in the opposite direction.

Emergent phenomena simply do not show up in EBMs, but knowing about them can be crucial. As an example, Greenwald and Kephart [3,6] showed that while intuition suggested that frequent price updates would allow firms to steal extra profits from their competitors, in fact it would lead to damaging price wars; and [1] showed how an agent-based model identifies effects of changes in rent-control policy that are beyond the reach of EBMs. Such findings are also echoed in ecology [4,13] where agent-based models (under the name "individual-based models") have been used for some years.

As others have described [2,9], it is possible to generate agent-based models from more traditional models. Figure 1 shows the process by which an agent-based model can be derived from an equation-based model. Presumably, the equation-based model (labeled box "B") was created after performing statistical analysis on a raw data set (box "A"). By definition, the statistical equation will be able to capture regularities in the data set and will provide a snapshot view of the environment or phenomena which it models. The agent-based model (box "C") is created by taking each of the variables in the equation-based model and the distribution of each of the variables, and then by defining agent behaviors that will produce results falling within this distribution. While single behaviors may contribute to one or two variables, the interaction between multiple behaviors can replicate the entire data set; and do so in an interactive environment that allows for experimentation.

The agent-based model can be verified by executing various scenarios iteratively, demonstrating that the parameter values stay within the expected confines and collecting statistical data on these experimental runs—the same category of values which were gathered to create the initial equation-based model. Then, statistical analysis is performed on this experimental data (box "D") to extract summary statistics (box "E") and these are then compared with the statistics derived from the original equation-based model (box "F"). If the two analyses agree, then the agent-based model has been verified. The fact that we can perform this validation is the reason that the work described here has been based on an existing model. Doing this grounds our agent-based model in reality (since the model we check it against was derived from census data), and gives us confidence that the results we obtain by predicting beyond mere validation are reasonable.

3   A Model of Human Capital

The model that we consider in this paper is drawn from a paper by Kremer [7], an article that derives a linear equation from US census data, and analyzes the aggregate behavior of the model. The original model was derived to identify the effect of the tendency for human societies to stratify by level of education—so-called *human capital*. The reason that the model is important in our wider work on modeling aspects of the education system is that it provides a mechanism, derived from data and verified against that data in [7], by which agents choose a level of education to attain. It can therefore act as a driver for the models we have previously developed [11,12].

The model from [7] gives the level of human capital $z_{i,t+1}$ of members of the $t + 1$th generation of the ith dynasty as being:

$$z_{i,t+1} = k_{t+1} + \alpha \left(\frac{z_{i,t} + z'_{i,t}}{2} \right) + \beta \left(\frac{\sum_{j=1}^{n} z_{j,t}}{n} \right) + \epsilon_{i,t+1} \qquad (1)$$

The notion of "dynasty" and "generation" that we use here are based on the definitions in [7]. Each generation of the ith dynasty has two children, one male and one female. Each is assumed to then become the spouse of an opposite sex member of another dynasty, forming a family which in turn produces one male and one female child. One family from a given generation of the ith dynasty remains in the ith dynasty, and one becomes part of another dynasty (the non-ith dynasty of the corresponding partner). Thus there is a constant number of members of each generation, and of each dynasty at each generation.

Breaking down the rather simple linear model from (1) we have:

$$k_{t+1} \qquad (2)$$

which is constant across dynasties, but may vary in time to capture exogenous trends in education—for example legislation that requires a certain number of years of additional schooling for given generations. This represents the basic level of education that every individual has to undergo ("education" and "human capital" are used more or less interchangeably in this model). Kremer [7] gives $k_{t+1} = 6.815$, and that constant value is what we adopt.

$$\alpha \left(\frac{z_{i,t} + z'_{i,t}}{2} \right) \tag{3}$$

measures the effect on the level of education of the $t + 1$th generation of the education of its parents in the t-th generation. The effect of the term is to assign to each child the average human capital of its parents, modified by α. Kremer [7] computes a baseline value of α to be approximately 0.39, based on census data. $z_{i,t}$ is the human capital of a member of the previous generation of the ith dynasty, and $z'_{i,t}$ is the spouse of $z_{i,t}$.

The next term:

$$\beta \left(\frac{\sum_{j=1}^{n} z_{j,t}}{n} \right) \tag{4}$$

does something similar to (3) but based upon the level of education of the parents' neighbors rather than the level of education of the parents themselves— these are the j in the summation, and n is the size of the neighborhood. Kremer [7] measures the baseline value of β to be around 0.15.

The final term in (1) is

$$\epsilon_{i,t+1} \tag{5}$$

which captures a specific "shock" to the human capital in a specific generation of a specific dynasty—for example the early death of a parent, requiring the children to curtail their education (though this value can be positive as well as negative). Once again we follow [7] in picking $\epsilon_{i,t+1}$ from a normal distribution with mean 0 and standard deviation 1.79.

4   Agent-Based Simulation

We have developed an agent-based model that is derived from the equation-based model given above. The agent-based model is concerned with a fixed number of agents, m in each generation, with $m/2$ dynasties, and 2 children per family. For simplicity, each family has one male child and one female child. The basic simulation loop, which executes once for each generation, has three steps given in Table 1. The result of Step 1 is fixed by (1), and Step 3 is fixed by the requirement to produce one male and one female child in each generation. Clearly the results are going to depend on the way in which Step 2 is implemented, and our model includes a number of variations.

The core of [7] is to determine, or measure, the extent to which *sorting* (that is, the tendency for people to choose both spouse and neighbors with similar levels of human capital) affects divergence in human capital between given dynasties as generations proceed. The agent-based model includes two mechanisms by which this sorting can mimic these choices: choice of spouse and choice of neighbor. For choice of spouse, there are three models that an agent can employ:

Table 1. The basic agent lifecycle

```
1. Establish level of z based on:
   (a) Parents
   (b) Neighbors of parents
2. Establish factors that influence z for children
   (a) Spouse
   (b) Neighbors
3. Generate children
```

No sorting: Agents pick partners at random.

Sorting: An agent with human capital z attempts to pick a partner with a human capital value in $[0.9z, 1.1z]$. If there are no such agents that are unmarried, the original agent picks the eligible agent with the highest human capital.

Max-matching: Agents pick as their partner the agent with the human capital value closest to their own.

In our experiments we need to be able to manipulate the correlation between married agents' human capital values. We achieve this by setting the probability p_s that a given agent uses a sorting method to choose a spouse. If $p_s = 0$, then, all agents will pick a partner at random. If $p_s = 1$, then every agent will use one of the sorting methods to pick a spouse. Figure 2(a) shows how varying p_s changes the correlation between spousal human capital. As elsewhere in this paper, the error bars indicate one standard deviation above and below the mean value. Here, and throughout the paper, the choice the agent makes with p_s is between no sorting and max-matching.

Given that the model in [7] is based upon census data, and that this has built into it a geographic notion of neighborhood, that is the kind of neighborhood used in the agent-based model[1]. Each dynasty has a unique location. Initial positions for dynasties are picked randomly, and as each generation goes through Step 2(a), the female child stays in the dynastic location, and the male child "moves" to the position of the spouse. The dynastic location is allowed to change between generations, modeling "sorting" between neighborhoods. Again we have three possibilities:

No sorting: Step 2(b) involves no operation—dynasties do not move relative to one another.

Sorting: Step 2(b) allows the families established in Step 2(a) to move to the neighborhood with the highest human capital value that has room for a dynasty to move in.

Max-matching: Dynasties move to the neighborhood that has the human capital value closest to the parental average and has room for a dynasty to move in.

---

[1] As opposed, for example, to a "social neighborhood" based on the acquaintances of the parents, which might not coincide with the geographical neighbors.

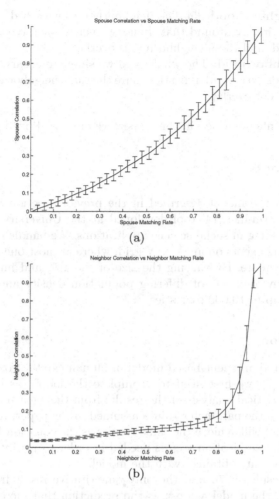

Fig. 2. The effect of p_s and q_s. (a) The relationship between p_s and the correlation between spouse agents' human capital values. (b) The relationship between q_s and the correlation between neighbor agents human capital values.

The human capital value of a neighborhood is the average value of the human capital of the agents located in that neighborhood.

Again, we control the sorting effect probabilistically, with each dynasty having a probability q_s of moving at a given generation. $q_s = 1$ means that all dynasties will move, and $q_s = 0$ means no dynasty will move. This probability, just like p_s, can be used to manipulate the correlation between the human capital of neighbors, and this relationship is plotted in Figure 2(b). For all the experiments in this paper, q_s chooses between no sorting and max-matching.

The impact of these different sorting policies will clearly depend on the nature of neighborhoods. We incorporated two types of neighborhood in the model:

1. **Moore neighborhood:** [5] The neighborhood for each dynasty is the set of locations directly around that dynasty—hence each dynasty has its own neighborhood, and these neighborhoods overlap.
2. **Fixed neighborhood:** The whole area we simulate is carved up into fixed neighborhoods, so several dynasties share the same neighborhood, and neighborhoods do not overlap.

For the experiments described in this paper, we only used fixed neighborhoods.

5   Experiments

We implemented the model described in the previous section in REPAST [10], a Java-based Swarm-like [14] tool developed at the University of Chicago for agent-based modeling in social science applications. We handled the geographic aspects by placing agents on an $N \times N$ grid, where at most one dynasty "lives" in a single grid-square. By varying the size of the grid and number of agents we can create environments of differing population density and have modeled communities of up to 10,000 dynasties.

5.1   Verification

Having constructed an agent-based model of human capital from the equation-based model in [7], we first need to "complete the loop" (as in Figure 1) by performing a statistical analysis of the results from the agent-based model, obtained when using the parameter values assumed in the paper, to show that our agent-based model will achieve the same results as the equation-based model we started with. This verification step is needed in order to justify further experimental results that are obtained with the model.

The central result of [7], and the only quantitative result from [7] that we can use to check the model against, is the prediction that increasing sorting—which the paper takes to mean increasing the correlation between the human capital values of the parent agents of a generation—will only cause an increase in inequality—which the paper takes to mean that the standard deviation of the human capital distribution grows generation by generation—when the value of α is large. [7] demonstrates this by showing the effect of changing correlation from 0.6 to 0.8 for various values of α. This result can be established though a steady-state analysis of (1), and this is done in full detail in [7]. Since the latter paper is based on census data, we take this as the experimentally determined truth against which we compare the predictions of our agent-based model.

Our agent-based model does not give us direct control of the correlations, but as we have already shown, we can, rather imprecisely, change the value of the correlations by changing the value of p_s. Running experiments on a 50×50 grid—which allows us to deal with a population that is considerably larger than the 1500 individuals analyzed in [7]—we find that our model gives good agreement with the predictions made in [7].

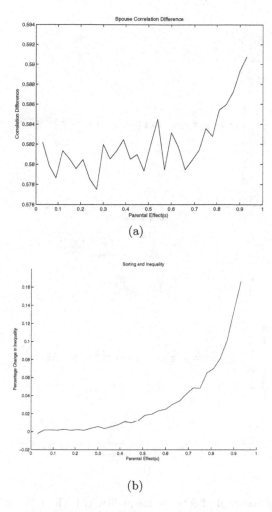

Fig. 3. Parental effect on inequality. (a) The relationship between the parental effect α and relative change in the standard deviation of the human capital distribution when sorting is increased. (b) The relationship between the parental effect α and the percentage change in inequality.

First, we plot the value of α against the change in the standard deviation of the human capital distribution (expressed as a fraction of the standard deviation) caused by switching from $p_s = 0.75$ (which is a correlation between parental capital of 0.6) to $p_s = 0.88$ (a correlation between parental capital of 0.8). This gives us Figure 3(a), which shows that the increase in standard deviation of the human capital distribution, and hence inequality, that is caused by increased sorting doesn't start to grow until α exceeds 0.8. We can also plot the effects in terms of the percentage change in inequality (as defined in [7]) rather than the

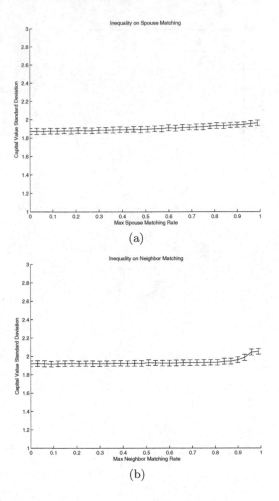

Fig. 4. Other than parental effects on inequality. (a) The relationship between p_s, the probability of agents picking partners based on capital value, and the percentage change in inequality. (b) The relationship between q_s, the probability of agents picking location based on capital value, and the percentage change in inequality.

increase in standard deviation of the human capital distribution. For $p_s = 0.88$, we get the relationship between α and inequality plotted in Figure 3(b).

To check that this change in inequality was really due to the change in α, and not due to some other parameter in the model, we examined how inequality changes when we vary such parameters. Figures 4 and 5, for example, show that for α held at 0.39 and β held at 0.15, there is no significant change in inequality if we change p_s, q_s and population density.

Note that the changes in inequality that we observe due to changes in α hinge on the value of $\epsilon_{i,t+1}$, the term in (1) that does not depend on the capital values of parents or neighbors. If we run our model with $\epsilon_{i,t+1}$ set to zero for

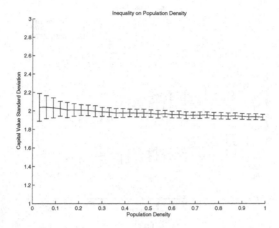

Fig. 5. Other than parental effects o inequality. The relationship between population density and the percentage change in inequality.

all dynasties and all generations, then inequality does not grow. Indeed, the standard deviation of the capital distribution falls over time until all agents have the mean value. This "seeding" effect of $\epsilon_{i,t+1}$ is another prediction that can be made from the analysis of (1).

Together these results—where statistics that can be extracted from the original, equation-based model match against the predictions made by the agent-based model—suggest that the agent-based model we have constructed adequately replicates the essence of the model it was designed to capture.

5.2   Identifying New Features

As we discussed above, one of the advantages that agent-based models have over equation-based models is that one can examine the model in greater detail. Whereas equation-based models can only really be studied in terms of broad statistical features—such as the results from [7] examined above—we can probe agent-based models in considerable detail, discovering what happens to individuals as well as to classes of individual. We have carried out such an investigation into the human capital model.

The main result from [7], replicated by our agent-based model, is that *on average* inequality in terms of human capital grows over generations. The widening standard deviation of the human capital distribution suggests that rich dynasties get richer and poor dynasties get poorer. However true this may be at a population level, it is interesting to ask whether it is true for all (or even most) individual dynasties, or whether there is some mobility between dynasties with different levels of human capital. It turns out that such mobility exists.

We divided our dynasties up into three "classes"—the quotes reminding us that this terminology, while convenient, conflates human capital, basically years

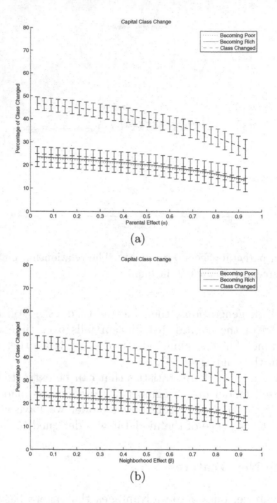

Fig. 6. Parental effect on "class". (a) The relationship between the percentage of dynasties that change "class" and α. (b) The relationship between the percentage of dynasties that change "class" and β.

of formal schooling, with monetary capital and social status. We call dynasties that fall within one standard deviation above or below the average human capital for the population *middle class*, we call those more than one standard deviation below average *poor*, and those more than one standard deviation above average *rich*. We then examined whether dynasties moved between classes.

The results are given in Figures 6(a) and 6(b), which show the way that the number of dynasties that are mobile in this sense changes for two different values of α and β, respectively. When α changes, β is held constant and vice-versa. These graphs show the total percentage of dynasties that move, and the percentage that become richer and poorer. They show that, no matter what the value of α and β, there is some mobility (at least 25% of the population, and

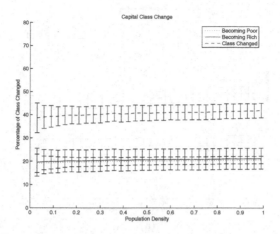

Fig. 7. Other than parental effect on "class". The relationship between the percentage of dynasties that change "class" and population density.

as much as 45% of the population changes class). Furthermore this change is symmetrical.

Note that this effect is separate from the growing inequality—because "middle class" is always defined in terms of the *current* standard deviation, if inequality was the only effect, the percentage of dynasties changing class would be lower than the figure we find. What we see here is the result of mixing. That is, individuals are choosing partners or neighbors who are sufficiently far above or below them in human capital terms so that their offspring move from one class to another.

We can follow up this investigation with a subsidiary one, checking to see whether additional factors have an effect on the class mobility of dynasties. One of the factors that we can imagine having an impact on the results we obtain in the model is the *density* of the agent population. In terms of the model, population density relates to the number of agents that are placed on the grid. Since the neighbor effect is based upon a geographic notion of neighborhood, and since neighbors certainly have an effect on class mobility — for example as shown in Figure 6 (b) — then one might imagine that changing the density of the population might have some effect on class mobility as well. However, this is not the case. As Figure 7 shows, population density has no systematic effect on class mobility. Carrying out similar investigations for the effects of p_s and q_s, Figures 8(a) and 8(b) respectively, again show no systematic effect on class mobility.

6   Summary

This paper set out to construct an agent-based model from a traditional, equation-based model, and to show that (i) this model could be verified against

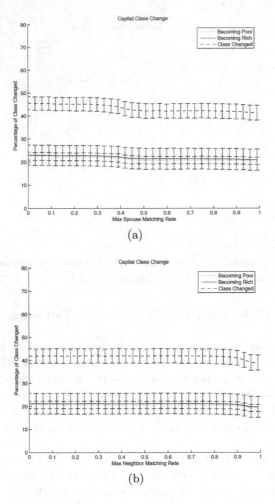

Fig. 8. Other than parental effect on "class". The relationship between the percentage of dynasties that change "class" and (a) p_s, the probability that a given agent chooses a partner by human capital value, (b) q_s, the probability that a given dynasty chooses its location by human capital value.

the predictions make by the equation-based model; and (ii) this model could identify new predictions that could not be obtained directly from the equation-based model. Both these aims have been achieved.

This work fits into our wider effort to model aspects of the education system [11,12], with the overall aim of being able to establish the impact of changes in education policy (rather as [1] does for the case of rent control). As described in [12], we have developed a number of models, including a model of interactions in classrooms [11]—which, for example, shows the effects of different pedagogical techniques to overcome absenteeism—and a model of school districts—which, for example, shows the effect of policies like "No child left behind". Our current work is to tie these models together, and, more ambitiously, to tie them into a comprehensive simulation of the way that education fits into the economy. This latter can be done, for example, by using the model in [8], a model that relates education and student ability with their lifetime productivity, and our interim results can be found in [15].

Acknowledgments. This work was partially supported by funding from NSF #REC-02-19347. Many thanks to the anonymous referees for their helpful comments.

References

1. Bernard, R.N.: Using adaptive agent-based simulation models to assist planners in policy development: The case of rent control. Working Paper 99-07-052, Sante Fe Institute (1999)
2. Bonabeau, E.: Agent-based modelling: Methods and techniques for simulating human systems. Proceedings of the National Academy of Science 99(3), 7280–7287 (2002)
3. Greenwald, A., Kephart, J.: Shopbots and pricebots. In: Proceedings of the Sixteenth International Joint Conference on Artificial Intelligence, pp. 506–511, Stockholm, Sweden (August 1999)
4. Grimm, V.: Ten years of individual-based modeling in ecology: what have we learned and what could we learn in the future? Ecological Modeling 129–148 (1999)
5. Hegselmann, R.: Cellular automata in the social sciences: Persepectives, restrictions and artefacts. In: Hegselmann, R., Mueller, U., Troitzsch, K.G. (eds.) Modelling and Simulation in the Social Sciences From the Philosophy of Science Point of View, ch. 12, Kluwer Academic Publishers, Dordrecht (1996)
6. Kephart, J., Greenwald, A.: Shopbot economics. Autonomous Agents and Multi-Agent Systems 5(3), 255–287 (2002)
7. Kremer, M.: How much does sorting increase inequality? The Quarterly Journal of Economics 112(1), 115–139 (1997)
8. Laitner, J.: Earnings within educational groups and overall productivity growth. The Journal of Political Economy 108(4), 807–832 (2000)
9. van Dyke Parunak, H., Savit, R., Riolo, R.L.: Agent-based modeling vs. equation-based modeling: A case study and users' guide. In: Sichman, J.S., Conte, R., Gilbert, N. (eds.) Multi-Agent Systems and Agent-Based Simulation. LNCS (LNAI), vol. 1534, pp. 10–25. Springer, Heidelberg (1998)
10. http://repast.sourceforge.net
11. Sklar, E., Davies, M.: Multiagent Simulation of Learning Environments. In: Proceedings of the Fourth International Conference on Autonomous Agents and MultiAgent Systems (AAMAS-2005), pp. 953–959 (2005)
12. Sklar, E., Davies, M., Co, M.S.T.: SimEd: Simulating Education as a MultiAgent System. In: Proceedings of the Third International Conference on Autonomous Agents and MultiAgent Systems (AAMAS-2004), pp. 998–1005 (2004)
13. Sole, R.V., Gamarra, J.G.P., Ginovart, M., Lopez, D.: Controlling chaos in ecology: From deterministic to individual-based models. Bulletin of Mathematical Biology 61, 1187–1207 (1999)

14. http://www.swarm.org/
15. Tang, Y., Parsons, S., Sklar, E.: An Agent-based Model that Relates Investment in Education to Economic Prosperity. In: Proceedings of the Sixth International Conference on Autonomous Agents and MultiAgent Systems (AAMAS-2007) (2005)
16. Wooldridge, M., Jennings, N.R., Kinny, D.: The gaia methodology for agent-oriented analysis and design. Autonomous Agents and Multi-Agent Systems 3(3), 285–312 (2000)

Contrasting a System Dynamics Model and an Agent-Based Model of Food Web Evolution

Emma Norling

Centre for Policy Modelling
Manchester Metropolitan University
norling@acm.org

Abstract. An agent-based model of food web evolution is presented and contrasted with a particular system dynamics model. Both models examine the effects of speciation and species invasion of food webs, but the agent-based approach focuses on the interactions between individuals in the food web, whereas the system dynamics approach focuses on the overall system dynamics. The system dynamics model is an abstract model of species co-evolution that shows similar characteristics to many natural food webs. The agent-based model attempts to model a similarly abstract food web (in which species are characterised by abstract features that determine how they will fare against any other species). The ultimate aim of this exercise is to explore the many of the assumptions inherent in the system dynamics model; the current challenge is to simply replicate the system dynamics results using agent-based modelling. Preliminary studies have revealed some underlying assumptions in the system dynamics model, as well as some intrinsic difficulties in linking the two different approaches. The paper discusses the key difficulties in linking these different types of models, and presents some discussion of the limits and benefits benefits that each approach may bring to the analysis of the problem.

1 Introduction

Traditional models of predator-prey relationships, such as the Lotka-Volterra equations, focus narrowly on single predator-single prey relations. Natural ecosystems however typically involve a large number of species: one hundred and eighty-two were identified in what is widely regarded as the most comprehensive study to date: that of Little Rock Lake, Wisconsin [1]. In these large food webs, a species may be basal, in which case it 'feeds' solely from the environment, but may have multiple species preying upon it; it may be a top species, having no predators but possibly several species upon which it preys; or it may be intermediate, in which case it would have one or more each of predator *and* prey species. Figure 1 illustrates an example simplified food web of this type. These different possibilities for interaction give rise to a dynamic *network* as well as population, where the dynamics of the population affects the structure of the network and vice versa. Several models of network structure for these large food

L. Antunes and K. Takadama (Eds.): MABS 2006, LNAI 4442, pp. 57–68, 2007.
© Springer-Verlag Berlin Heidelberg 2007

webs have been proposed, as summarised by Dunne [2, Box 1], but these models have been *static* structures, reflecting the network at a given point in time, but not responding to any changes that might arise due to the population dynamics. The system dynamics model introduced by Caldarelli et al. [3] and refined further in [4,5,6,7], henceforth referred to as Model A, goes one step further than most models in that it attempts to capture both population and network dynamics. Furthermore, it allows the introduction of new species to the web, which can be seen either as evolved species (small variation on existing species within the web) or invading species (completely new species, arriving for example on ocean currents, or – more commonly – introduced by man).

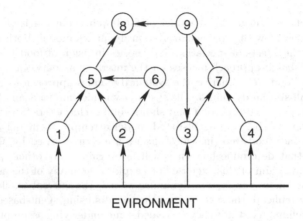

Fig. 1. An illustrative example of a food web. Species 1, 2, 3 and 4 are basal species, 5, 6, 7 and 9 are intermediate species, and 8 is the sole top species.

As noted by Parunak et al., agent-based models compete with "equation-based" (system dynamics) models in many domains [8]; the domain of predator-prey relations is no exception. (In truth, the two approaches should not be seen as competing, but complementary. The work described here is one example of a collaboration that is attempting to bridge the gap between the two approaches, and explore their relative strengths and weaknesses.) Two-species predator-prey relationships are commonly used as introductory assignments for agent-based modelling (often presented as 'wolves and sheep,' or 'foxes and rabbits'), and are also often explored in the context of multi-agent learning (for example, Grefenstette's work[9]). However as with the more traditional system dynamics approaches, agent-based models of food webs rarely consider more than a handful of species, and although they do allow for dynamic network structures, they do not consider the introduction of new species to the web. While contrasting agent-based and system dynamics models of predator-prey relations, Wilson's work should be noted [10], which resolved discrepancies between an individual-based model (of the cellular automata variety) and "reaction-dispersal" (that is, system dynamics) models of a single prey, single predator environment. This paper describes a similar attempt to create an agent-based model of (multi-species) food web dynamics that relates directly to a particular system dynamics model. The ultimate aim of the agent-based model is to explore the effects of the assumptions of heterogeneity (both between species and within species) that are enforced by the system dynamics model.

Agent-based modelling provides an alternate means for exploring the implications of the assumptions encoded in the equations of Model A. Some of these assumptions have been explicitly stated by the authors of that model; others have become apparent when decisions have had to be made during the construction of the agent-based models. A third set of assumptions have become apparent when considering the discrepancies between the two models, and these are particularly the subject of ongoing investigations. The next section of this paper will introduce the equations that govern the dynamics of Model A, which will be followed by a description of the agent-based model. Section 4 looks at the results of the models, before a discussion in Sect. 5 of some of the possible reasons for the differences that appear and areas of ongoing investigation.

2   The System Dynamics Model

The description of the systems dynamics model that is presented here is an abbreviated version of that given in [3]. As mentioned previously, this model has been refined further in later work, but as the 1998 publication presents the most simple form, this was selected for the initial study. The model is based upon traditional models of predator-prey dynamics, but extended to deal with multi-way interactions between species – for full details, readers should refer to the original work.

The model has two distinct phases: the population dynamics for a particular set of species in a food web, and the introduction of a new or mutated species to the food web. The species that are used in the model do not correspond to those in any particular natural ecosystem, but are stylised species, each defined by a set of morphological or behavioural features. These features are themselves abstract – represented by numerical values whose only purpose are to generate the scores which determine what eats what as described below – but can be conceptualised as things such as 'sharp teeth' or 'fast runner;' features which could potentially give the species an edge over other species.

The model has a pool of K of these possible features, and each species is assigned a subset of L of these features. In the majority of experiments using this model, K was set to 500 and L to 10. A $K \times K$ matrix of scores is constructed, where the value $m_{\alpha\beta}$ at any position in the matrix describes how 'useful' feature α is against feature β. The matrix is constructed at the start of a simulation run, is antisymmetric (that is $m_{\alpha\beta} = -m_{\beta\alpha}$), has diagonal set to 0 (so any feature has no benefit (or disadvantage) when used against the same feature) and consists of random Gaussian values with mean zero and unit variance.

The score of one species i against another species j is then defined as

$$S_{ij} = \max\left\{0, \frac{1}{L}\sum_{\alpha \in i}\sum_{\beta \in j} m_{\alpha\beta}\right\} \tag{1}$$

where α runs over all the features of species i and β runs over all the features of species j. A positive score S_{ij} indicates that species i is adapted from predation on species j. At the start of a run, the world is assigned a set of L features, and this determines which species can be basal. Species with a positive score against the world are adapted to feed directly from its resources, which are input at a constant rate R and distributed amongst species as a function of their score, while those with a zero score against the world must prey upon other species in order to survive.

At the start of a run the population is seeded with a single individual of a random species (that is, with a random selection of K features from L). The population of that species grows according to the equations described below until a new 'evolutionary time step' is reached. This occurs at the first of either 1) the entire population drops to zero, 2) the entire population stabilises (there may be fluctuations, but these are cyclical), or 3) a set maximum number of time steps elapses without population stabilisation. At this point, a single individual in the existing population is removed, a single feature of the species of that individual is replaced by another, and a single individual of that new species is put back into the population. This species may become extinct, may cause other extinctions, or the food web may simply adapt to accommodate it. This process continues over time, allowing the food web to grow and evolve.

The short-term population dynamics of a species is given in terms of the population sizes of the other species in the ecosystem

$$N(n, t+1) = \gamma_{n,0}R + \sum_{n'}\gamma_{n,n'}\lambda N(n', t) + \gamma_{n,n}\lambda N(n, t) \tag{2}$$

where $N(n,t)$ is the number of resources (assumed to be equal to the number of individuals) of species n and λ is the fraction of the resources of the prey that is converted into resources of the predator (the ecological efficiency). $\gamma_{n,n'}$ is the fraction of resources of species n' that is obtained by species n, and is used to capture the idea that the most efficient predator of a given species will be the most successful at gaining resources from that species; other predators will gain relatively little. To achieve this, the *main predator* of species n' is defined as the one with the best score against n':

$$S_{n'}^{M} = \max\{S_{n,n'}\} \tag{3}$$

where n is a predator of n'. The predators of n' will obtain a share of the available resources according to

$$F_{n,n'} = \max\left\{0, \left(1 - \frac{S_{n'}^{M} - S_{n,n'}}{\delta}\right)\right\} \tag{4}$$

where δ is a parameter of the model that determines the strength of competition between species – the smaller δ, the stronger the competition. $\gamma_{n,n'}$ is then defined as:

$$\gamma_{n,n'} = \frac{F_{n,n'}}{\sum_m F_{m,n'}} \tag{5}$$

$\gamma_{n,n}$ is however a special case, being equal to -1 if n has at least one predator species, or 0 otherwise.

2.1 Explicit Assumptions in this Model

A key assumption in the model is that the constants (δ and λ) and equations for all species are equal. This was a deliberate decision of the authors, in part for simplicity but also because they wanted flexibility for species to take any position in the food web and for that position to change as the web evolved.

The value of the ecological efficiency was kept constant for the majority of the experiments, at $\lambda = 0.1$. The value of δ, the competition parameter, was selected by observing that all scores $S_{n,n'}$ are of the order 1, and that when a single feature is changed, the score changes by an amount of the order of $1/L$. Thus δ should be roughly this size. (If $\delta \gg 1/L$, even very uncompetitive species will be allocated some resources, whereas as $\delta \to 0$, only the main predator will gain resources.) For the experiments presented in [3], values of δ from 0.05 to 0.2 were used. R, the total number of resources in the environment, was also varied over the runs, from 10^3 to 10^6.

As stated previously, the model assumes that $N(n,t)$ represents both the number of resources in total of species n and also the number of individuals of species n. This turns out to be one of the key difficulties in reconciling the system dynamics model and the agent-based model, as will be discussed in Sect. 5.

The resource distribution equation, used to ensure that the strongest predators gained the majority of a species' resources, was noted by the authors of this model to have been too simplistic: the food webs that were evolved using this equation developed into impervious webs that could never be invaded by new species – something that is not seen in nature. Later refinements of the model (introduced in [4]) used a more sophisticated means of resource distribution, introducing further parameters and assumptions. While agent-based analogues of these refined equations have also been explored, they did not produce significantly different results to those presented here, so these remaining assumptions are ignored here.

3 The Agent-Based Model

One of the aims when constructing the agent-based model was to capture the system dynamics model as closely as possible. However in an agent-based simulation the system-level behaviour should emerge from the interactions of individual agents, whereas the system dynamics approach attempts to explicitly encode the system-level behaviour. Thus the aim here was not to try to directly translate the equations from Model A into behaviours for the agents in these models, but rather to encode the motivations behind the equations. The match between the model presented here and Model A is not yet fully successful, although some likely causes for this have been identified, as will be discussed in Sect. 5, and are being investigated as part of the ongoing work on this project.

In the agent-based model, R, the number of resources added per time step, is used as it is in the system dynamics model. Similarly, λ, the ecological efficiency, is used to determine the number of resources an agent receives from a 'kill'. δ is also used in the agent-based model, but whereas in Model A this is used to determine the fraction of resources obtained from a species, in Model B it is used to 'truncate' the score of one agent against another, in that an agent of species i can only eat an agent of species j if $S_j^M - S_{i,j} < \delta$.

Model B uses a $K \times K$ matrix of feature scores in the same way as Model A, with species being defined by their particular set of L features. This matrix is also used to generate species scores in the same manner as in Model A, using (1).

A single time step in the Model B consists of the following sequence of events:

1. If the population is 0, a new individual is created, with a random new species. (This happens both at the start of the simulation and also if all species become extinct.)
2. If this is the start of a new evolutionary time step (that is, current population is stable or a fixed number of steps have elapsed), do a mutation. This involves selecting an individual and randomly modifying a single one of its L features.
3. The agents in the population are shuffled, then for each agent
   (a) The agent randomly selects a prey, or the world, upon which it will feed, with weighting of prey versus world corresponding to the total population versus number of world resources.
   (b) If the agent can feed upon its prey (or the world as the case may be), the prey (or a fraction of the world's resources) is consumed, with the agent receiving a proportion, λ of the prey's resources.
   (c) If the agent received enough resources while feeding (that is, its total resources > 1), it will reproduce. Offspring are given the agent's excess (over 1) resources; the agent is left with 1 resource in its stores.
   (d) The agent's age (which as yet is unused) is incremented.
4. After each agent has been stepped in this manner, any agents that were born during this process are added to the main population.
5. Any agents which died (due to being killed by a predator) are removed from the population.

This is the most simple form of the model, forming a starting point for further exploration.

4 Preliminary Results

Before considering the model results, a few comments on the measures of comparison. Firstly, as noted by many ecologists (see [11]), there are considerable difficulties in getting reliable data on real food webs. One of the difficulties is the issue of defining 'an ecosystem.' Typically, an ecosystem is said to encompass some geographic region such as a lake, a desert or an island, but there will always be species within the food web of such an ecosystem that do not adhere to these geographic boundaries, and thus may feed upon (or be preyed upon by) species that are outside the considered ecosystem. Furthermore there are tremendous difficulties in gathering data on food webs even for limited geographic domains. Nevertheless the authors of Model A have used data from a number of experimentally studied food webs (see [3, Tab. 3]) for comparison against their own. The measures of interest are: number of species, number of links, links per species, average level (where the level is defined by the shortest number of links to environmental resources), maximum level, percentage of basal, intermediate and top species, percentage of links between different species types (i.e. TB, IB, II, TI), and ratio of prey to predators.

Caldarelli et al compare their model against a range of real world data [3]. In that analysis, the authors report plausible food webs emerging after 250,000 speciation steps (where a 'step' is when a new species is introduced) for values of R in the range of 10^3–10^4, although it is noted that there is an inverse relationship between λ and R – that is, if R is increased while λ is decreased, the structure of the resulting food web has the same basic properties.

One of the downsides of the agent-based approach is the computational complexity of the system – the more individuals that there are, the longer it will take to run. In Model B, the time taken for similar size runs seems comparable to that of Model A, however as the complexity of each individual's calculations increases, agent-based models slow down. While the agent-based model gives the possibility for exploring heterogeneity, this will have a performance cost, but it is hoped that it will be possible to limit this to a linear increase in time taken.

The early stages of Model B runs show some promise, with multiple species managing to co-exist. Figure 2 shows the time series of populations on two different runs. The first run is one in which the environment is relatively benign (that is, many species are able to feed upon the environment). The second has a more harsh environment, in which most species cannot feed directly from the environment – they must prey upon the few species that can. The first case particularly illustrates some characteristic behaviour of population change. Many new species never find a niche in the existing food web, but some do, sometimes causing the extinction of other species as a result. The benign environment particularly demonstrates how the introduction of a new species can change the balance of a population. Even when it exists only in small numbers, it can cause the population of other species to vary significantly, such as seen at around time step 12,500, when species 16 is introduced, allowing the population of species 8 to increase.

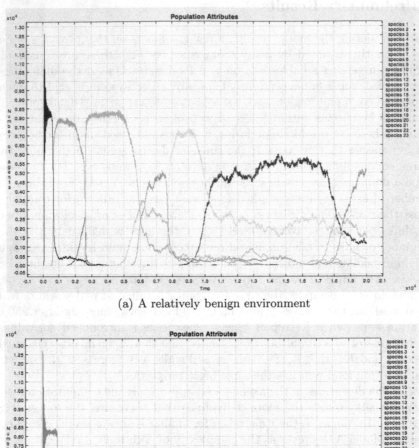

(a) A relatively benign environment

(b) A harsh environment

Fig. 2. Population dynamics for two different runs of Model B

Figure 3 shows snapshots of the food webs of the same two runs at $t = 20000$. The numbers on each node represent the unique identifier of the species and, in parentheses, the number of individuals of that species. Rectangular species are those getting at least some of their resources directly from the environment; those with solid colours are feeding off at least one other species. In the benign environment, three basal species co-exist with one that feeds both on the environment and one of the other basal species. It should be noted that this is only at a particular point in time: at the next time step, they may all feed only from the environment, or other species may be eaten. In the harsh environment, a predator-prey relationship has evolved. As can be seen from Fig. 2, this is just one in a series of such relationships, with previous predators being driven out by the new one. (There are also many species that have not had any impact on the food web.)

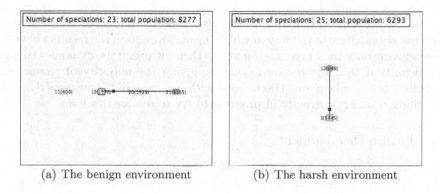

(a) The benign environment   (b) The harsh environment

Fig. 3. The food web structure for the same two runs at $t = 20000$

The problem with Model B is that complex food webs (containing more than two levels) do not arise, even for runs over extended periods. Reasons for this are discussed in the next section. This issue must be resolved before the exploration of heterogeneity in species and/or agents is undertaken.

5 Discussion

Model B is deliberately an extremely simplistic agent-based model of a food web. In particular, the decision to use a non-spatial representation for agents was driven by the fact that Model A does not have a spatial representation. However in an agent-based approach it does not make sense to have a global view of the system, and so agents should not use global knowledge in selecting their prey. The problem is that the random sampling used in Model B can give an individual agent a distorted picture of the population, and this leads to over-predation of species, and a lack of stratification of the food web.

Nevertheless, Model A does not include any notion of a spatial representation, yet it manages to produce a realistically-structured food web. Furthermore, experiments that introduced a form of spatial representation to Model B did not produce significantly different food webs to those produced by Model B. This slavish emulation of what might be seen as a fault of Model A might seem counter-productive, but one of the purposes of this research is to draw a bridge between the two approaches. The aim is to first replicate the behaviour of Model A, and then examine how variations (such as spatial distribution or heterogeniety) impact upon this behaviour.

What appears to be of far greater importance is the discretisation that is enforced by the agent-based model. In Model A, there is no distinction between the number of resources in a species and the number of individuals in a species. In Model B, each agent represents an individual of a particular species – thus a discrete number of individuals – but each agent has a continuous variable representing its resources. Because each agent gains only 10% of the resources of its prey, the number of resources at any given time step will almost certainly *not* be equal to the number of individuals. This is reflected in the fact that the model is *extremely* sensitive to the way in which agents reproduce: the results above had agents giving only their excess resources to their offspring; the dynamics changed significantly if this was reversed (that is, giving the majority of resources to offspring) or shared equally. Discussions with members of the systems dynamics modelling team are currently in progress to try to resolve this issue.

5.1 Future Development

One enhancement that has been considered is to treat the system as closed, so that rather than resources being added to the system at each time step, the system is initialised with a certain number of resources and these must be maintained in one form or another within the system. Thus environmental resources would be consumed by first level individuals, which would in turn be consumed by individuals of higher level species, with the excess (since the predator gets only a fraction of the prey's resources) being returned to the environment. Preliminary experiments have shown that this variation has little impact on the system behaviour, nevertheless it is something that many ecologists consider to be important, and will be explored further when the differences between the models have been resolved.

Another variation is to allow agents to store resources, giving them a buffer which would allow them to survive in the event of a scarcity of prey. Tied in with this would be the idea that agents require some resources simply to survive, which would be consumed at each time step whether or not they found food. In the current model, an agent can survive until it reaches old age in the absence of prey, even if it does not harvest any resources. This seems unreasonable, but the preliminary experiments which have added this concept of subsistence resources and a buffer have not produced markedly different outcomes.

However perhaps the most important potential of the agent-based system is the possibility of heterogeneous behaviour. To date this concept has not been explored, but it would seem reasonable that different species could and should have different parameters to represent a range of characteristics. For example, different species could have different average life spans, ecological efficiencies, subsistence levels and, if spatial representation is added, movement abilities.

These variations in parameters could be linked to the feature set of the species so that, for example, an agent that scored particularly well against a range of species might have a higher subsistence level than average (representing a larger body mass or higher metabolism perhaps). Beyond this variation in parameters, different species might even have different behaviours (for example, different foraging strategies).

6 Conclusions

The agent-based model that has been presented here represents the first steps in replicating and extending the systems dynamics approach to food web modelling of Caldarelli et al. While there are still some issues to be resolved, the preliminary model shows a certain level of correspondence to the system dynamics model, and the key issue in relating the two – that of discrete versus continuous measures – has been identified. Ongoing work is aimed as resolving this issue in order to progress to the next stage of studies.

The agent-based model will allow the exploration of a range of variations that would be difficult (if not impossible) to encode in the system dynamics model. The system dynamics model has provided some results that are of interest to ecologists (for example, it appears to indicate that catastrophic extinctions are *extremely* unlikely); agent-based modelling provides a tool for further exploration of these results, and possibly an understanding at the micro level of why they are so. Furthermore, the agent-based models provide the opportunity to examine the impact of the assumptions that are encoded in the system dynamics model.

Acknowledgements

The work in this paper has been undertaken as part of the "NANIA" project, funded by the EPSRC "Novel computation, coping with complexity" initiative. Many people from within that project and at the Centre for Policy Modelling have contributed to discussions that fed into this work, most notably Bruce Edmonds (who wrote an earlier, loosely-related agent-based simulation of food web evolution), Alan McKane (the common co-author of papers on the system dynamics model), and Craig Powell. The feedback of reviewers for and participants at the MABS 2006 workshop also provided useful insights for the ongoing work.

References

1. Martinez, N.D.: Artifacts or attributes? Effects of resolution on the Little Rock lake food web. Ecological Monographs 61(4), 367–392 (1991)
2. Dunne, J.A.: The network structure of food webs. In: Pascual, M., Dunne, J.A. (eds.) Ecological Networks: Linking Structure to Dynamics in Food Webs, pp. 27–86. Oxford University Press, Oxford (2005)
3. Caldarelli, G., Higgs, P.G., McKane, A.J.: Modelling coevolution in multispecies communities. Journal of Theoretical Biology 193, 345–358 (1998)

4. Drossel, B., Higgs, P.G., McKane, A.J.: The influence of predator-prey population dynamics on the long-term evolution of food web structure. Journal of Theoretical Biology 208, 91–107 (2001)
5. Drossel, B., McKane, A.J., Quince, C.: The impact of nonlinear functional responses on the long-term evolution of food web structure. Journal of Theoretical Biology (229), 539–548 (2004)
6. Quince, C., Higgs, P.G., McKane, A.J.: Deleting species from model food webs. Oikos (110), 283–296 (1995)
7. Quince, C., Higgs, P.G., McKane, A.J.: Topological structure and interaction strengths in model food webs. Ecological Modelling (187), 389–412 (2005)
8. Parunak, H.V.D., Savit, R., Riolo, R.L.: Agent-based modeling vs. equation-based modeling: A case study and users' guide. In: Sichman, J.S., Conte, R., Gilbert, N. (eds.) Multi-Agent Systems and Agent-Based Simulation. LNCS (LNAI), vol. 1534, pp. 10–25. Springer, Heidelberg (1998)
9. Grefenstette, J.J.: The evolution of strategies for multi-agent environments. Adaptive Behavior 1, 65–89 (1992)
10. Wilson, W.G.: Resolving discrepancies between deterministic population models and individual-based simulations. The American Naturalist 151(2) (1998)
11. Cohen, J.E., Beaver, R.A., Cousins, S.H., DeAngelis, D.L., Goldwasser, L., Heong, K.L., Holt, R.D., Kohn, A.J., Lawton, J.H., Martinez, N., O'Malley, R., Page, L.M., Patten, B.C., Pimm, S.L., Polis, G.A., Rejmanek, M., Schoener, T.W., Schoenly, K., Sprules, W.G., Teal, J.M., Ulanowicz, R.E., Warren, P.H., Wilbur, H.M., Yodzis, P.: Improving food webs. Ecology 74(1), 252–258 (1993)

Roost Size for Multilevel Selection of Altruism Among Vampire Bats

Mario Paolucci and Rosaria Conte

ISTC-CNR, Via San Martino della Battaglia 44, 00185 Roma, Italy
mario.paolucci@istc.cnr.it
http://www.istc.cnr.it/labss/

Abstract. Abstract. In this paper we analyse the roosting effect among artificial vampires as a way to preserve altruism from cheaters exploitation. We simulate the formation and maintenance of new social structures (roosts) from initial populations as a consequence of both demographic growth and social organisation. Food-sharing among vampire bats (Desmodus Rotundus) is a well-known form of altruism, necessary for the survival of this species, supported by wide ethological evidence. By means of simulation, we study the performance of the system under varying mutation rate (giving rise to cheaters that exploit the altruistic mechanism) and roost size. Results show that the roosting effect can cope with sensible mutation levels. Moreover, the most robust size of roosts indicated by our simulations is shown to be comparable with the size actually found in nature.

1 The Sociobiological Debate

According to Group Selection Theory (GST), biological evolution can operate also on groups, and not only on individual organisms. Aggregates are considered so that the fitness value for individuals become the sum of an individual contribution and of a group contribution; in the interesting cases in which these parts are in contrast, it is the context to decide the one to prevail. Popular until the mid-sixties [16], GST underwent severe critiques from among sociobiologists [13]. Inspired by the principle of inclusive fitness, which looked at individuals as vehicles for genetic reproduction, some theorists [9] explained non-kin altruism in terms of reciprocity, i.e. the probability of donors being reciprocated when needy, rejecting any solution in terms of group. Later, GST has been re-proposed [15], in a variant defined as multilevel selection theory. While standard evolution takes place at individual level, groups defined by a common set of characteristics may compete on the same evolutionary stage, and act as units of selection. A given habit or trait characterising one group may increase its fitness and therefore its preservation.

2 Altruism and the *Roosting Effect*

In nature, examples of altruism abound [2]. Inter-specific mutualism was documented among lycaenid butterfly larvae and ants [6]. Between mammals the

L. Antunes and K. Takadama (Eds.): MABS 2006, LNAI 4442, pp. 69–79, 2007.
© Springer-Verlag Berlin Heidelberg 2007

most famous example of pro-social behaviour is blood-sharing in vampire bats [10],[12], a behaviour in favour of starving, unlucky hunters. Ethological observations and even experiments [11] are often interpreted as supporting the inclusive fitness explanation, based on the evidence that animals - in this case, vampire bats - give help to recognised individuals (possibly once-donors, or at least potential helpers).

However, this explanation is not fully satisfactory. How to tell the difference between individual vs. in-group recognition, by means of natural experiments, if a group is small enough as to allow individuals to meet all others at least once? The species studied by Wilkinson lives in Central America, in small groups (a few dozen individuals) inhabiting the cavity of trees. These basic units are called roosts. As all tree-roosting bats, vampires live in multiple roosts located on different trees in a highly dynamic social environment, moving in subgroups between several roosts on a regular basis, even every few days. Their diet consists of ingesting each day an amount of fresh blood, which they suck from herbivores. However, each night about 7% of the adults find no prey to parasite. In these occasions, they can survive thanks to luckier fellows regurgitating for them a portion of the food ingested. Wilkinson, who studied this species in its natural settings, states that such behaviour depends equally and independently of relatedness and an index of opportunity for reciprocation. Moreover, from the ethological literature we know that:

1. relatedness within the roost is quite low (around .11);
2. females live in groups with all their children (all-mothering) and only the alpha male has access to this group. Bachelors stay in a group of their own.
3. a vampire bat will share food only if it has spent at least 60% of its time with the recipient.

In a previous simulative work [3],[8], we argued that roosting can blindly shelter altruists. In the simulations, even a small percentage of non-helping individuals can bring to extinction a population composed by a single group. But the natural division of the population into small units (roosts), apparently due to environmental constraints (size of the tree cavities), allows for local variation in the rate of non-altruists. As a consequence, a subset of the roosts, those that are inhabited by a large majority of altruists, will survive the others, reproduce and soon colonise the population. We defined this phenomenon as roosting effect. In the case of vampire bats, the simulations showed that the roosting effect might have been sufficient to eliminate an initial (even quite large) rate of cheaters. However, roosting in nature does not seem such a black-and-white phenomenon as was assumed in our previous simulations. In general, bats tend to be loyal to small defined areas and to given individuals within these areas, but they also display what has been named a fission-fusion [14] model of social behaviour: on a given night, the colony would consist of multiple roosting subgroups, spread among different trees within the roosting area. Indeed, according to [14], tree-roosting bats are known to switch roosts every few days, but the same authors admit that the motivation underlying roost-switching is not well understood. Subgroups may break apart and mix as they move to different trees within the roosting area. How to combine the defence of altruism with a more dynamic social organisation?

3 The Simulation

In the study of the evolutionary bases of social behaviour, analytical reasoning and ethological findings have been found insufficient: the former cannot provide generative [4] and out-of-equilibrium explanations of phenomena observed among heterogeneous entities [1]; the latter instead do not easily allow for controlling and manipulating experimental variables. An innovative turn was impressed with a systematic and extensive application of multi agent-based modelling and simulation (MABS), that has more in common, methodologically, with the natural sciences and engineering disciplines than with deductive logics or mathematics. Indeed, it is closer to experimental than formal science [5]. Simulation is also considered as a new tool that can contribute to cope with the well known theoretical difficulties for explaining and predicting the behaviour of complex systems.

We have already begun to show the impact of rigid roosts on the evolution of food sharing among artificial vampires. Far from being interested in the ethological debate around the life of vampire bats per se, our goal is to model altruism at an abstract level and in a non-arbitrary way. Starting from ethological data [8], we developed a simulation platform to analyse the key features of altruistic behaviour among Desmodus Rotundus. In a previous work, we have shown the initial results: roosts can play the important role of eliminating a massive initial presence of cheaters. However, in that work only rigid roosts were implemented, and since no mutation was allowed in the composition of new roosts, cheaters could not appear in altruistic roosts. In this work, instead, we will observe the roosting effect with mutation.

3.1 Simulation Details

Agent behaviour. Every agent in the simulation was designed to reproduce the essential traits of the hunting and social activity of vampire bats. Each simulation time step, representing 24 hours of real time, included one daily and one nightly stage. In the night, bats hunt. In substance, each night 93% of the population finds food to survive until the next hunt, while the remaining 7% begin to starve. Vampire bats do not accumulate resources: hunt is performed only for short-term food consumption. Even if the average lifetime of these animals measures around 14 years, starvation and death are a constant menace to them, since each good hunt gives them no more than 60 hours autonomy. As a consequence, for a bat in isolation, two failures in a row are fatal. These are the harsh conditions characterising the life of vampires, which face infrequent but lethal food scarcity. In the simulation, agents perform about 1.65 episodes of double unsuccessful hunt per animal per year. The only way to prevent starvation and death is receiving help from fellows, under the form of regurgitation, which is what these animals appear to do in nature. During the daily stage, the simulated animals perform social activities (grooming and food-sharing). In detail, the following actions can be performed:

Groom. The condition for this action is that two agents are sorted out from the same roost. In this simulation, grooming plays the only role of allowing for help requests.

Ask for help. If an agent (the requestor) is starving, that is, went through two consecutive hunting failures, it will request help to the current grooming partner. The effect of a request will be either donation or denial. In the former case, the requestor will ingest some blood and gain some hours of autonomy. In the latter, it will die and be removed from the simulation.

Donate. This action can be activated only on request from the grooming partner. Under normal conditions, the potential donor will honour the request when possible, that is, if returning from a successful hunt. The effect is that the donors lifetime is reduced and the recipients is increased. In accordance with physiological data, donation is a non-zero sum interaction: the receiver gains more time than the donor loses.

Deny help. The condition is that agent received a request for help. The effect is the requestors death. In the simulation, an average bat will deny help only if unable to donate - that is, if it failed hunting in the previous night. Some agents, the cheaters, will instead always refuse help.

Each day, grooming pairs are formed by randomly coupling agents from the roost population. As in the real world, in our model grooming has the effect of increasing the probability of food-sharing among in-roosts: a starving bat will turn to its grooming partner for help, and will avoid death if the partner is found to be full (having had a good hunt). Because of the bats metabolism, the donor will lose much less time than is gained by the recipient. In the simulation, the donor loses an amount of energy allowing it to survive for six hours; this amounts to losing a chance to ask for help during the next day, in case two failures in a row follow the last donation. In this set of experiments, we set the number of partners per day - for grooming and for eventual help request - to one.

In nature, female vampire bats may give birth to one single child per time; they reproduce about every ten months. New-borns leave the roost as soon as they are able to care for themselves. In the simulated experiment, individual are identical at birth and sexless. They reproduce by cloning every ten months, starting from the twentieth, in order to model the juvenile phase. To obtain a reasonable rate of reproduction, at each occurrence each agent has 50% probability to clone. Although poorly realistic, this is a minimal condition allowing for roost formation, which is the focus of our study.

Roost behaviour. As seen above, roosts define and limit the subset of agents that one has the chance to interact with. The only interesting behaviour of roosts is their splitting (the equivalent, at group level, of agent reproduction). In our model, the only change in roost population (except for birth and death of in-roosts) is the formation of new roosts when a critical mass of new individuals is reached. In the ethological literature this threshold is known to be in the range of a few dozens in-roosts. The rationale underlying roost formation was made to consist of their reproductive success: the more the in-roosts, the higher the number of new roosts formed.

Parameters. The numbers obtained in the baseline experiment (with no cheaters) match with what is known by ethological observations in presence of help: the yearly rate of death for adults is about 24%. But what is even more interesting, they also correspond to the results of a simulation carried on by Wilkinson [11] in absence of help. As said above, help is rare but critical: roosts in which all individuals deny help reduce their population by 82% in a year.

For simulation purposes, we have also introduced a carrying capacity, which sets a limit to the number of agents present at the same time. With this parameter we mean to simulate the filling up of an ecological niche, and to avoid overgrowth of the system. In substance, when the number of individuals in a simulation - independent of the number of roosts - is reached, agent reproduction is inhibited and permitted again when owed to natural death - the number of agents falls below the carrying capacity. In simulations with carrying capacity, the population either becomes extinct, remains in the middle, or oscillates around the carrying capacity. From our observations, if the carrying capacity is high enough (from experience, 200 agents are enough) no destructive effect occurs in the community of agents: once the population has reached the maximum, extinction never follows. Comments received during the workshop induced us to examine also the effects of this parameter, and in the following we add also a set of experiments with a carrying capacity value of 500; these confirm our supposition.

The case under study presents two peculiarities. In the species under study, any kind of wealth accumulation is impossible. Energy coming from a meal is dissipated after two nights, so that there can be no such thing as a wealthy individual. The lucky hunter of today has the same chances as everybody else to starve tomorrow. Moreover, direct retaliation is simply impossible in the present setting. The victim of cheating dies on the spot; asking for help is the last resort, and with the further restriction we have introduced of one helping partner per night, a cheater is a dangerous killer that is really difficult to find out. As a consequence, no explicit mechanism for the punishment of cheaters has been implemented. In the simulations, only starving animals asked for help, and were helped by their addressees if these were both altruist and satiated. No bluff was allowed. Agents had no memory of past interactions and could not calculate the probability of reciprocation. Under these conditions, solutions seem to reside in incentives or enforcement mechanisms, which are usually obtained by means of cognitive artefacts like image or reputation. But is such a cognitive complexity the only way out? In our previous work, in order to explore the effect of groups on the evolution of altruism, simulations with mixed populations (altruists and cheaters in variable combination) initially distributed over a given number of roosts were run. During the simulation, roosts can either grow or collapse, depending upon the survival and reproduction rates of their members. Without mutation, altruists and cheaters compete for the same niche, based only on they initial ratio. Roosts give rise to new roosts if the number of young individuals reached a given threshold, which we called launch size. This was meant as an operational simplification of the notion of group selection and reproduction. Roost reproduction leads a new roost being created, which contains one half (rounded down) of the bats inhabiting the original roost; those selected for the new roost are the younger bats. In that study [8], the phenomenon of roosting was found to allow for roost selection in favour of the most altruistic roosts. The presence of even one single cheater proved clearly disadvantageous as mirrored by the rate of roost reproduction. The roosting effect, in the end, eliminates groups containing selfish vampires. These have a better in-roost fitness, but play a destructive role by gradually reducing the reproductive capacity of their roosts until extinction. When some demographic catastrophe (triggered by cheaters themselves) leads by chance to an earlier extinction of cheaters, the reproduction of altruists takes off again and the number of roosts grows rapidly and indefinitely.

3.2   Implementation

The simulation model has been implemented on the *Repast* platform. Data analysis and visualization have been performed with *R*. Data and code are available on request from the first author.

4   Evidence from Simulations: Resistance to Mutation and Ideal Roost Size

In this study, our purpose is to analyse the effect of introducing mutation in bats reproduction, in inter-action with the roost reproduction mechanism. We already know that roost reproduction can drive away a substantial percentage of cheaters, but what about a cheating trait that reappears randomly in the population? Cheating behaviour could appear in nature in one of several ways - genetic mutation, imitation or contagion, individual reasoning, vertical transmission - the latter being implausible among bats. To simulate the return of cheaters, we will use a generic mutation rate, leaving open the interpretation about where the mutation could be originated. What is relevant from the evolutionary point of view, of course, is that the cheating behaviour implies increased individual fitness, what should contribute to its diffusion and fixation in the population. In our previous work, the efficacy of the roosting mechanism was explained by the random appearance of an all-altruistic roost, whose spawns will have a reproductive advantage on all mixed (cheater-altruistic) roosts. In this way, the initial population of cheaters will be driven out and the ecological niche soon occupied by altruists only. However, this explanation leans on the impossibility for the cheater trait to return once the initial population has been driven away. In this paper, instead, we will allow cheaters to return through mutation. The spawn of altruists will be a cheater with a fixed probability - the mutation rate.

4.1 Hypotheses

This study was aimed to test the effect of mutation rate on the roosting effect that we know to be sufficient to drive out a relatively large (up to 30%) sub-population of cheaters, thus supporting a multilevel interpretation of the evolution of altruism, both in terms of individual and group fitness. The reference example in the real world is the vampire bats food-sharing. As previously recalled, this species offers a clear evidence of the advantages of altruism on life expectancies. However, it is unclear whether and to what extent vampires take measures against cheaters. Wilkinsons findings refer to the comparison between an all-cooperators condition Vs an all-defectors condition. What happens in intermediate conditions? Which is the minimal share of altruists for obtaining an increase of the survival rate with regard to the all-defectors condition? Moreover, does the survival rate increase effectively correspond to an increase of donors fitness, or is it redistributed over the entire population? And if so, are individual donors always refunded or do they sustain a share of the costs of redistribution? The latter question is crucial since if donors are not always reciprocated in person or along their future generations, there is reason to question the reciprocal altruism interpretation, and to look for another concurrent explanation. To actually support group selection (or, more appropriately, multi-level selection), the simplification of inserting only an initial percentage of cheaters must be removed. In such a perspective, if the altruism trait, even if not beneficial for the individual, can be accounted for in terms of its contribution to the fitness of the group, even on the presence of mutation, we will have a much stronger ground for supporting an explanation in terms of multi level selection. In other words, vampires food-sharing could be seen as a habit that evolved thanks to its positive effects on the fitness of roosts taken as wholes, rather than on the individual fitness of donors. The first hypothesis that will be tested by means of simulation will then be that our simulated system is actually able to survive in presence of a mutation that allows the cheating trait to return. Moreover, we will try to find out the maximum mutation rate that the system is able to endure.

To test the second hypothesis, we observe that we have been using a fixed roost size for starting the roost split (or reproduction) - what we call the launch size. We employed a launch size of 20, which would imply an average roost size of 10, roughly corresponding to what is found in ethological observations. Now the question is, does this size have to do with physical constraints only (bats live in tree holes, that have a limited capacity), or does it have something to do with altruism? The second hypothesis is then: ideal roost size exists, and is roughly correspondent to roost size found in nature. The first part of this hypothesis states that there is an ideal size, that is, a roost size that can resist better than any other to all levels of mutation. The second part of the hypothesis states that this size is comparable - at least in order of magnitude - to the one actually found in nature.

4.2   Findings

First Hypothesis: resistance to mutation. To find out the maximum tolerance of the system to mutation, several batches of simulations have been run showing, as expected, that survival rate of agents is inversely related to mutation rate. To show more precisely how this happens, we collected results from 1000 simulations with launch size fixed at 20, and mutation ranging from 2% to 4%. The maximum number of agents present in the simulation is limited from a carrying capacity of 200 agents. We report the number of living agents after 50000 simulation steps as a function of mutation rate. As can be seen in Fig.1, despite the wide variation between single experiments with the same parameter value, a clear trend emerges. Findings clearly show support for our first hypothesis: the system is able to withstand mutation rate, in this case up to 3.3%.

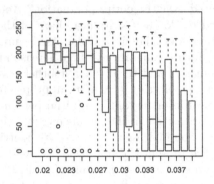

Fig. 1. Box-plot of the number of living agents at the end of simulation (vertical) by mutation rate (horizontal). Launch size fixed at 20, 50000 steps. Averages are represented by the central line; boxes and lines give the five numbers summary, dots are outliers.

Second Hypothesis: Ideal roost size. To support the second hypothesis, we run a first set of 3509 simulations, exploring a square of parameters where the mutation rate changes from 0 to 0.5 and the launch size from 20 to 300. To visualize how agents react to the change of parameters, as a first step we calculate the average number of living agents at fixed parameter combinations, and show the result in a level plot (Fig. 2) from which it is evident how the area where the system survives and expands (light) is decreasing with the increase of the launch size. When the launch size approaches 200 (corresponding to the carrying capacity), only mutation rates less than 1% can be tolerated, while in the lower area, down to a launch size of 20, mutation can be tolerated up to 4%. What about the ideal roost size? If there is a decreasing survival potential when launch size grows over 20, we can also argue that the situation must change when going to lower values, at least when the roost size reaches one, when no roost will be present in the system, that will extinguish even without mutation.

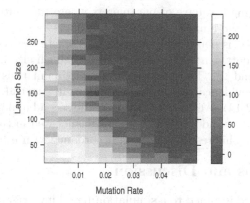

Fig. 2. Level plot of average number of living agents by launch size and mutation rate. More agents correspond to lighter colours. Each area is the average of 11 simulations. There is a clear decrease of survival for high values of launch size.

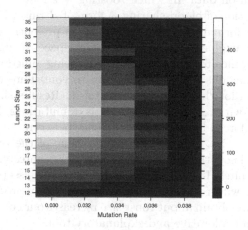

Fig. 3. Level plot of average number of living agents, in a zoomed area. More agents correspond to lighter colours. Each area is the average of 200 simulations. Note the maximum survival area for values of launch size comprised between 17 and 27.

As a consequence, the resistance to mutation as a function of launch size needs to have a maximum in above one and - as can be seen from Fig. 2 - not too far from 20.

Looking for this maximal value, we represent, in Fig. 3, the median of the agents living after 50000 steps. This time, we zoom in the parameter space to obtain a finer view of what is happening in the interesting area, that is, when the launch size is around 20. In addition, this set of simulations has been obtained by raising the carrying capacity of the system from 200 to 500, in answer to a request presented in the MABS workshop presentation of this work. As resulting from out tests, the modification of the carrying capacity is neutral with respect to the claims of this paper. In Fig. 3, we show results from a run set of 24000 simulations, exploring a square of parameters where the mutation rate changes from 3% to 4% and the launch size from 12 to 35.

From the figure, it is definitively how an area where the system as a whole is more resistant to mutation can be identified for launch size in a range between the values of 17 and 27. The shape of this maximum resistance area is also underlined by the evidence of a sudden decrease in survival rates in the lower launch size area (12-14). We can thus say that the second hypothesis is confirmed also in its second part, and the ideal roost size is located in the area between 17 and 27 individuals. This result is fully in accordance with ethological data.

5   Conclusions and Discussion

The model presented is aimed to a simulation-based investigation of the roosting effect among tree-roosting bats as a road to altruism. Food-sharing among vampire bats (Desmodus Rotundus) is a well-known form of altruism, necessary for the survival of this species, and supported by wide ethological evidence. Driven by previous simulation data, in which roosting was found to significantly contribute to the evolution of blood-sharing -a form of altruism vital for the species- we simulated roost formation and maintenance in presence of mutation and for variable roost size, exploring a large parameter space, to find out the borders of the system resistance to mutation. Far from being aimed to find explanation specific to the Desmodus Rotundus, we aim to contribute to the basis of the general explanation for the evolution of altruism. Results show that the roosting effect can cope with reasonably high levels of mutations. Moreover, they are confirmed and reinforced by the correspondence between the calculated and the observed ideal roost size. What is the added value of the present work? From previous work, we know that the roosting effect eliminates groups initially containing selfish vampires. In this study, we reinforce this assertion by saying that this effect can cope with returning cheaters, as internally produced by mutation. The confirmation we obtain about roost size increases our confidence in the value of simulation as an explorative and explanatory tool.

This work is a first step in the direction of a defence of altruism based on multilevel selection and at the same time compatible with a more dynamic social organisation. On one side, we actually believe that altruism in intelligent agents (including humans) should be also explained in terms of high-level cognitive constructs. Intelligent altruism should be studied as such, and should not be reduced to automated punishment or implicit reciprocation, as stated by game theory, nor accounted for in terms of more or less fixed group structures. On the other side, this line of research cannot do without a deeper understanding of the simpler evolutionary pressures, of which we propose one aspect, which can effectively shape the foundations of intelligent altruism.

Acknowledgements

We would like to thank the participants in MABS '06 for the useful comments and for the encouragement in further pursuing the exploration of the parameter space. Thanks to Gennaro di Tosto and Antonietta Di Salvatore for helpful comments and support, and to the MABS organizers, Luis Antunes and Keiki Takadama, for their helpful attitude towards the authors and their tendency to fight with deadlines. This work was partially supported by the European Community under the FP6 programme (eRep project, contract number IST-FP6-028575).

References

1. Arthur, B.W.: Out-of-Equilibrium Economics and Agent-Based Modeling. In: Tesfatsion, L., Kenneth, L.J. (eds.) Handbook of Computational Economics. Agent-Based Computational Economics, vol. 2 (2006)
2. Brembs, B.: Chaos cheating and cooperation: potential solutions to the Prisoners Dilemma. Oikos 76, 14–24 (1996)
3. Conte, R., Paolucci, M., Di Tosto, G.: Vampire Bats and the Micro-Macro Link. In: Billari, F., Fent, T., Prskawetz, A., Scheffran, J. (eds.) Proceedings of the topical workshop on Agent-Based Computational Modelling, Physica-Verlag, Heidelberg (2006)
4. Epstein, J.M.: Remarks on the Foundations of Agent-Based Generative Social Science. In: Tesfatsion, L., Kenneth, L.J. (eds.) Handbook of Computational Economics. Agent-Based Computational Economics, vol. 2, North Holland (2006)
5. Hales, D., Rouchier, J., Edmonds, B.: Model-to-Model Analysis. JASSS 6(4) (2003)
6. Leimar, O., Axn, A.H.: Strategic behavior in an interspecific mutualism: interactions between lycaenid larvae and ants. Anim. Behav. 46, 1177–1182 (1993)
7. Milinski, M., Kulling, D., Kettler, R.: Tit for Tat: sticklebacks (Gasterosteus aculeatus) ÓtrustingÓ a cooperating partner. Behav. Ecol. 1, 7–11 (1990)
8. Paolucci, M., Di Tosto, G., Conte, R.: Reciprocal Versus Group Altruism among Vampire Bats. In: AGENT 2003 Conference on Challenges in Social Simulation. Argonne National Laboratory (2003)
9. Trivers, R.: The evolution of reciprocal altruism. Q. Review of Biology 46, 35–37 (1972)
10. Wilkinson, G.S.: Reciprocal food sharing in the vampire bat. Nature 308, 181–184 (1984)
11. Wilkinson, G.S.: Social Grooming in the Common Vampire Bat, Desmodus rotundus. Animal Behaviour 34, 1880–1889 (1986)
12. Wilkinson, G.S.: Food Sharing in vampire bats. Scientific American 2, 64–70 (1990)
13. Williams, G.C. (ed.): Group Selection. Aldine, Chicago (1971)
14. Willis, C.K.R., Brigham, R.M.: Roost switching, roost sharing and social cohesion: forest-dwelling big brown bats, Eptesicus fuscus, conform to the fissionfusion model. Animal Behaviour 68(3) (2004)
15. Wilson, D.S., Sober, E.: Reintroducing group selection to the human behavioral sciences. Behavioral and Brain Sciences 17(4), 585–654 (1994)
16. Wynne-Edwards, V.C.: Animal Dispersion in Relation to Social Behaviour. Oliver & Boyd, Edinburgh (1962)

Tactical Exploration of Tax Compliance Decisions in Multi-agent Based Simulation

Luis Antunes, João Balsa, Ana Respício, and Helder Coelho

GUESS/Universidade de Lisboa, Portugal
{xarax,jbalsa,respicio,hcoelho}@di.fc.ul.pt

Abstract. Tax compliance is a field that crosses over several research areas, from economics to machine learning, from sociology to artificial intelligence and multi-agent systems. The core of the problem is that the standing general theories cannot even explain why people comply as much as they do, much less make predictions or support prescriptions for the public entities. The compliance decision is a challenge posed to rational choice theory, and one that defies the current choice mechanisms in multi-agent systems. The key idea of this project is that by considering rationally-heterogeneous agents immersed in a highly social environment we can get hold of a better grasp of what is really involved in the individual decisions. Moreover, we aim at understanding how those decisions determine tendencies for the behaviour of the whole society, and how in turn those tendencies influence individual behaviour. This paper presents the results of some exploratory simulations carried out to uncover regularities, correlations and trends in the models that represent first and then expand the standard theories on the field. We conclude that forces like social imitation and local neighbourhood enforcement and reputation are far more important than individual perception of expected utility maximising, in what respects compliance decisions.

1 Introduction

Tax evasion is a serious problem in most economies, especially those in transition to democracy. Evasion undermines the central government budgets and expenditures, harming public welfare, and creates a sense of unfairness that can ultimately generate further evasion.

Interestingly, the scientific field that addresses tax evasion is known as *tax compliance* [2]. The decision to comply or evade is individual. When we consider rational individuals, who pursue their self-interest, we expect that the common behaviour would be to evade. However, in the real world, the numbers of compliance are quite high. Indeed, the literature of the field is mainly centered around discovering the adequate models to explain *why do people pay their taxes* [1,8,17,20]. Of course, central authorities would like to fully grasp the mechanisms underlying tax compliance and evasion, in such a way that they could ultimately promote evasion reduction [2].

Economists traditionally model individual tax evasion as if the individual is just adding one more risky asset to her household's portfolio [2]. Nevertheless,

L. Antunes and K. Takadama (Eds.): MABS 2006, LNAI 4442, pp. 80–95, 2007.

this theoretical approach fails to explain the behaviour that real societies display: households comply far more than could be predicted in this theory. For instance, in the USA, although fine value (or rate) can be neglected, and even though less than 2% of households were audited, the Internal Revenue Service (IRS) estimates that 91.7% of all income that should have been reported was in fact reported (numbers from 1988-1992-1995, cited from [2]).

In multi-agent systems, most accounts of agents assume limited rationality, that is, agents decide in such way to pursue their self-interest, based upon an idea of utility, and maintaining some degree of autonomy [9]. The deepest insight to approach the tax compliance issue by multi-agent based simulation comes from Simon's famous sentence "people have reasons for what they do" [18]. Each person/agent has her own limited rationality, and the notion of rationality here prescribed can be described as "multi-varied, situated, and individual" [4].

In this paper, we put together the methodologies behind multi-agent based simulation with rationally-heterogeneous agents and tackle the tax compliance problem. Our aim is to understand the mechanisms behind the compliance decision, both at the individual and collective (social interactions) level. Agent technology and exploratory simulation provide us with tools and methodologies that allow for the rehearsal of mechanisms to try out different design scenarios. Agent heterogeneity and individuality provide a more realist account of the rational decisions that determine the overall behaviour of the society.

Next section presents the broad context of this research. In section 3, we propose a hierarchy of models to explore expansions and alternatives to the standard theory. We describe how our models partially cover the design space, and propose a strategy for its exploration. Section 4 presents Ec_0, a model that represents the standard theories, which we use to introduce the concepts and terminology used on the field. In the following sections we introduce several enhancements to this basic model: Ec_0^τ, Ec_3^{*i}, and Ec_4^*. We examine their respective constraints, and report on experiments and simulations done over them. In section 9 we present the environmental setting we used, and in section 10 we conclude and discuss prospects for future work.

2   Context of Research

With the agent-view on computer intelligence, a lot of social issues gained relevance and built a huge source of metaphors and inspirations for societies of artificial agents. It was later that this collaboration between social scientists and computer scientists started to be fruitful for both sides. Since at least the first SimSoc workshop [12], most fields of social science began to endure the idea that computer agent societies could provide a powerful tool to conduct experiments in controlled environments in a principled way. Multi-agent based simulation was developed as a field where the inherently complex issues could be subject to controlled exploration, most of the times not to build or prove theories, but rather to find the "right" hypotheses, conjectures, intuitions, with which to carry on the scientific work [13,10]. The scientific questions to be answer are no longer only "what happened?" and "what may have happened?" but also "what are the necessary conditions for a given result to be obtained?" In exploratory simulation, the descriptive character is not a simple reproduction of the real social phenomena, and the prescriptive character cannot be simplistically resumed to an optimisation. To put things simply, the subject of research expands from the target phenomenon, and now includes its modelling, and not only real societies can be studied, possible societies can be studied as well.

In some recent papers ([6,3]) we argued that for characterising existing societies with enough realism as to allow solid explanatory power, and enough predictive power to permit policy recommendations, there exists the need for heterogeneous and adaptive rationality. In the tax compliance scenario, we have proposed some models of individual agents and of societies, and have been experimenting with them to gain insights into this complex issue, as well as set the grounds for theories that can be used both to explain individual and social behaviour, and to recommend central authority policies.

The classical problem of individual tax compliance, as well as the problem of determining the correct tax enforcement policy, have constituted for decades a challenge for economics, public finance, law enforcement, organisational design, labour supply, and ethics [2], because it presents both theoretical and practical problems that are hard to be dealt with. It is also an interesting problem for MAS practitioners, since it presents a clear case where the limits of situated rationality are put to test, and the neo-classical economics approach of maximising expected utility remains wanting in face of the empirical results available. Because of its inherently complex social character, tax compliance is also a great issue to test out agent based simulation methodologies and techniques, and to perform exploratory simulations that can help tackle the hot questions themselves, while gaining in experience and improving the necessary methodologies for experimentation with self-motivated agents.

The idea of a society constituted by agents with heterogeneous rationalities is central in the research we are conducting. This view opposes the traditional endeavour of economics and particularly game theory, where all the agents follow the same general law, and societies are homogeneous in rationality and therefore, *qualitatively*, in trends for individual behaviour. This means that the sources of complexity in global behaviour are limited to circumstances of the world, and parametric features of the agent's minds. Rather, with heterogeneous, self-motivated agents, societies are orders of magnitude more complex, since in every individual decision there is a potential for new, unpredictable behaviour. This is our bid for truly taking on the *open systems* challenge, as was proposed by Carl Hewitt in the 1970s [14,15].

Experimentation with such heterogeneous rational agents will foster different lines of research:

-i- Cognitive modelling: mind design is being experimentally challenged, especially in what concerns decision and motivation;

-ii- Multi-agent based simulation: social simulations where the central unit is the individual agent is a recent field, and with each new problem addressed, more is discovered about the potential of this methodological approach to experimental social science. The issue of tax compliance is a rich research field for this approach. Exploratory simulation together with agent heterogeneity and individuality, will provide reasonability, realism, and the possibility to rehearse mechanisms and try out different scenarios;

-iii- Tax compliance modelling and policy: we can explore more accurate and realist models of the individual decision by the tax payer, and its consequences on the overall global society, particularly in what concerns policy decisions;

-iv- Methodology for experimentation with self-motivated agents: the validity of results obtained through simulation is always debatable, and it has been argued that self-motivation only makes the case worse [4]. By conducting simulations that span over a broad field of applications, analysing their results, and proposing theory refinements and agents' mind re-engineering, we will gather information that can inform a full-fledged methodology for experiments and simulations whose meaning can have an impact in the real target phenomena. This is especially important when there is the need to provide policy recommendations and expect their outcomes to be accurate.

3   The e*plore Methodology

The idea of using a collection of models to proceed with the exploration of the tax compliance problem has been used to illustrate a methodology for such problems. The base steps of this methodology come originally from Gilbert's lifecycle of simulation research [11]. The main ideas that go beyond those are centred around back and forth journeys to provide robustness and ensure exploration; progressive deepening of mechanisms in a broad but shallow design of agents, societies and experiments; and face complexity through exploration of model variability.

These are the steps of the e*plore methodology [5]:

i. *identify the subject* to be investigated, by stating specific items, features or marks;

ii. *unveil state-of-the-art* across the several scientific areas involved to provide context. The idea is to enlarge coverage before narrowing the focus, to focus prematurely on solutions may prevent the in-depth understanding of problems;

iii. *propose definition* of the target phenomenon. Pay attention to its operationality;

iv. *identify relevant aspects* in the target phenomenon, in particular, *list individual and collective measures* with which to characterise it;

v. if available, *collect observations* of the relevant features and measures;

vi. *develop the appropriate models* to simulate the phenomenon. Use the features you uncovered and program adequate mechanisms for individual agents, for interactions among agents, for probing and observing the simulation. Be careful to base behaviours in reasons that can be supported on appropriate individual motivations. Develop visualisation and data recording tools. Document every design option thoroughly. *Run the simulations*, collect results, compute selected measures;

vii. return to step iii, and *calibrate everything*: your definition of the target, of adequate measures, of all the models, verify your designs, validate your models by using the selected measures. Watch individual trajectories of selected agents, as well as collective behaviours;

viii. *introduce variation* in your models: in initial conditions and parameters, in individual and collective mechanisms, in measures. Return to step v;

ix. After enough exploration of design space is performed, use your best models to *propose predictions*. Confirm it with past data, or collect data and validate predictions. Go back to the appropriate step to ensure rigour;

x. Make a generalisation effort and *propose theories and/or policies*. Apply to the target phenomenon. Watch global and individual behaviours. Recalibrate.

4   A Structure of Models to Explore the Tax Compliance Problem

The classical approach to tax compliance, as well as the main concepts and terminology of the field, are summarised in [2]. In [3], we have modelled the traditional agent in the income tax setting, and the corresponding society model: Ec_0. The details of this model are described in the next section.

A number of unrealistic assumptions were on the basis of Ec_0, and those could explain its little predictive power and accuracy in face of real world data. Significant changes were there proposed to the basic agent model of Ec_0, resulting in a series of models Ec_1, Ec_2, etc. Figure 1 depicts the structure of these models, and helps to illustrate the kind of trajectory we are attempting in our exploration of the space of possible designs. The idea behind this trajectory is to successively remove overcome the shortcomings of Ec_0, and use each new experiment to get a deeper insight into the problem and eventually converge on an appropriate model to face real data.

In the first models, the agent would resort to more complex reasoning to deliberate towards her compliance decision, by keeping track of past events, or

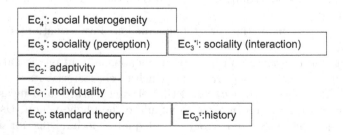

Fig. 1. Structure of designs for exploratory simulations in the tax compliance problem

accessing her individual characteristics. However, the decision was kept individual, as no social perceptions or interactions were taken into account in decision making.

In Ec_1 the agent possesses some wealth, and consumes it at a certain rate (γ). The agent's wealth determines its propensity to comply or not to its tax duties. Agents also have their own tendency towards evading, which we crudely represented with a real number $\epsilon \in [0,1]$. The decision to comply takes these individual features into account. Ec_1 is the first model where the agent can be said to have some kind of (limited) individuality.

In Ec_2 we added some adaptivity. Ec_2 agents possess some evolution capabilities, namely, their tendency towards evading (or not) is dynamic, and evolves towards non-compliance at a given rate (δ). Some times agents are caught evading, and this tendency to non-compliance is completely canceled for a period of time we call memory, an individual agent parameter.

In Ec_3^* we introduced social perceptions as part of the data to be considered in decision. Agents have a global perception about the level of evasion in the society, and decide to comply or not according to their individual tolerance towards this perception.

The picture of the models to be considered is now completed with new models that encompass critical observations on the previous ones introduced in [3]. These new models and respective results will be introduced in subsequent sections of this paper, so here we only place them in the overall picture, as a way to deploy our strategy of exploration. In the remainder of this paper we will be concerned with tactical placement and setting of the models herein introduced.

So, in the next section we summarise the concepts, terminology and notations we used for Ec_0. Then we extend Ec_0 with history, introducing Ec_0^τ. This model slightly changes the standard theory to consider a criticism we produced in [3], that when an agent is caught evading the central authority will investigate not only the current year but also previous ones. We then present Ec_3^{*i}, a model where we explore the concept of imitation, and study how a core of stubborn agents can influence a whole society towards the behaviour they adopt, and how the distribution of two cores of stubborn agents with opposing behaviours can produce global effects. Finally, we introduce Ec_4^*, a model where two different breeds of agents are used to model tax payers and tax enforcers. Geography and locality become especially relevant in this latter model, as results are particularly dependent on initial conditions and performance circumstances of the simulation.

5 Ec_0: Modelling the Standard Theory

We now present model Ec_0, the basis of our pyramid of increasingly complex models. This model was introduced in [3] and we use it here to introduce the important concepts, terminology and notations, as well as to have a reference framework of ground results against which to compare our subsequent models.

The terminology used in [1] has become standard for the area. A taxpayer has exogenous income y, facing a tax rate t. The amount reported to the government is $x \leq y$, leaving $z = y - x$ unreported, and paying tax tx. The tax authority does not know the true income y, and has to enforce compliance through a policy of audits and penalties. The model goes on to assume that the enforcement policy is known to the taxpayer and depends on a probability p, with $0 < p < 1$. Further assumptions are that p does not depend on x, and that the tax authority is always able to discover the true value of y. Then, if θ is the penalty to be paid for every unit of income evaded, the cheating taxpayer will additionally have to pay $\theta z + tz$. Given this, and assuming the taxpayer is risk averse, and that $u(\cdot)$ is the utility of money, it can be shown that her expected utility if she decides to evade is [2,20]:

$$(1 - p)u[y(1 - t) + tz] + pu[y(1 - t) - \theta z)] \tag{1}$$

For experimentation with Ec_0, we used a slightly simplified version of this formulae, concentrating only on what the agent saves by not complying. So, the evading decision is taken by each agent if the following inequality holds:

$$(1 - p)u(tz) + pu(-\theta z) > 0 \tag{2}$$

The results produced by experimentation with Ec_0 are pretty much what could be expected from direct analysis of the decisions involved. Only in extreme and unrealistic conditions will the agents choose to comply. Observing that z (≥ 0) does not influence inequality 2, we conclude that tax payers evade when the following (all equivalent) inequations are satisfied:

$$p < \frac{t}{t + \theta} \qquad \theta < \frac{1 - p}{p}t \qquad t > \frac{p}{1 - p}\theta \tag{3}$$

Note that the decision is independent of the income value (y). Table 1 shows the turning point of individual decisions for usual values of the parameters. For instance, in the first section of the table we observe that for a tax of 30% and a fine of 50%, we need to inspect more than 38% of the tax payers to ensure compliance.

Table 1. Ec_0: Evasion point for usual values of θ, t, and p. Each cell contains, for each of the inequations 3, the point in which the truth value changes.

$\theta \setminus t$	0.10	0.20	0.30	0.40
0.25	0.29	0.44	0.55	0.62
0.50	0.17	0.29	0.38	0.44

$p \setminus t$	0.10	0.20	0.30	0.40
0.01	9.90	19.80	29.70	39.60
0.05	1.90	3.80	5.70	7.60
0.10	0.90	1.80	2.70	3.60

$\theta \setminus p$	0.01	0.05	0.10
0.25	0.0025	0.0132	0.0278
0.50	0.0051	0.0263	0.0556

As expected, the numbers that promote compliance are quite stressful. For instance, for a tax rate of 40% and with a fine of 50%, the central authority would have to inspect over 44% of the tax returns to ensure overall compliance. Or, for an average tax rate of 30% and a probability of inspection of 1%, the fine would have to be above 2970% over the evaded amount. Or still, for a fine rate of 50% and a probability of inspection of 1%, the tax rate would have to be less than 0.51% to encourage compliance. None of these values is the least reasonable in face of what happens in real life. It remains to be captured by the model *what* leads people to comply.

6 Extending Ec_0 with History

One criticism that was quite prominent in [3] was that it would be rather awkward for the central authority to discover an evader agent and not investigate previous years. In fact, the common practice is that once a tax payer is inspected once, not only she will be investigated for her past, but also she will continue to be investigated in the future, even if she did not evade at all (although we are not considering the future in the model).

Model Ec_0^τ incorporate the previous history of the agent in her own utility calculations. Instead of considering θz, the amount of penalty will be $\theta(z_\tau + z_{\tau-1} + z_{\tau-2} + \ldots + z_{\tau-n})$, where τ is the current year. In most European countries, tax reports can be scrutinised reaching 10 years back, so we picked $n = 9$.

If, on top of this, interests are charged on past due taxes and/or fines, the compliance equation above significantly changes, and could indeed produce the tax compliance behaviour we observe on most Western countries. To simplify, we show only calculations for the simplified compliance rule:

$$(1 - p)u(tz_\tau) + pu[-\theta \sum_{i=0}^{n} (z_{\tau-i}) - \sum_{i=0}^{n} ((1+r)^i tz_{\tau-i})] > 0 \qquad (4)$$

where r is the going interest rate for delayed payments. Note that the decision is taken in year τ, but only the 10-year aggravated penalties need be included in the decision, as the gains were already taken into account in the previous year's decisions. The decision to evade was already taken, there is nothing to be gained in year τ about that money, only to be risked. There are also some more simplifying assumptions, for instance, the interest rate is fixed over the years, as well as the fine rate, the tax rate and the probability of inspection. In a stable economic setting these options do not distort in any way the results of simulation, but in unstable settings, refinements must be made for the sake of realism.

In table 2 we can see the point in which the decision of whether to comply or not changes, for fixed usual values of the parameters. In the top part of the table, we fix some values for the tax and fine rates, and point out the smallest value for the probability of inspection that ensures full overall compliance. We note that there is a substantial decrease in the percentage of tax returns to be

Table 2. Ec_0^T: Point in which the decision to comply changes for usual values of θ, t, and p

$\theta \setminus t$	0.10	0.20	0.30	0.40
0.25	0.23	0.31	0.36	0.39
0.50	0.15	0.25	0.28	0.31

$p \setminus t$	0.10	0.20	0.30	0.40
0.01	9.81	19.61	29.41	39.21
0.05	1.81	3.61	5.41	7.21
0.10	0.81	1.61	2.41	3.21

audited. For instance, for an average tax rate of 30% and a fine of 25%, we pass from 55% (in table 1) to 36% tax returns to be audited in order to ensure full compliance.

In the bottom part of table 2, we fix usual values for the tax rate and the probability of inspection, and we observe the smallest value of the fine rate that ensures full overall compliance. Here, the decrease in the fine rate is proportionally very small. It is obvious that any individual taxpayer is indifferent between a fine rate of 570% and another of 540% when deciding about compliance.

We conclude that these modifications alone do not have a very significant impact in the behaviour of tax payers, much less the overall behaviour of the society. For any reasonable values of p, t and θ, percentages of complying agents are quite small and far from reality.

Table 3. Evolving the percentage of evaders by changing θ, p, and n simultaneously

	$n = 10$		$n = 15$
	$p = 0.01$	$p = 0.02$	$p = 0.01$
$\theta = 0.5$	85%		
$\theta = 2$		24%	
$\theta = 4$	73%	5%	6%

However, when experimenting with increasing the probability of inspection p by very small amounts, we noticed that everything else being equal, the impact on the number of compliers of passing from $p = 0.01$ to $p = 0.02$ was far more significant than if we passed from, say, $p = 0.1$ to 0.2. So, we tried to manipulate more than one variable at the same time. In table 3 we have results that show some promise. By passing from $p = 0.01 \wedge \theta = 0.5$ to $p = 0.02 \wedge \theta = 2$, the number of evaders decreases from 85% to only 24%. More impressively, a very high fine rate of $\theta = 4$ will only conduct to 27% of compliers when $p = 0.01$, but for $p = 0.02$ it will yield 95% of compliers. And even for the smallest $p = 0.01$ (we cannot forget that it is expensive to conduct audits, far more than to increase fines), we can achieve 94% of compliance by examining tax returns back 15 years, instead of 10. The problem here would be that a simple strategy of 'killing' companies and founding new ones with the same assets could have the effect of 'cleaning up' the dirty past and getting on.

In any case, there remains an important gap to be covered by our models. We should note nonetheless that for any agent decision model M we can produce the corresponding history-aware model M^τ and enhance our coverage. However, the promise of Ec_0^τ is that perhaps there are still individual decision mechanisms to be explored in the classical theory and that the social front is not the only one to be considered. We will surely conduct further investigations along these ideas.

7   Stubbornness and Imitation

There is a considerable amount of literature about formation of consensus among homogeneous and heterogeneous agents. In multi-agent systems, the issue has been studied by Kaplan [16], and later by Urbano [19]. Urbano showed that a mechanism of imitation together with a small percentage of stubborn agents (agents that would not change opinion whatever happened) could be enough to promote a global societal change. In this section we propose to adopt this mechanism to model Ec_3^* [3]. The resulting model is called Ec_3^{*i}. In Ec_3^{*i} our population is divided into three subgroups: the stubborn compliers (SC), the stubborn evaders (SE), and the imitators (I).

Agents travel randomly in a square grid, and meet with other agents. For the decision, the agent will follow Ec_2 rules, which consider the ethical attitude $\epsilon \in [0, 1]$, such that whenever $\epsilon = 1$ the agent always complies and where $\epsilon = 0$ the agent always evades. So, the agent will pay her taxes if $\epsilon \geq \frac{1}{1+\theta} \frac{\omega}{\overline{W}}$, where ω is the wealth of the agent, and $\overline{W}$ is the average of wealth of all agents. If the agent evades and is caught, her ϵ will be updated to 1. In the opposite case, her ethical attitude decays by a quantity δ (regulating the memory of having been caught evading). The idea of using factor $\frac{\omega}{\overline{W}}$ amounts to consider that agents whose wealth is above the average will more easily risk larger amounts of money than poorer agents. Agent's income is consumed at a rate γ, the remaining amount is added to her personal wealth.

Along the spirit of Urbano's investigation, we propose very simple and immediate mechanisms for imitation. The agent's individual attitude is publicly known (we will remove this constraint later on, and investigate on how the agent's behaviour can be affected by the reputation it renders), and agents imitate others following one of these rules:

:i: The agent looks at the other agents in the same square, and adopts as her new ethical attitude (ϵ) the average of their ethical attitudes.

:ii: The agent looks at the other agents in the same square, and adopts the ethical attitude of the more committed agent (the one that potentially has the highest influence on others), that is, of the agent that has her ϵ closest to one of the extremes of interval $[0, 1]$.

:iii: The agent keeps track of the previous n encounters, and takes on the average of the involved agents' attitudes;

:iv: The agent only considers the other agents' ϵ if they have a higher energy (for simplicity's sake, say wealth).

Using rule i, we conducted simulations with typical values: $\theta = 50\%$, $p = 1\%$, and $t = 30\%$. Our aim was to find out the combination of reasonable features that could ensure some stable equilibrium with an acceptable amount of overall compliance.

After some preliminary runs, it was clear that in such a highly social setting, the model was very responsive to variations in population density. So, in table 4 we present, for imitation rule i, the amount of evasion found in the equilibrium state (about 2000 iterations of the simulation), considering no stubborn evaders, and different proportions of stubborn compliers. In the line labelled "% ev. sc" we have the outcomes for a scarcely crowded society, where the average imitation rate per iteration is around 3.8%. Line "% ev. mc" displays the same numbers for a medium crowded society, where the average imitation rate is 9.7%. Line "%ev. hc" represents a highly crowded society, and the average imitation rate is 23.7%.

Table 4. Ec_3^{*i} Rule i: Variation of evasion over different proportions of Stubborn Compliers for different population densities

Rule i$|t = 0.3\ \theta = 0.5\ p = 0.01\ \delta = 0.01\ \gamma = 0.99\ SE = 0\%$

SC	0	10	20	30	40	50	60	70
% ev. sc	74	63	52	45	34	29	22	16
% ev. mc	78	65	48	37	28	25	16	11
% ev. hc	86	60	35	20	15	11	4	2

Figure 2 depicts the results of these series of experiments. It is clear that if all the society is composed of only imitators (no stubborns), the main trend is to evade, and agents imitate each other, hence reinforcing that trend. The introduction of a small proportion of stubborn compliers (say 20%) produces substantial effects in compliance for any density of population. In general, when we increase the relative number of stubborn compliers, the corresponding increase in compliance is always greater by a significant amount. This effect is particularly dramatic in highly crowded societies.

We conducted more experiments with the different imitation rules (ii, iii, and iv), but the results were not as exciting. An important parameter in the experiments is δ, the degradation of the memory of being caught evading. We remade the above experiments with $\delta = 0.10$ and the outcome was far worse. Agents seem to forget too soon that they were caught and start evading again. The consumption rate γ is quite high, about 99%. This means that agents do not save enough to be prepared to face a high penalty, and are better off complying. As happened in the previous series of experiments, increasing either the inspection (p) or the fine (θ) rates greatly reduces evasion. For instance, with $p = 10\%$ and $\theta = 100\%$, a stubborn compliers proportion of 20% yields an overall evasion rate below 5%.

From table 1 we can observe that for a fine of 50% and a tax rate of 30%, the minimum inspection rate to ensure total compliance is 38%. Here, with an

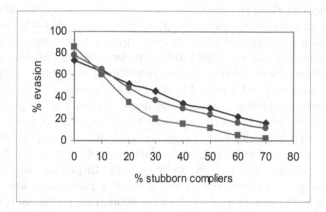

Fig. 2. Evolution of evasion when the fixed percentage of stubborn compliers varies. The square-dotted line represents a highly crowded society. The dotted line represents a medium crowded society. The diamond-dotted line represents a sparse society.

inspection rate of 1%, we can assure 65% of compliance with 20% of stubborn compliers, or even 89% of compliance with 50% of stubborn compliers.

This phenomenon we observed can explain why more people comply than standard theories predict. Stubbornness can be explained by personal characteristics, education, ethical stance, moral imperatives, social motivations, or even by some other mechanisms to be explored, such as reputation, imitation itself, altruism, fear, shame, political beliefs, etc.

The policy implications of these conclusions are substantial. If the stubborn compliance is appropriately encouraged (e.g. by offering prizes, such as tax reductions) and spread out, it will have a multiplying effect on overall compliance. In this case, it could pay off to bet on investing great efforts in building up a core of stubborn compliers, instead of dividing those efforts undiscriminantly over the whole population. The idea would be to *induce* or *favour* stubborn behaviour rather than *recognise* and *enhance* it, as it would be very difficult to distinguish a stubborn behaviour from an imitator with a very high threshold[1].

8   I Fought the Law and the Law Won

We now introduce an expansion of our previous models into Ec_4^*. In this model, we introduce a new breed of agents, the tax enforcers, or inspectors. An agent is only audited if she meets with one of these tax inspectors, and the inspector decides to audit her. This decision is taken autonomously, and so the whole concept of p ceases to be a number to be adopted blind by some anonymous central authority, and becomes an overall subjective goal of that authority, one that depends on individual decisions of the inspectors.

---

[1] We are thankful to an anonymous reviewer for pointing this out to us.

Geographical location (representing, more generally, complex social distances) becomes also an important issue, as well as trajectories that both tax payers and inspectors will go through. We keep trajectories random, using an uniform distribution to select among the eight candidates for each individual step. Later on, we will investigate mechanisms such as imitation of neighbours, clustering and flocking, to examine how these will influence the patterns of overall behaviour.

For tax-paying behaviour, we use the decision model of Ec_2. As to tax inspectors, their decision to inspect an agent is based on the following criteria. Central authority has a limited budget for auditing and inspectors, taken out of the whole amount of collected taxes. Each inspector receives a fixed amount of money per period, c_f, and each audit costs c_a. Inspectors are then assigned a personal budget b by the central authority. For now, these are obtained by dividing equally the overall budget B of the central authority by the number of inspectors.

When deliberating about whether or not to inspect an agent i, the inspector considers how much money he has got left from his budget, how much the audit will cost, and how much due tax and fine the audited taxpayer is expected to provide. These calculations are based on individual experience (frequency of successes in previous audits) and on the wealth of the inspected agent. If the information is available about previous evasions, the inspector can take that into account. For this purpose, inspectors exchange information among them about previous caught evaders. This exchange happens only when inspectors meet with other inspectors in their trajectories. Machine learning techniques can also be used to improve inspectors' performance.

With this inspection policy, we eliminate further criticisms of Ec_0 [3]: that audits are determined by a probability; that the probability of an agent being audited is independent of the past; that the probability of an agent being audited is independent of the probabilities of other agents being audited; that the cost of an audit is irrelevant and there is no limit for the number of audits to be carried out.

Experiments with Ec_4^* are reported in [7]. Our findings show that the overall compliance behaviour can be quite high in this new setting, given the appropriate fine tuning. Moreover, the distribution of the prerogative to audit tax payers from the central authority to autonomous inspectors can help meet the conditions for compliance in other models. However, individual decision mechanisms should still be enhanced, possibly through the use of context dependent adaptive functions. On top of that, the complexity and multiplicity of social distances must be taken into account in the simulation.

9   Experimental Environment

The experiments here reported have been programmed in NetLogo 3.0, of the Center for Connected Learning and Computer-based Modelling of the Northwestern University (Illinois). Figure 3 is a screen shot of our application running an experiment with Ec_3^{*i}.

The typical simulation would have a square world with 100×100 slots, where 500 agents would evolve. Then it would run until some equilibrium was found, which would happen at most around iteration 200 for the first experiments and around iteration 2000 for the simulations of section 6.

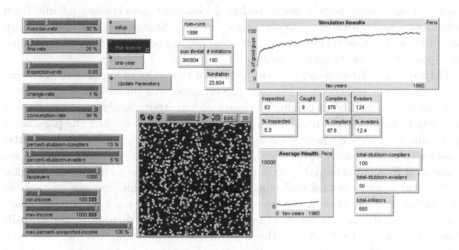

Fig. 3. A snapshot of application Ec^* running model Ec_3^{*i}

Development under the NetLogo 3.0 environment was gentle and swift, and the collection of data was straightforward. The results we present in the paper are mostly taken from typical runs, although sometimes we run several experiments and averaged the result. The exploration of the model parameters to obtain some desired outcome was conducted mainly by setting usual values for some parameters while thoroughly spanning over the remaining ones. In order to find which are the key parameters, as future work we intend to conduct a sensitivity analysis.

10   Conclusions

Tax compliance is a challenge posed to each individual in a society, and one that defies the standing proposals for explaining rational behaviour, as well as (re)produce it in artificial agent experimental settings. When the issue is looked upon from a social standpoint, experimental complexity grows steeply and comprehension of the observed phenomena becomes harder and even more defying.

We take on this challenge from the multi-agent based simulation standpoint. Our proposal is to consider situated, multi-dimensional, adaptive and individual decision models as a means to provide a richer representation of the actors in a simulation. In this paper, we report some exploratory simulations that have allowed us to have a deeper insight of the mechanisms involved in both the individual decision and the dynamics of societal behaviour.

We propose models that promote the explanation of compliance mechanisms to a level that the classical theories could not achieve. This is the first step towards a robust approach to tax compliance, able to predict real outcomes, and eventually to propose policy recommendations, for central authorities. This is particularly important in countries where public deficits and tax evasion are very high. Among these models, we introduced historical inspections and imitation behaviours, and obtained particularly good results. Stubbornness and leadership can nurture a stable equilibrium with good overall compliance levels, provided the appropriate constraints are assured.

Future work will focus on the completion of the series of experiments, as well as calibrating some new models and mechanisms. An important step towards this calibration will be to conduct a thorough sensitivity analysis on the models we already have run in our simulations: it is important to explore the parameter space and investigate whether we can be located in special niches or particular locations in that space. In particular, we will investigate how our models are influenced by the particular distribution of income we use to model our agents.

We also want to obtain real empirical data to help this fine tuning task, as well as validate our present results and design options. We also plan to compare our tax simulations with other compliance behaviours, such as public transit. Another idea is to stretch out the kind of choice functions we use, and consider prospect theory, infinite penalties, moral imperatives, and other individual sources of decision. Mechanisms for spreading of reputation and social stigma will also be investigated.

Acknowledgements

The authors wish to express their gratitude to the anonymous reviewers who throughout successive revisions of this paper contributed to its clarification and improvement.

References

1. Allingham, M.G., Sandmo, A.: Income tax evasion: A theoretical analysis. Journal of Public Economics 1(3/4), 323–338 (1972)
2. Andreoni, J., Erard, B., Feinstein, J.: Tax compliance. Journal of Economic Literature 36(2) (1998)
3. Antunes, L., Balsa, J., Moniz, L., Urbano, P., Palma, C.R.: Tax compliance in a simulated heterogeneous multi-agent society. In: Sichman, J.S., Antunes, L. (eds.) MABS 2005. LNCS (LNAI), vol. 3891, Springer, Heidelberg (2006)
4. Antunes, L., Coelho, H.: On how to conduct experiments with self-motivated agents. In: Lindemann, G., Moldt, D., Paolucci, M. (eds.) RASTA 2002. LNCS (LNAI), vol. 2934, Springer, Heidelberg (2004)
5. Antunes, L., Coelho, H., Balsa, J., Respício, A.: e*plore v.0: Principia for strategic exploration of social simulation experiments design space. In: Proceedings of The First World Congress on Social Simulation, Kyoto, Japan (2006)

6. Antunes, L., Del Gaudio, R., Conte, R.: Towards a gendered-based agent model. In: Proceedings of Agent 2004 Conference on Social Dynamics: Interaction, Reflexivity and Emergence, Chicago, USA (2004)
7. Balsa, J., Antunes, L., Respício, A., Coelho, H.: Autonomous inspectors in tax compliance simulation. In: Proceedings of the 18th European Meeting on Cybernetics and Systems Research (2006)
8. Boadway, R., Marceau, N., Mongrain, S.: Tax evasion and trust. Technical Report 104, Center for Research on Economic Fluctuations and Employment, Université du Québec à Montréal (February 2000)
9. Castelfranchi, C.: Guarantees for autonomy in cognitive agent architecture. In: Wooldridge, M.J., Jennings, N.R. (eds.) Intelligent Agents. LNCS, vol. 890, Springer, Heidelberg (1995)
10. Conte, R., Gilbert, N.: Introduction: computer simulation for social theory. In: Gilbert, N., Conte, R. (eds.) Artificial Societies: the computer simulation of social life, UCL Press, London, UK (1995)
11. Gilbert, N.: Models, processes and algorithms: Towards a simulation toolkit. In: Suleiman, R., Troitzsch, K.G., Gilbert, N. (eds.) Tools and Techniques for Social Science Simulation, Physica-Verlag, Heidelberg (2000)
12. Gilbert, N., Doran, J. (eds.): Simulating Societies: the computer simulation of social phenomena. Proceedings of SimSoc 1992. UCL Press, London (1992)
13. Gilbert, N., Doran, J. (eds.): Simulating Societies: the computer simulation of social phenomena. UCL Press, London (1994)
14. Hewitt, C.: Viewing control as patterns of passing messages. Artificial Intelligence 8 (1977)
15. Hewitt, C.: The challenge of open systems. Byte (April 1985)
16. Kaplan, F.: The emergence of a lexicon in a population of autonomous agents (in French). PhD thesis, Université de Paris 6 (2000)
17. Myles, G.D., Naylor, R.A.: A model of tax evasion with group conformity and social customs. European Journal of Political Economy 12(1), 49–66 (1996), http://ideas.repec.org/a/eee/poleco/v12y1996i1p49-66.html.
18. Simon, H.: Rationality in psychology and economics. In: Hogarth, R.M., Reder, M.W. (eds.) Rational choice: the Contrast Between Economics and Psychology, Univ. of Chicago Press (1987)
19. Urbano, P.: Decentralised Consensus Games (in Portuguese). PhD thesis, Faculdade de Ciências da Universidade de Lisboa (2004)
20. Wintrobe, R.: K. Gërxhani. Tax evasion and trust: a comparative analysis. In: Proceedings of the Annual Meeting of the European Public Choice Society – EPCS 2004 (2004)

Learning to Use a Perishable Good as Money

Toshiji Kawagoe

Future University - Hakodate, 116-2 Kameda Nakano cho, Hakodate, Hokkaido,
041-8655 Japan
kawagoe@fun.ac.jp

Abstract. In this paper, a variant of Kiyotaki and Wright's model of
emergence of money is investigated. In the model, each good has different
durability rather than storage cost as in Kiyotaki and Wright's model.
Two goods are infinitely durable but one is not durable. With certain
conditions, non-durable good can be money as a medium of exchange.
But equilibrium condition may be sensitive to the time evolution of the
distribution of goods that each agent holds in its inventory. We test, with
several learning models using different level of information, whether or
not the steady state in this economy can be attainable if the distribution
of goods is far from the steady state distribution. Belief learning with full
information outperforms the other models. The steady state equilibrium
is never attained by belief learning with partial information. A few agents
learn to use non-durable good as money by reinforcement learning which
does not use information about distribution of goods. It is surprising
that providing partial information is rather detrimental for attaining
emergence of a non-durable good money.

1 Introduction

In this paper, Cuadras-Morató [6]'s model of perishable money as a medium of
exchange, a variant of Kiyotaki and Wright [13]'s model of emergence of money,
is investigated. In the model, each good has different durability while each good
has different storage cost in Kiyotaki and Wright [13]'s model. In our setting,
two goods are infinitely durable but one is perishable.

With certain condition, a perishable good can be money as a medium of exchange in the stationary equilibrium. In the mathematical analysis, the stationary equilibrium has been derived by assuming that the economy has been near
the stationary equilibrium. To the best of our knowledge, there is no discussion
about the process of how the economy converges to the stationary equilibrium
if the economy is initially far from the steady state. As the equilibrium condition may be sensitive to the time evolution of the distribution of goods in the
economy, it is necessary to check whether the economy which is far away from
the stationary equilibrium can converge to the equilibrium.

We test whether stationary equilibrium is attainable by artificial agents which
follow several learning models in the economy where a perishable good can be
money. Especially we would like to compare belief learning model a la fictitious

L. Antunes and K. Takadama (Eds.): MABS 2006, LNAI 4442, pp. 96–111, 2007.
© Springer-Verlag Berlin Heidelberg 2007

play[1] with reinforcement learning model[2]. In the belief learning, agent utilizes the information of current state of the distribution of goods explicitly. On the other hand, in the reinforcement learning, agent pays attention to its own experience only and never looks at what the other agents do. In other words, agent never utilizes the information about the distribution of goods in the reinforcement learning. So belief learning and reinforcement learning represent two extreme cases of how information of the other agents' behaviors is treated in the learning process [3]. By comparing these models, we would like to see which degree of information is necessary to attain the stationary equilibrium in Cuadras-Morató [6]'s model when the economy is far from the steady state equilibrium.

For attaining a steady state in the economy with perishable money, our simulation result shows that belief learning with full information of the distribution of goods outperforms reinforcement learning. In the reinforcement learning, agent learns not to use a perishable good as a medium of exchange immediately. Moreover, interestingly, it is theoretically shown that belief learning with partial information of the distribution of goods never learns to use a perishable good as a medium of exchange. In the belief learning with partial information, each agent is provided only aggregate information of the distribution of goods in the economy. So this means that providing partial information is rather detrimental for attaining a steady state equilibrium in the economy with perishable money.

The organization of the paper is as follows. In the next section, the structure of Cuadras-Morató [6]'s model and its equilibrium prediction are explained. In the section 3, the simulation design and models of belief and reinforcement learning are shown, and then simulation results are summarized in section 4. Conclusions are given in the final section.

2   Model

Jevons [12] gives a list of requirements that any object should have in order to be suitable to perform the functions of money. Among others, portability, homogeneity, divisibility, stability of value, cognizability, and durability are regarded by him as desirable qualities of any commodity performing the role of money. Before Jevons wrote his book, Karl Marx [15] gave a similar list of desirable properties of money for hoarding. The passage of Peter Martyr's book cited in his work is of particular interest for us.

> The high specific value of precious metals, their durability, relative indestructibility, the fact that they do not oxidize when exposed to the air and that gold in particular is insoluble in acids other than aqua regia. All

---

[1] For a general reference to belief learning, see Fudenberg and Levine [11].
[2] For reinforcement learning, see Sutton and Barto [19] and Young [20].
[3] Some experimental economists compare belief learning with reinforcement learning in game theoretic settings. See Camerer and Ho [4], Cheung and Friedman [5], and Feltvich [10].

these physical properties make precious metals the natural material for hoarding. Peter Martyr, who was apparently a great lover of chocolate, remarks, therefore, of the sacks of cocoa which in Mexico served as a sort of money.

"Blessed money which furnishes mankind with a sweet and nutritious beverage and protects its innocent possessors from the infernal disease of avarice, since it cannot be long hoarded, nor hidden underground!" (De orbe novo [Alcala, 1530, dec. 5, cap. 4].24)

Hence, a perishable good such as a cocoa was used as money in Mexico in those days. But Marx didn't ask the question of why a perishable good such as a cocoa could be money even when it was lacking one of the desirable properties, durability, that money should have. When we look back in the history of money, there have been a number of cases reported by anthropologists and historians in which perishable goods appear to be used as mediums of exchange. For example, eggs in Guatemala, butter in Norway, tobacco, rice, grain, beef, peas and so on in the USA (see, for example, Einzig [9]). To explore the economic foundation of emergence of money as a perishable medium of exchange might be interesting for study of the historical evolution of money.

In Cuadras-Morató [6]'s model, there are infinitely many agents of three types who lives infinitely long periods. Type i agent enjoys utility, U, when it obtains a good i and consumes it, then it produces a good $i+1$ (modulo 3) with production cost, D, in the next period. Each agent can have at most one good at a time. While good 1 and 2 are infinitely durable, good 3 is perishable and loses its value within two periods after it is produced. We call a good 3 at the first period as 3_0, and a good 3 at the second period as 3_1. It is assumed in the theory that each agent also commonly knows the distribution of goods that each agent holds at each period. They meet at random at the market and then decide whether they would like to exchange their goods. If they mutually agree to exchange their goods, transactions between agents take place. If the trading partner holds same good, transaction never takes place. If agent of type i obtains a good i in its transaction, it will produce a new good $i+1$ (modulo 3) at the beginning of the next period. If agent of type i did not obtain a good i in its transaction, it continues to keeps the good that it has already held asa far as it is a durable good. If agent holds a good 3_1 and fails to obtain a good i , it has to dispose the good 3_1, then must produce a new good $i+1$ (modulo 3) in the next period. Each agent i tries to maximize its expected lifetime utility with the discount factor $\beta(0 < \beta < 1)$. Here, denote V_{ij} as the agent i's expected lifetime utility when it participate in the market with a good j.

Fig. 1 shows a trading process in which type 1 agent exchanges a good 2 with a good 3_0 that type 2 agent holds, then type 1 agent exchanges his good 3_1 with a good 1 that type 3 agent holds. Thus, if a good 3 can circulate successfully among these agents during two periods, every agent can obtain goods that they desire for their consumption. In this way, a good 3 can be money as a medium of exchange. In this trading process, it is trivial that type 1 agent and type 3 agent offer to trade because both of them have goods that their trading partners desire

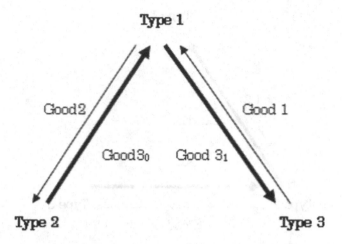

Fig. 1. Good 3 can be a medium of exchange

to consume. But a trade between type 1 and 2 agents is not trivial because type 1 agent does not desire a good 3_0 for its consumption.

But if $V_{13_1} > V_{12}$ holds, it is desirable for type 1 agent to exchange its good 2 with 3_0 because it may earn higher expected utility with a good 3_1 in the next period than it keeps a good 2 in its storage. So, it is optimal for type 1 agent to exchange its good 2 with good 3_0. V_{12} and V_{13_1} are given by Bellman equation respectively as follows.

$$V_{13_1} = \frac{\beta}{3}[-D_1 + V_{12} + p21(-D_1 + V_{12}) + p_{23_0}(-D_1 + V_{12})$$
$$+ p_{23_1}(-D_1 + V12) + p_{31}(U_1 - D_1 + V_{12}) + p_{32}V_{12}]$$
$$V_{12} = \frac{\beta}{3}[V_{12} + p_{21}(U_1 - D_1 + V_{12}) + p_{23_0}V_{13_1} + p_{23_1}V_{12}$$
$$+ p_31V_{12} + p_{32}V_{12}]$$

Thus, if the following equation (1) is positive, type 1 agent would like to trade its good 2 for a good 3_1.

$$V_{13_1} - V_{12} = \frac{(p_{31} - p_{21})(U - D) - 2D}{1 + \frac{\beta}{3}p_{23_0}} \tag{1}$$

where p_{ij} is the fraction of type i agent who holds a good j in the economy[4].

For type 2 agent, by calculating its expected lifetime utilities with the discount factor, the following equation holds,

---

[4] The detail of deriving the expected life time utility is partially given in Cuadras-Morató [6]. The full analysis is provided upon request. In addition, I will show an example for deriving the expected life time utility in an another setting in the section 3.3.

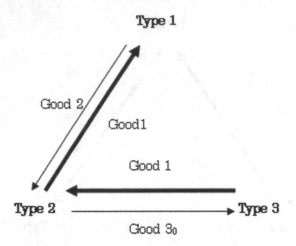

Fig. 2. Good 1 can be a medium of exchange

$$V_{21} - V_{23_1} = \frac{\beta}{3}[p_{12}U + (1 + p_{13_1})(V_{21} + D - V_{23_0})] \tag{2}$$

It is always positive whenever $p_{32} = 0^5$.
Finally, for type 3 agent,

$$V_{31} - V_{32} = \frac{\beta}{3}[V_{31} - V_{32} + p_{12}(V_{31} - V_{32})] \tag{3}$$

From this, we obtain $V_{31} - V_{32} = 0^6$. Thus, as type 3 agent starts its transaction with a type 1 good, it is indifferent between type 1 and 2 goods, we assume that it never hold a type 2 good. Thus, $p_{32} = 0$.

From these results, we can see that trading strategy for type 2 and 3 agent is not affected by the time evolution of the distribution of goods. Steady state distribution of the goods implied by these agents' behaviors is $p^* = (p_{12}, p_{23_0}, p_{21}, p_{31}) = (0.8967, 0.3456, 0.5272, 1.0)^7$. Vice-versa, If the distribution of goods is p^*, it is best response for type 1 agent to trade a good 2 for a good 3_1 if and only if $\frac{U}{D} > 5.2301^8$. If this condition is satisfied, even if a good 3 is perishable, it can be money as a medium of exchange in this economy. This is an equilibrium prediction of this model.

In the same way, we can calculate the conditions that a good 1 can be money. The necessary and sufficient condition for that a good 1 can be money is $V_{21} > V_{23_1}$ as shown in Fig. 2. In fact, as we have already shown, the condition $V_{21} >$

---

[5] As explained below, we assume that $p_{32} = 0$ always hold.
[6] If $V_{31} - V_{32} \neq 0$, it must be $\frac{\beta}{3} + \frac{\beta}{3}p_{21} - 1 = 0$. This implies $3 = \beta(1 + p_{12}) < 2$, a contradiction.
[7] The detail of deriving the steady state is partially given in the appendix of Cuadras-Morató [6]. The full analysis is provided in the appendix A in this paper.
[8] Substituting for p^* and rearranging, $V_{13_1} - V_{12} > 0$ holds if and only if $U/D > 5.2301$.

Table 1. Optimal trading strategy for type 1 agent

	Good held by trading partner			
Good held by type 1	good 1	good 2	good 3_0	good 3_1
good 2	1	0	1	0
good 3_0	1	0	0	0
good 3_1	1	1	1	0

Table 2. Optimal trading strategy for type 2 agent

	Good held by trading partner			
Good held by type 2	good 1	good 2	good 3_0	good 3_1
good 1	0	1	1	0
good 3_0	1	1	0	0
good 3_1	1	1	1	0

V_{23_1} always holds regardless of the values of U and D and the distribution of goods. So, good 1 can always be money as a medium of exchange in this economy. On the other hand, the necessary and sufficient condition for that a good 2 can be money is $V_{32} > V_{31}$, while the condition $V_{32} > V_{31}$ never hold for any values of U and D. Thus, good 2 is never money as a medium of exchange.

Thus, in summary, depending on the values of U and D for type 1 agent, there are two equilibria in this economy.

(**Equilibrium A**) Both good 1 and 3 can be money.
(**Equilibrium B**) Only good 1 can be money.

If the condition for Equilibrium A is satisfied, type 1 agent's trading strategy can be summarized in the Table 1. In each cell of the table 1, 1 means that type 1 agent would like to trade and 0 means that it would not, depending on the good that the trading partner holds. Apparently, it is impossible that type 1 agent participates in the transaction with a good 1 because it certainly consumes it. So, that case is omitted. If the trading partner holds a good 1, type 1 agent offer to trade regardless of the good it holds, so every cell in the first column should be 1. If the trading partner holds a good 3_1, type 1 agent never offer to trade whatever good it holds, so every cell in the fourth column should be 0. If type 1 agent holds a good 3_1, it would like to offer to trade whatever good its trading partner holds, so every cell in the fourth row should be 1. By the assumption, if the trading partner holds same good, transaction never take place, so every cell in the diagonal should be 0. Finally, type 1 agent would like to exchange its good 2 with a good 3_0, not vice-versa. This is an optimal trading strategy under complete information for type 1 agent. Similarly, optimal trading strategies under complete information for type 2 and 3 agents are given in Table 2 and 3 respectively.

Table 3. Optimal trading strategy for type 3 agent

	Good held by trading partner			
Good held by type 3	good 1	good 2	good 3_0	good 3_1
good 1	0	0	1	1

3   Simulation Design

We compare the following four behavioral models in our simulation.

3.1   Model 1. Theoretical Model

All the agents follow the optimal trading strategy under complete information derived from theoretical prediction as shown in Table 1, 2, and 3. This model is used as a baseline for comparing performances of the other learning models. But, unlike in the theoretical model mentioned in section 2, as the economy in this simulation starts with the initial condition far from the steady state equilibrium, it is still uncertain whether the steady state is attainable even though agents follow this model. So one need to check it by a simulation and we did it.

3.2   Model 2. Belief Learning with Full Information

Belief learning has a long history in theory of games. Brown [2] proposed it as a numerical algorithm for finding a minimax solution in a two-person zerosum game and Robinson [16] proved that the algorithm proposed by Brown, called fictitious play learning, always converges to a minimax solution in a two-person zero-sum game. On the other hand, if that learning algorithm is applied to a nonzerosum game, such convergence result does not always hold. In fact, Shapley [18] shows a counter example of a non-zerosum game that fictitious play learning does not converge to an equilibrium but circulates among some non-equilibrium outcomes. Recently, a number of researchers in experimental economics use fictitious play learning to replicate subjects' behaviors in laboratory experiments. They showed that fictitious play learning outperforms reinforcement learning in some cases (see Camerer and Ho [4], Cheung and Friedman [5], and Feltvich [10].).

   In belief learning such as fictitious play learning, agent forms a belief of the other agents' behaviors from the past experiences. Given that belief, agent tries to maximize its expected payoff. Basically that belief is derived from frequency of the strategy choices by the other players in the previous periods.

   Next we consider how to apply fictitious play learning in our modeling. First of all, note that the frequency of the strategy choices by the other players are represented in the distribution of goods in the previous period, $p^{t-1} = (p_{12}^{t-1}, p_{23_0}^{t-1}, p_{21}^{t-1}, p_{31}^{t-1})$. So type 1 agent who follows belief learning tries to maximize its life time expected payoff given p^{t-1}. Thus each type 1 agent calculates $V_{13_1}(p^{t-1}) - V_{12}(p^{t-1})$ at the beginning of period t and trades its type

2 good for a type 3 good in the period t if $V_{13_1}(p^{t-1}) - V_{12}(p^{t-1}) > 0$. From equation (1),

$$V_{13_1}(p^{t-1}) - V_{12}(p^{t-1}) > 0 \Leftrightarrow (p_{31}^{t-1} - p_{21}^{t-1})(U - D) - 2D > 0 \qquad (4)$$

Thus, if $U > D$ and $p_{31}^{t-1} = 1$, this condition implies[9],

$$p_{21}^{t-1} < \frac{U - 3D}{U - D} = f(U, D) \qquad (5)$$

This condition is depicted in Fig. 3. The gray area is the parameter space in which type 1 agent would like to trade its type 2 good for a type 3 good.

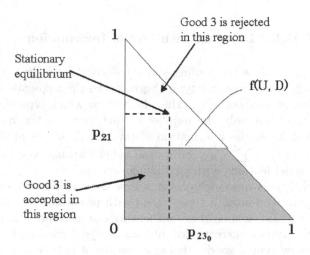

Fig. 3. Parameter space for type 1 agent

As each type 1 agent knows every agents' transaction in the past in this case, we call this type of belief learning 'belief learning with full information'.

Note that even if the equilibrium condition of Equilibrium A, $\frac{U}{D} > 5.2301$, is satisfied, that equilibrium might not be attainable. Now suppose that the economy is far from the steady state, for example, somewhere in the gray area in Fig.3. As type 1 agent trades its type 2 good for a type 3 good in the gray area, the proportion of type 2 agent who holds type 1 good, p_{21}, moves up toward the steady state of Equilibrium A. But when the state of economy just goes across the borderline of $f(U, D)$, type 1 agent doesn't accept a type 3 good, however. Even if the equilibrium condition $\frac{U}{D} > 5.2301$ is hold, this can be the case because the condition (5) is violated. In other words, even if $\frac{U}{D} > 5.2301$ is hold, as p_{21}^{t-1} is higher than $f(U, D)$, agent who follows belief learning with full

---

[9] Thus, from $(1 - p_{21}^{t-1})(U - D) - 2D > 0$, we have $(1 - p_{21}^{t-1}) > \frac{2D}{U-D}$. Then $1 - \frac{2D}{U-D} > p_{21}^{t-1}$. Finally, we have $\frac{U-3D}{U-D} > p_{21}^{t-1}$.

information would not like to trade a type 2 good for a type 3 good. Then before reaching the steady state of the economy, p_{21} goes down toward the gray area. Again, as the state of economy is in the gray area, type 1 agent accept a type 3 good and then p_{21} goes up. Thus eventually the economy circulates around the borderline of $f(U, D)$ and does not converge to the steady state. This is a similar phenomena of a counter example shown by Shapley [18] in a simple matrix game.

So, we would like to know whether equilibrium A can be attained with belief learning if we start the economy with the initial condition that the distribution of goods is far from the steady state.

As type 2 and 3 agents' optimal trading strategies are not affected by time evolution of the distribution of goods, we assume in our simulation that these types always follows optimal strategies in Table 2 and 3.

3.3   Model 3. Belief Learning with Partial Information

Type 2 and 3 agents follow the trading strategy derived from theoretical prediction as in Model 2. We assume that type 1 agent knows the aggregate information of the distribution of goods only, i.e., they don't know which type of agent holds which type of good but only the number of each good in the market. Thus type 1 agent only know the information of (p_1^t, p_2^t, p_3^t), where $p_1^t = \sum_{i=1}^{3} p_{i1}^t$, $p_2^t = \sum_{i=1}^{3} p_{i2}^t$, and $p_3^t = \sum_{i=1}^{3} p_{i3}^t$. So we call belief learning based on this type of information 'belief learning with partial information'.

In this model, type 1 agent who holds a type 2 good believes that it meets with another agent who holds a type 1 good with probability p_1^t. If that agent is type 2 (here we also assume that, without loss of generality, it occurs with probability 0.5^{10}), type 1 agent trades, obtains a type 1 good and consumes it, and produces a new type 2 good, otherwise that agent is type 3, so transaction never takes place. Type 1 agent who holds a type 2 good believes that it meets with another agent who holds a type 2 good with probability p_2^t and transaction never take place. Type 1 agent who holds a type 2 good believes that it meets with another agent who holds a type 3 good with probability p_3^t and transaction never take place. Then the expected life time utility with the discount factor β for type 1 agent who holds a type 2 good is as follows.

$$V_{12} = \frac{\beta}{3}[\frac{p_1^t}{2}(U - D + 2V_{12}) + (p_2^t + p_3^t)V_{12}] \tag{6}$$

Similarly, the expected life time utility with the discount factor β for type 1 agent who holds a type 3_1 good is as follows.

$$V_{13_1} = \frac{\beta}{3}[\frac{p_1^t}{2}(U - D + 2V_{12}) + p_2^t(-D + 2V_{12}) + p_3^t(-D + 2V_{12})] \tag{7}$$

---

[10] The conclusion does not change unless we consider quite an extreme case. Such an extreme case, of course, possibly arises, but it's a quite rare case.

Hence,

$$V_{13_1} - V_{12} = \frac{\beta}{3}[(p_1^t + p_2^t + 2p_3^t)(-D)] < 0 \qquad (8)$$

Therefore, a perishable good is never a medium of exchange when agent follows belief learning with partial information. As we prove that Equilibrium A is never attainable when agent follows belief learning with partial information, we didn't run any simulation of this model and we will not provide any result for that model.

3.4   Model 4. Reinforcement Learning

In reinforcement learning model, each agent doesn't care for what the other agent do but care for its own payoff in each period. So, the distribution of goods doesn't matter in reinforcement learning. Each agent changes its behavior in accordance with its local information. So this is the lowest information condition compared with belief learning models.

Propensity of holding a type 3_1 good for type 1 agent, $R_{13_1}^t$, is updated by the following rule.

$$R_{13_1}^{t+1} = \delta R_{13_1}^t + I_1^t(U - D) + I_2^t(-D) \qquad (9)$$

Where $\delta(0 < \delta < 1)$ is forgetting parameter, $I_1^t = 1$ if the agent trades a good 3 for a good 1, and otherwise $I_1^t = 0$, $I_2^t = 1$ if the agent does not trades, disposes its type 3 good and produces a new good 2, and otherwise $I_2^t = 0$. Thus if $I_1^t = 0$ and $I_2^t = 0$, the agent trades its good 3 for good 2. In similar way, propensity of holding a type 2 good for type 1 agent, R_{12}^t, is

$$R_{12}^{t+1} = \delta R_{12}^t + I_{12}^t(U - D) \qquad (10)$$

With these propensities, type 1 agent trades its good 2 for a good 3_1 with the following probability in the logit form,

$$P_{13_1}^t = \frac{\exp(\lambda R_{13_1}^t)}{\exp(\lambda R_{13_1}^t) + \exp(\lambda R_{12}^t)} \qquad (11)$$

where $\lambda \geq 0$ is the precision parameter.

3.5   Other Simulation Settings

In our simulation, parameters, U, D and p_{21}, affect learning behavior of each agent in belief learning. As for utility and cost, we fix $D = 100$ and vary the value of U among 400, 523, and 800 when belief learning is tested. $U = 523$ is chosen because it is the borderline of the equilibrium requirement. Two relatively high and low values for or against attaining Equilibrium A, $U = 800$ and $U = 400$, are chosen for comparisons. For reinforcement learning, we use $U = 523$ only because reinforcement learning cannot be affected by these parameters as we explained before. As for the distribution of goods, we choose two extreme initial distributions of goods for type 2 agent, $p_{21} = 0$ and $p_{21} = 1$. δ affect only the speed of learning, so we fix $\delta = 0.9$ without loss of generality. Although we also varied λ among the values $\{0.5, 1.0, 2.0, 4.0\}$, agent's behavior did not change qualitatively. So we take $\lambda = 1.0$ as a representive case. There are totally 300 agent in the market where 100 agents are assigned for each type. Each run of simulation consists of 50 periods, and 20 run of simulations are conducted.

4   Results

Table 4 shows the aggregate information of the number of transactions that type 1 agents made.

At the first look, proportions of type 1 agent accepting a good 1 are almost same among these four models. But proportions of type 1 agent accepting a good 3, a perishable good, are different among these four models. For belief learning with full information, type 1 agent trades a good 2 for a good 3 more frequently when $U = 523$ and 800. Type 1 agent had opportunity to trade a good 2 for a good 3 totally 9932 (10060) times. Then they actually made such trades 6151 (10052) times when $U = 523$ (800). Note that even the equilibrium condition of Equilibrium A, $\frac{U}{D} > 5.2301$, is satisfied, agent who follows belief learning with full information does not trades a good 2 for a good 3 in 40% of times. On the other hand, no such trade occurred in belief learning with full information model when $U = 400$ and only a few trades occurred in reinforcement learning model when $U = 523$ (0.37% of the total trades). This means that good 3 can be money as the medium of exchange when each agent follows belief learning with full information and utility from consuming a good is relatively high.

Table 4. The aggregate information of the number of type 1 agent's transactions

	Belief $U = 523$	Belief $U = 800$	Belief $U = 400$	Reinf. $U = 523$
type 1 agent trades good 2 for good 3_0	6151 / 9932 (61.9%)	10052 / 10060 (99.9%)	0 / 9984 (0.0%)	362 / 9783 (0.37%)
type 1 agent trades good 2 for good 1	16636 / 48232 (34.5%)	16383 / 46428 (35.3%)	17195 / 50586 (34.0%)	17199 / 50546 (34.0%)

To measure the degree of convergence to the steady state, we employ the Euclidian distance between the distribution of goods in each time period and one in the steady state, i.e.,

$$d^t = \sqrt{(p_{12}^t - p_{12}^*) + (p_{21}^t - p_{21}^*) + (p_{23_0}^t - p_{23_0}^*) + (p_{31}^t - p_{31}^*)} \quad (12)$$

as a measure of convergence.

Fig. 4 shows time series data of the Euclidian distance in each case. The Euclidian distance for belief learning with full information soon converges around

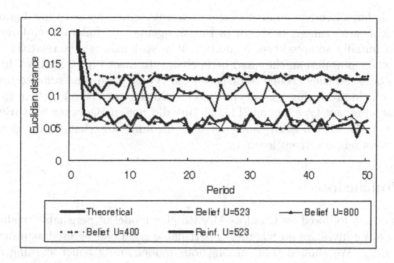

Fig. 4. Euclidian distance between the distribution of goods in each period and in the steady state

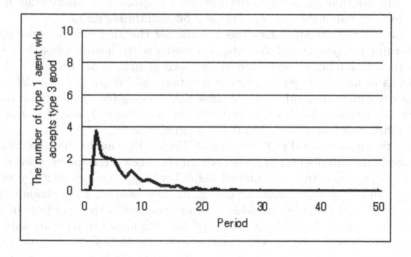

Fig. 5. The number of type 1 agents who accept type 3 good in reinforcement learning

the equilibrium, within Euclidian distance of 0.05 when $U = 800$. It performs well as in theoretical model. On the other hand, when $U = 400$ belief learning with full information performs as worse as reinforcement learning, it stays away from the equilibrium with Euclidian distance 0.13 in average. Finally, when $U = 523$, the performance of belief learning is in between these cases. Thus, this also confirms that agent who follows belief learning with full information can learn to use a perishable good as a medium of exchange when the utility for consuming a good is relatively high.

Fig. 5 shows average number of type 1 agents who accepted type 3 goods in reinforcement learning. As shown in Fig. 5, agents who followed reinforcement learning initially accepted type 3 goods. But as such agents were relatively fewer in the whole population, they had little chance to meet type 3 agents who held type 1 goods. So they needed to dispose their type 3 goods and suffered production cost D in producing a new type 2 goods. Such experiences led them to learn to refuse to accept type 3 good. This picture did not change when we varied the value of λ. So, type 3 good could not be a medium of exchange among agents who follows reinforcement learning.

5   Conclusions

In this study, followed by Cuadras-Morató [6]'s model of perishable medium of exchange, we investigated whether a perishable good can be used as a medium of exchange. We showed that, among four models, only belief learning model with full information learns to use a perishable good as money in this economy. Reinforcement learning performs relatively poor. But, interestingly, worst model among four is belief learning with partial information. This means that providing partial information is rather detrimental for attaining a steady state in the economy with perishable money. This is a bit unintuitive for us.

So far, several attempts have been made for checking whether speculative equilibrium in Kiyotaki and Wright [13]'s model is attained in laboratory environment with human subjects and in multi-agent simulation. Brown [3], Duffy and Ochs [7] and Duffy [8] investigate Kiyotaki and Wright [13]'s model in the laboratory with human subjects and show that speculative equilibrium is hardly observed. Marimon, McGrattan, and Sargent [14], Başçı [1] and Rouchier [17] also confirm this result in the multi-agent simulation.

Note that it is assumed in Kiyotaki and Wright [13]'s model that the information about the distribution of goods is common knowledge among agents. But no one in previous studies examined belief learning, which explicitly uses the information of the distribution of goods, in their studies. Even though Duffy and Ochs [7] and Duffy [8] provided such information to their subjects in their laboratory studies, they did not use belief learning model to replicate subjects' behaviors in their simulation. One could ask that the difficulty of attaining speculative equilibrium in the simulation may be due to the lack of the information of the distribution of goods. In other words, simulation studies remove two basic assumptions in Kiyotaki and Wright [13]'s model, (1) perfect rationality of agents and (2) complete information of the distribution of goods, and then replace them with (1) bounded rationality of agent and (2) informational uncertainty of the distribution of goods. One may think that lacking of both basic assumptions is too much for testing the theory.

Our results in Cuadras-Morató [6]'s model may indicate that if we would provide full information about the distribution of goods in the Kiyotaki and

Wright [13] economy, speculative equilibrium can be attained even by boundedly rational agents who follow belief learning. We would like to prove this conjecture in the future research.

References

1. Başç, E.: Learning By Imitation. Journal of Economic Dynamics and Control 23, 1569–1585 (1999)
2. Brown, G.W.: Iterative Solutions of Games by Fictitious Play. In: Coopmans, T.C. (ed.) Activity Analysis of Production and Allocation, Wiley, Chichester (1951)
3. Brown, P.M.: Experimental Evidence On Money As A Medium Of Exchange. Journal of Economic Dynamics and Control 20, 583–600 (1996)
4. Camerer, C., Ho, T.H.: Experience-weighted Attraction Learning in Normal Form Games. Econometrica 67, 827–874 (1999)
5. Cheung, Y.W., Friedman, D.: Individual Learning in Normal Form Games: Some Laboratory Results. Games and Economic Behavior 19, 46–76 (1997)
6. Cuadras-Morató, X.: Can Ice Cream Be Money?: Perishable Medium Of Exchange. Journal of Economics 66, 103–125 (1997)
7. Duffy, J., Ochs, J.: Emergence Of Money As A Medium Of Exchange: An Experimental Study. American Economic Review 89, 847–877 (1999)
8. Duffy, J.: Learning To Speculate: Experiments With Artificial And Real Agents. Journal of Economic Dynamics and Control 25, 295–319 (2001)
9. Einzig, P.: Primitive Money. Pergamon Press, Oxford
10. Feltvich, N.: Reinforcement-Based vs. Belief-Based Learning Models in Experimental Asymmetric-Informatio Games. Econometrica 68, 605–641 (2000)
11. Fudenberg, D., Levine, D.K.: The Theory of Learning in Games. The MIT Press, Cambridge (1998)
12. Jevons, W.S.: Money and the Mechanism of Exchange. Henry S. King and Co, London (1875)
13. Kiyotaki, N., Wright, R.: On money As A Medium Of Exchange. Journal of Political Economy 97, 927–954 (1989)
14. Marimon, R., McGrattan, E., Sargent, T.J.: Money As A Medium Of Exchange In An Economy With Artificially Intelligent Agents. Journal of Economic Dynamics and Control 14, 329–373 (1990)
15. Marx, K.: A Contribution To The Critique Of Political Economy (1859)
16. Robinson, J.: An Iterative Method of Solving a Game. Annals of Mathematics 54, 296–301 (1951)
17. Rouchier, J.: Re-implementationo Of A Multi-Agent Model Aimed At Sustaining Experimental Economic Research: The Case Of Simulations With Emerging Speculation. Journal of Artificial Societies and Social Simulation 6(4) (2003)
18. Shapley, L.: Some Topics in Two-person Games. In: Dresher, M., Shapley, L.S., Tucker, A.W. (eds.) Advances in Game Theory, Princeton University Press, Princeton (1964)
19. Sutton, R.S., Barto, A.G.: Reinforcement Learning An Introduction. MIT Press, Cambridge (1998)
20. Young, H.P.: Strategic Learning And Its Limit. Oxford University Press, Oxford (2004)

A   Deriving the Steady State Distribution of Equilibrium A

In this appendix, we will show how to derive the steady state distribution of Equilibrium A. First, we check how the distribution of goods evolves if the condition of Equilibrium A holds and every agent follows optimal trading strategies in Table 1, 2, and 3. With this consideration, we construct a Markov process of the evolution of the distribution of goods. Then we have the steady state distribution corresponding to Equilibrium A.

Let's consider how type 1 agent trades if it follows optimal trading strategy.

Case 1a. Type 1 agent who holds a type 2 good still holds a type 2 good in the next period if
1. it meets another type 1 agent and does not trade,
2. or it meets a type 2 agent who holds a good 1, trade, and produces a new type 2 good,
3. or it meets a type 2 agent who holds a good 3_1 and does not trade,
4. or it meets a type 3 agent who holds a good 1, trades, and produces a new good 2,
5. or it meets a type 3 agent who holds a good 2 and does not trade.

Case 1b. Type 1 agent who holds a type 2 good holds a type 3_1 good in the next period if it meets a type 2 agent who holds a good 3_0 and offers to trade.

Case 2a. On the other hand, type 1 agent who holds a type 3_1 good holds a type 2 good in the next period if
1. it meets a type 3 agent who holds a good 1, trades, and produces a new good 2,
2. or it meets a type 3 agent who holds a good 2 and trades,
3. or it meets another type 1 agent or type 2 agent, does not trade, and its type 3 good perishes, then it produces a new type 2 good.

Case 2b. Type 1 agent who holds a type 3_1 good still holds a type 3_1 good in the next period is impossible.

Thus, the evolution of $p_1 = (p_{12}, p_{13_1})$ consists a Markov chain, and its transition matrix is as follows.

$$\Pi_1 = \frac{1}{3} \begin{pmatrix} p_{12} + p_{13_1} + p_{21} + p_{23_1} + p_{31} + p_{32} & p_{23_0} \\ 3 & 0 \end{pmatrix}$$

Analogously, we can derive the transition matrix for type 2 agent.

$$\Pi_2 = \frac{1}{3} \begin{pmatrix} p_{13_1} + 1 + p_{31} & p_{12} + p_{32} & 0 \\ p_{31} & p_{12} + p_{32} & p_{13_1} + 1 \\ p_{31} & 2 + p_{32} & 0 \end{pmatrix}$$

where we used $p_{12} + p_{13_1} = 1$ and $p_{21} + p_{23_0} + p_{23_1} = 1$.

As we have shown, type 3 agent never receive type 2 good, so we have already obtained it's steady state distribution.

$$p_{31} = 1 \tag{13}$$

The condition for the steady state for type 1 agent is $p_1 \Pi_1 = p_1$. From this, we have

$$p_{12}(1 + p_{21} + p_{23_1} + 1) + 3p_{13_1} = 3p_{12} \tag{14}$$

$$p_{12}p_{23_0} = 3p_{13_1} \tag{15}$$

The condition for the steady state for type 2 agent is $p_2 \Pi_2 = p_2$, where $p_2 = (p_{21}, p_{23_0}, p_{23_1})$. From this,

$$p_{21}(p_{13_1} + 1 + p_{31}) + p_{31}(p_{23_0} + p_{23_1}) = 3p_{21} \tag{16}$$

$$p_{21}(p_{12} + p_{32}) + p_{23_0}(p_{12} + p_{32}) + p_{23_1}(2 + p_{32}) = 3p_{23_0} \tag{17}$$

$$p_{23_0}(p_{13_1} + 1) = 3p_{23_1} \tag{18}$$

Thus, the steady state distribution of the goods implied by these strategies

$$p^* = (p_{12}, p_{23_0}, p_{21}, p_{31}) = (0.8967, 0.3456, 0.5272, 1.0000)$$

is obtained by solving equations (13) to (18) numerically.

A Holonic Approach to Model and Deploy Large Scale Simulations

Sebastian Rodriguez, Vincent Hilaire, and Abder Koukam

Université de Technologie de Belfort Montbéliard,
90010 Belfort Cedex, France
`sebastian.rodriguez@utbm.fr`
Tel.: + (33) 384 583 009

Abstract. Multi-Agent Based Simulations (MABS) for real-world problems may require a large number of agents. A possible solution is to distribute the simulation in multiple machines. Thus, we are forced to consider how Large Scale MABS can be deployed in order to have an efficient system. Even more, we need to consider how to cluster those agents in the different execution servers. In this paper we propose an approach based on a holonic model for the construction and update of clusters of agents. We also present two modules to facilitate the deployment and control of distributed simulations.

1 Introduction

Multi-Agent Based Simulations (MABS in the sequel) are based upon the analogy between real world entities and autonomous and interacting agents. This is a natural and intuitive approach for problem simulation.

However, for real world problems, MABS frequently leads to a great number of agents. Any MAS platform, such as FIPA-OS[18], JADE[1] or MadKit[14], inherits operating system and hardware layers constraints e.g. memory, cpu and thread number limits.

In this context we are forced to consider how Large Scale MABS can be deployed in order to have an efficient system. A possible solution is to profit from MAS' intrinsic decentralized nature to distribute agents on several computers.

Two issues have then to be considered. First, how to group agents that will execute in the same machine. And second, how do we deploy and control a distributed system or simulation.

In order to support the decentralized characteristic of the agent paradigm, we need to provide the MAS with a platform that enables distributed interactions in a transparent way from the agent's point of view. To face this problem, we propose two plugins for the MADKIT platform [14] that facilitate MAS deployment and the control of a distributed simulation.

We also discuss the issue of how to create the clusters of agents that will be sent to the machines. Indeed, before distributing the MAS, we need to find means to create clusters of agents that will execute in the same machine. To

L. Antunes and K. Takadama (Eds.): MABS 2006, LNAI 4442, pp. 112–127, 2007.

tackle this problem we define a distribution logic using the holonic paradigm. This distribution follows the holon organizational structure.

Holons were defined by Koestler [15] as self-similar structures composed of holons as substructures. They are neither parts nor wholes in an absolute sense. The organizational structure defined by holons, called holarchy, allows the modelling at several granularity levels. Each level corresponds to a group of interacting holons.

The paper is organized as follows: section 2 presents our approach for holonic modelling and illustrates it with the traffic simulation model of a big plant. Section 2 presents the principles of the MadKit platform and the two plugins we have created to handle large scale MABS. Section 4 details the plant traffic simulation and section 5 concludes.

2 Holonic Modelling of Large Scale Simulations

One of the issues discussed in this paper is: how do we create the clusters of agents that will be sent to the machines?

In our approach we will base that decision on the holarchy. In the next section we briefly introduce our framework for holonic MAS. For a complete definition of this framework see [22,23]. [21] presents an approach for environment modelling using this framework and in [20] we have proven pertinent properties about this framework.

2.1 Holonic Framework

Holonic MAS have attracked recently much interest of the DAI community. These types of systems have been applied to a wide range of domains such as Transports [3], Manufacturing Systems [25,16], etc.

However most of the frameworks proposed to model them are strongly related to their domain of application. This renders the approach sometimes difficult to apply to other problems. In an attempt to solve this drawback, we based our framework in an organizational approach [23]. The framework uses then organizations to model the status of the members (sub-holons) in the composition of higher level holons (super-holons) and to model the interactions of the members to achieve their goals/tasks.

We have adopted a moderated group structure for holonic MAS[12]. This decision is based on the wide range of configurations that are possible by modifying the commitments of the members toward their super-holon. In a moderated group, we can differentiate two status for the members. First, the *moderator* or *representative*, who acts as the interface with non-member holons, and, second, *represented* members, who are masked to the outside world by their representatives. Even if we use the name *"Moderated Group"* for compatibility with earlier works in this domain, it can be misleading. As we see it, the structure does not necessarily introduced any authority or subordination. The name makes reference to the different status found in the group. We can then adapt this organization by giving the representatives specific authorities according to the problem or constraints.

In order to represent a moderated group as an organization we have identified a set of roles that can represent these concepts. We have chosen to use four roles to describe a moderated group as an organization: Head, Part, Multi-Part and StandAlone. The three first roles describe a status of a member inside a super-holon. The Stand-Alone role represents, on the other hand, how non-members are seen by an existing holon.

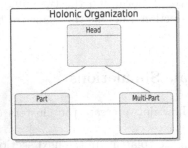

Fig. 1. RIO Diagram of the holons members

Fig. 2. RIO Diagram of the Merging Organization

As shown in the figure 1 the representatives of the super-holon play the *Head* role. A *Head* member becomes then part of the visible face of the super-holon. This means that the *head* becomes a kind of interface between the members of the holon and the outside world. The *head* role can be played by more than one member at the same time.

The members can confer the *head* a number of rights or authorities. According to the level of authority given to *heads*, super-holon can adopt different configurations. Thus, the *Head* role represents a privileged status in the super-holon. *Heads* will generally be conferred with a certain level of authority. However, these members have also an administrative load. This load can be variable depending on the selected configuration.

It is important to remark that when a set of holons merge into a super-holon a new entity appears in the system. In this case, they are not merely a group of holon in interaction as in "traditional" MAS theory. The super-holon is then an entity of its own right. Thus, it has a set of skills, is capable of taking roles, etc. At the same time, as *Heads* constitute the interface of the super-holon, they are in charge of redistributing the information arriving from the outside. And, thus to "trigger" the (internal) process that will produce the desired result. The *Part* role identifies members of a single holon. These members are represented by *Heads* within the outside world. While the holon belongs to a single super-holon, it will play this role. However, when the holon is not satisfied with its current super-holon it has two possibilities. The first is to quit its super-holon entirely and try to find a new holon to merge and collaborate with. The second is to try to merge with a second super-holon while remaining as a member of the first super-holon. In this case the holon will change his role to $Multi-Part$. The $Multi-Part$ role is an extension of the $Part$ role. It puts emphasis on a particular situation when a sub-holon is shared by more than one super-holon.

In order to support the integration of new member, we need to provide external holons with a "standard" interface so they can request their admission. From the super-holons point of view, external holons are seen as $StandAlone$ role players. When a super-holon is created, only $Heads$ belong to the interface of the super-holon. Thus, other members ($Part$ and $MultiPart$) should not be visible by external holons. This is modeled by the organization presented in figure 2. In this organization, $StandAlone$ holons may interact only with the $heads$ of the super-holon.

2.2 Holarchy Example

In order to illustrate our framework we take an example and describe it with holonic concepts. This example consists in a simplified University. Imagine that we model the university as composed of Departments and research Laboratories. They are in turn composed of Professors and Researchers respectively. If we isolate the Computer Science and Laboratory Holon and their components from the university example and we add these holonic roles, we obtain figure 3. $Part$ role players for the laboratory represent researcher that belong only to the laboratory, e.g. full time researchers. On the other hand, some researcher may, in addition to their activities in the laboratory, give lectures in the computer science department. These holons, like holon RP in figure 3, belong to both super-holons simultaneously and thus they play the $MultiPart$ role. In this example, the department and laboratory directors would be the $Heads$ of the C.S. Department and the laboratory respectively.

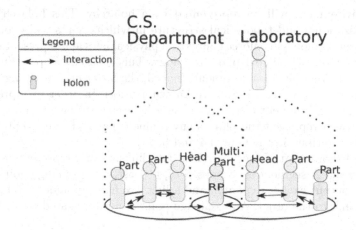

Fig. 3. Department and Laboratory Holons

As we mentioned earlier other organization will be used to specify domain dependant interactions (e.g. a *Lecture Organization* to describe how professors interact with their students) [23].

Based on these *holonic* roles –Head, Part and MultiPart– we have defined mechanisms to handle holons dynamics. They are based upon the affinity and satisfaction between holons. The notion of *Affinity* was inspired by a technique used for the Artificial Immune System [6]. The term *Satisfaction* has often been used to represent the gratification of an agent concerning its current state or the progress of its goals/tasks [5,24].

The affinity between holons must be defined according to the domain of the application. The affinity measures, according to the application's objectives, the compatibility of two holons to work together toward a shared objective.

The *compatibility* of two holons means that they can provide help to each other to progress towards their goals. Based on the application's objective, we define a set of rules that allow us to evaluate this *compatibility*. Generally speaking, we can say that two holons are compatible if they have shared goals and complementary services.

Using these two notions, holons are able to decide when they should join or leave a super-holon (satisfaction) and with which super-holon to merge with (affinity). Holons can then move from one super-holon to another as the system (in our case simulation) evolves.

2.3   PSA Simulation Model

We propose the use of holarchies for the modelling of simulation environments. In the Peugeot SA (PSA in the sequel) plant example we want to simulate the traffic within the plant. The environment of this simulation is defined by the topology of the plant. The agents will be the different vehicles driving through the plant.

The environment will be represented by a holarchy. This holarchy defines the organizational and topological structure in which agents will evolve. Each environmental holon will enforce contextual physical laws and represent a specific granularity level of the real plant topology. This holarchy is predefined as it represents the real plant environment. Indeed, the latter cannot change and the physical laws we need to enforce are known a priori. In order to represent the geographical environment of the plant as a holarchy we have to find recursive concepts which represent the plant's environment parts. The concepts we have chosen are described in the figures 4 and 5.

Figure 4 shows that a road is divided into links. A link represents a one way lane of a road. A segment is composed of, at least, two exchange points, called input and output exchange points, and a link. Exchange points let vehicles pass from one link to the other. An exchange point is always shared by at least two segments.

In the figure 5 we can see that the industrial plant is composed of a set of zones, that in turn contain Buildings and Segments. Buildings and Segments can also communicate through shared exchange points. Usually an exchange point

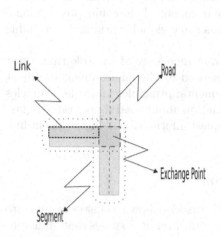

Fig. 4. Roads, Segments, Links and Exchange Points

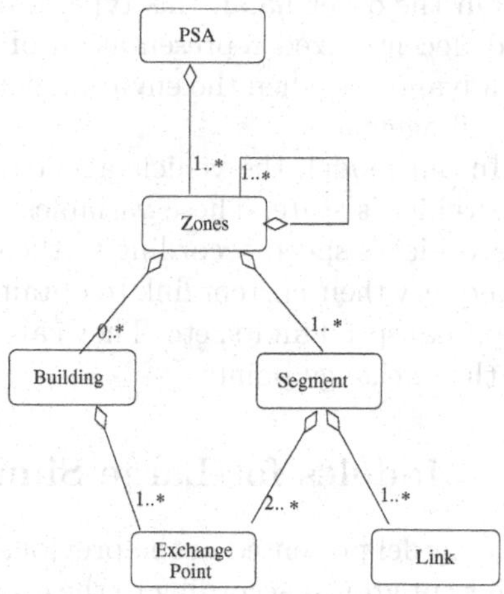

Fig. 5. Conceptual view of the plant

represents a crossroad, but in can also represent an entrance used by trucks to access buildings. A zone may also be decomposed in smaller zones which contains Buildings and Segments and so on recursively.

This decomposition also gives us important information about the roles involved. Let us consider the *ExchangePoint* role. This role represents an exchange point between physical entities such as roads and buildings. An Exchange-Point can then be specialized to respect certain constraints, for example, a door lets a human get into a building but it's impossible for a car to use it. As we can see the exchange point is a "special" role from the "holonic point of view" since the role is actually shared by more than one holon by definition. Note that this situation differs from the one where a particular holon plays the multi-part role. In this case, we know that the holon preforming this role will be shared by at least two holons prior to the simulation, even more, we can even know exactly to which two super-holons. Such a hierarchical decomposition of the environment presents several advantages when compared to a global representation. First, no size limit is imposed by the model, this enables us to use the same environment decomposition to simulate the traffic inside a city or a (much) smaller industrial plant. Some semantical information could be introduced, like this, instead of zones, we will represent quarter, block, etc. [7].

Second, all necessary information to simulate the traffic inside a link is local (other vehicles, roadsigns, etc). This makes the model easier to distribute in a network and leaves the door open to Real-time applications as well as Virtual Reality implementations.

It is important to notice that the decomposition may continue in order to provide a higher level of detail. It provides a simple way of decomposing different types of environments. For instance, a building itself can be decomposed in Rooms and Exchange Points(doors).

On the other hand, this type of decomposition imposes a highly hierarchical and decentralized representation of the environment. This could present some disadvantages when the environment presents some global "variables" accessible for all agents.

In our model, the vehicle agent is able to change a set of variable that affect the vehicle's state. These variables are later used by the environment to adjust the vehicle's speed according to the environmental principles and rules. Vehicles can query their current link to obtain information about road signs, traffic lights, maximal speed limits, etc. They can also request information about adjacent link to the exchange points.

3   Modules for Large Simulations

The model presented in the previous section considers how to cluster agents into coherent groups according to the application. However, it assumes that all holons in the system can communicate regardless of their physical location. To enable this behavior, we propose two plugins for the MADKIT platform. An overview is presented in figure 6. The first plugin (NetComm), presented in section 3.2, is in charge of generating and maintaining the "Virtual Community" between kernels. On top of that community the second plugin (SimSever), presented in section 3.3, offers the possibility to distribute and control a simulation.

Before we detail the architecture of these plugins, let us first briefly review MADKIT 's principles.

3.1   MadKit Principles

MadKit is built upon the AGR model [8] illustrated in figure 7. This model is based on the following organizational concepts: Agent, Group and Role. An

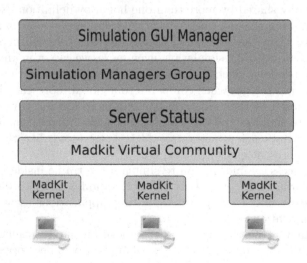

Fig. 6. Plugins Overview

agent is an active, communicating entity playing *roles* within *groups*. An agent may hold multiple roles, and may be a member of several groups. An important characteristic of the AGR model is that no constraints are placed upon the architecture of an agent or about its mental capabilities. Thus, an agent may be reactive as an ant, or deliberative with mental states.

A group is a set of agents sharing some common characteristics. A group is used as a context for a pattern of activities. Two agents may communicate if and only if they belong to the same group, but an agent may belong to several groups.

A role is the abstract representation of a functional position of an agent in a group. An agent must play at least a role in a group, but an agent may play several roles. Roles are local to groups, and a role must be requested by an agent. A role may be played by several agents.

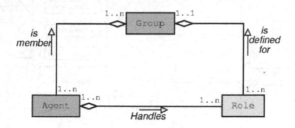

Fig. 7. AGR Model from [13]

The MADKIT platform proposes libraries to create/join groups, take roles, send messages to other agents via the roles they play, etc. It is written in JAVA using the micro-kernel principle. A MadKit kernel is created before agents are launched and intercept all service calls.

3.2 Transparent Connection of Kernels

One interesting characteristic of the MADKIT platform is that, from the agent's perspective, there is absolutely no difference between the communication with local agents and the communication with distant agents.

Even if MADKIT offered a plugin, called Communicator, to interconnect kernels, it presented a few disadvantages. Among them, the Communicator offers a single "hard coded" protocol for the communication between kernels. This approach restricts the network capabilities evolutions of the platform. It also required to know a priori the distant kernel's address and port.

To tackle these problems, we developed a new plugin for MADKIT called NetComm. This plugin presents a multi-agent design, allowing different protocol to be used and featuring an automatic detection and connection of existing kernels in the network.

The underlying idea of the NetComm Module is to have a group of agents that will manage all incoming and outgoing communication. Each foreign kernel will interact with one local agent in commonly selected protocol. This approach lets us envisage a number of different protocols, that will be selected according to the situation.

Following the MADKIT architecture, a specific agent must register as the Communicator, or Communication Responsible. In NetComm this agent is the NetAgent. The NetAgent is a sort of representative of all other agents in the communications module. We now briefly describe the main agents present in the module. Figure 8 shows the general structure of the NetComm Plugin.

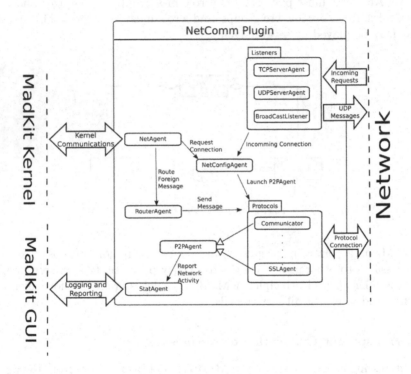

Fig. 8. NetComm Overview

The **NetAgent** can be called the main agent of Netcomm. This agent will represent the whole communication system in front of the local kernel.

The **RouterAgent** agent takes care of routing the messages received from the NetAgent to the P2PAgent responsible of the connection with the concerned Kernel.

The **NetConfig** agent is launched every time a new kernel is going to be connected. First the agent will try to know whether at the other end there is a CommunicatorAgent (the original communication module of MADKIT) or another NetConfigAgent. If the agent is interacting with a Communicator agent, an instance of the Communicator compatible agent will be launched. When interacting with a NetConfigAgent, a protocol is followed to establish a common protocol. If a common protocol is found, it will be sent and the corresponding P2PAgent will be launched.

The **P2PAgent** is the super class of the agents responsible for the connections with other kernels. Several types of P2PAgents exist like the SSLAgent enabling SSL communications.

The **StatAgent** keeps track of the network usage statistics. The statistics can be enabled or disabled in real-time by sending a NetConfigMessage. In the time being the StatAgent reports only through its graphical interface. However future work will enable this agent to log the network traffic in a file for later analysis.

Three different agents, the **Listeners**, are in charge of listening incoming requests, one per used protocol. Thus we have a TCP, UDP and Broadcast Listeners. Incoming request will start a new NetConfigAgent to configure the connection with the foreign kernel.

This plugin is concerned with the discovery of new kernels in the network and provides the *Virtual* MADKIT *Community* that we need to deploy our agents. It is important to notice, that the network may grow at runtime. Indeed, new kernels can be integrated to the community dynamically, since MADKIT 's kernels can synchronize their information.

3.3   Distribution of a Simulation

The NetComm plugin described previously gives us the possibility to consider that all kernels in the system are capable of automatically connecting, thus providing a unique virtual MADKIT Community. The second problem to tackle is the distribution of the agents themselves. A second module was developed for this purpose, called *SimServer*. In distinction with NetComm, it does not intend to be a generic plugin for any simulation. This plugin tries to reduce the development time to distribute a simulation for all those that do not need to introduce a migration mechanism into agents. Even if we used the NetComm plugin to interconnect the kernels, we could use any other means to connect the kernel, the communicator or a third module. This is to say that the SimServer plugin is completely independent of the NetComm plugin. In top of the MadKit "Virtual Community" a number of groups are created to control and observe the simulation. The first is the "Simulation Status". This group aims to provide statistics of the state of the servers in terms of memory, cpu load, etc. The organization consists of three roles: *StatusManager,StatusRequester* and *ServerInformer*. The **ServerInformer** is in charge of collecting the information of the server where it is running and informs the Status Manager. This information contains, but is not limited to, memory, cpu load, simulations running in the server and agents per simulation.

The **StatusManager** collects the information and formats it for logs and special request.

The **StatusRequester** role is played by agents willing to get information about a simulation or the status of the servers. It requests the information to the StatusManager. For instance, a simulator will typically have the possibility to show to the user information about servers where the user's simulation is running on. For this, an agent should play the StatusRequester roles to get the required information.

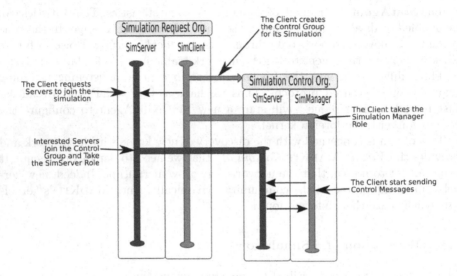

Fig. 9. Sequence diagram used to create a new Simulation

When a new simulation needs to be created a specific protocol must be followed. An *organizational sequence diagram* (this type of diagrams was presented in [9]) illustrates this protocol in figure 9.

1. An agent takes the *SimulationClient* role. This agent creates a group for the simulation. This group will be used to control the simulation itself.
2. The client broadcasts a message to all *SimulationServer* role players. This message informs the servers that a new Simulation needs to be created. The message contains information about requirements of the simulation, e.g. number of agents to be created, name of the group to control the simulation, etc.
3. Servers interested in participating in the simulation join the simulation management group created in step 1. This decision is based on the status of the server it represents, i.e. cpu and memory load, number of agent already running in the server, etc.
4. The SimulationManager (role of the Control group) distributes the required information to instantiate the agent required for the simulation, e.g. the agents identifiers, classes to load, etc.

5. Once all the servers acknowledge that they are ready to start, the SimulationManager may start sending Control messages to the server in its group, i.e. start, stop, etc.

The module contains a default implementation of the agents that provide a basic support. These agents are a generic implementation and make a number of assumptions. However, they can be used as starting point to develop a more suitable implementation, in particular for the simulation controllers.

4   Simulation

As presented in section 2.3, the environment is modeled as a holarchy. Each holon of this holarchy represents a specific context. For the PSA example it's a specific place in the plant. These places have different granularity levels according to their level in the holarchy. During the simulation, vehicle agents move from one holon to another and the granularity is chosen by execution or simulation constraints such as which features can be observed.

The dynamic choice of the environment granularity level during the simulation must be transparent for the agents. In order to do this, agents use our holonic framework and specifically *ExchangePoint* holons which enable the communication between holons of the same level and connected in the plant's topology. The figure 10 describes the sequence of messages exchanged between the *ExchangePoint*, a vehicle and the Segment's Head. The vehicle agent is moving along the segment 1 and requests the exchange point to forward a merging request. The exchange point forwards the request and receives a reply. The reply is forwarded to the vehicle. If the reply is positive the vehicle can merge with the segment 2 holon as shown in figure 11. These interaction sequences are a mean to represent the influence/reaction model [10]. Indeed, the agent emits influences in asking to merge with a specific holon. The environment is able to determine the eventual answer according to jams or environment properties.

Notice that using this mechanism does not require the environmental holons to execute in the same kernel (or machine). Indeed, the virtual community, created using the NetComm plugin, enables holons to communicate transparently. When vehicle holons move between segments, they also move to the segment's execution kernel. Like this, most frequent interactions (e.g. between the link and the vehicle and between vehicles in the same link) will always be executed locally. So, clusters of agents are created on different machines following the structure of the holarchy.

The whole simulation can be controlled and observered using the SimServer Plugin.

This approach enables one to describe the environment with multiple levels of granularity; examples are given in figures 12 and 13. In figure 12 we can view the simulation of several roads, crossroads and buildings. The figure 13 is a more fine grain simulation of a crossroad. Nevertheless the simulation of the rest of the plant is always running in the two cases.

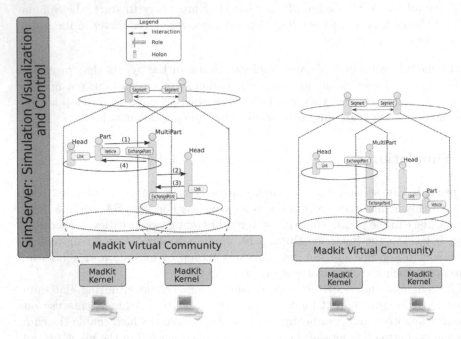

Fig. 10. Access request sequence

Fig. 11. If accepted, the vehicle moves to the next segment

Fig. 12. View of different crossroads and buildings

Fig. 13. Crossroad close up

5   Related Works

Two problems are frequently encountered during MABS [2]. First, how to model the agents and their environment to exploit inherent agents parallelism. Second, how to choose an appropriate grain size for the simulation. These two problems are related. Indeed, chosing an inappropriate grain size could hamper the distribution of the simulation [2].

In the sequel we compare our work with existing approaches combining concepts for the conceptual distribution of MABS with implementation support.

The PDES-MAS project approach [2] consists in partitioning the environment in zones called "interest areas" or "spheres of influence" concept similar to holons in our case. It is a specific locus of interaction and perception for agents. These clusters execute concurrently. The drawback of this approach is that it doesnt take into account multiple granularities.

The MACE3J architecture [11] is based on two modelling hypothesis. First, there exists an organizational structure called ActivationGroup which is a group of agents acting in relation with each another. This structure is implemented by an object which contains services such as: scheduler, time manager, environment, ... Second, agents havent any imposed architecture but must implement the Registerable JAVA interface which allows request from the ActivationGroup. These agents group result in a flat architecture such as the one use within the MadKit platform [14].

The MadKit platform [14] proposes mechanisms which ease the deployment of distributed simulations. We have already discussed in the section 3 the drawbacks of these mechanisms. The conceptual model of MadKit , namely AGR, does not propose any clustering concept except the organization. It may be difficult to take into account efficiency problems of a distribution only based upon organizations.

The RePast [4] agent simulation toolkit, which uses the ideas of the well-known SWARM platform [17], offers services to display and monitor simulations. To our knowledge there is no facility proposed for the distribution of simulations. The SPADES system [19] propose an architecture for deploying parallel or distributed simulations based on a discrete simulation engine. The agents must be based on a sense/think/act loop which is not a strong assumption. The drawback of this approach is that it supposes that events are centralized in a master process which has complete knowledge of all pending events. This hypothesis may hinder the scalability of MABS.

6   Conclusion

In this paper we have presented an approach to model and deploy large scale and variable scale MABS. This approach is based upon holonic MAS and is supported by two plugins which ease the distribution, monitoring and control of simulations hence reducing the complexity of deploying distributed MABS.

The distribution and clustering of agents follows the holarchy structure and thus reduces distant message passing. This issue is frequently discussed in approaches for distributed MABS. Each holon defines a cluster of agents executing on a same computer or part of a network. These agents share the same part of the environment. The interactions are thus mostly locals. Even more, agents may change their executing machine as they move in the environment. The distribution also allows the connection of the simulation to visualization tools such as Virtools as it is the case in figures 12 and 13.

The first plugin, NetComm, was designed to allow an automatic connection of the MADKIT kernels in a network. These connections allow the creation of a virtual community so that the distribution of kernels is transparent. NetComm also enables the creation of new kernels and or the relocation of existing kernels. The second plugin, SimServer, enables the distribution of agents, the management and monitoring of the simulation. By distribution of agents we mean that an agent must belong to a specific kernel which may change during its lifetime. This kernel change is illustrated by an example in figures 10 and 11. Management and monitoring facilities are provided in order to control the overall simulation and to be able to visualize the simulation results. Both are plugins for the MADKIT platform. These modules allows the execution of a great number of agents. Among the future works, we plan the integration of analytic tools in the plugins.

References

1. Bellifemine, F., Poggi, A., Rimassa, G.: Jade - a fipa-compliant agent framework. Technical report, CSELT (1999)
2. Logan, B., Theodoropoulos, G.: The Distributed Simulation of Multi-Agent Systems. Proceedings of the IEEE 89 (2001)
3. Bürckert, H.-J., Fischer, K., Vierke, G.: Transportation scheduling with holonic mas - the teletruck approach. In: Proceedings of the Third International Conference on Practical Applications of Intelligent Agents and Multiagents, pp. 577–590 (1998)
4. Collier, N.: Repast: Recursive porus agent simulation toolkit
5. Christine, K., Fernandes, C.e S.: Systèmes Multi-Agents Hybrides: Une Approche pour la Conception de Systèmes Complexes. PhD thesis, Université Joseph Fourier-Grenoble 1 (2001)
6. Dasgupta, D.: Artificial Immune Systems and Their Applications. Springer, Heidelberg (1998)
7. Farenc, N., Boulic, R., Thalmann, D.: An informed environment dedicated to the simulation of virtual humans in urban context. In: Proc. Eurographics '99, pp. 309–318, Milano, Italy (1999)
8. Ferber, J., Gutknecht, O.: A meta-model for the analysis and design of organizations in multi-agent systems. In: Demazeau, Y., Durfee, E., Jennings, N.R. (eds.) ICMAS'98 (July 1998)
9. Ferber, J., Gutknecht, O., Michel, F.: From agents to organizations: an organizational view of multi-agent systems. In: Giorgini, P., Müller, J.P., Odell, J.J. (eds.) Agent-Oriented Software Engineering IV. LNCS, vol. 2935, pp. 214–230. Springer, Heidelberg (2004)
10. Ferber, J., Müller, J.-P.: Influences and reaction: a model of situated multiagent systems. In: ICMAS'96 (December 1996)
11. Gasser, L., Kakugawa, K.: Mace3J: fast fllexible distributed simulation of large, large-grain multi-agent systems. In: AAMAS, pp. 745–752. ACM, New York (2002)
12. Gerber, C., Siekmann, J.H., Vierke, G.: Holonic multi-agent systems. Technical Report DFKI-RR-99-03, Deutsches Forschungszentrum für Künstliche Intelligenz - GmbH, Postfach 20 80, 67608 Kaiserslautern, FRG (May 1999)
13. Gutknecht, O.: Proposition d'un Modéle Organisationnel générique de systéme multi-agent. Examen de ses conséquences formelles, implémentatoires et méthodologiques PhD thesis, Université de Montpellier II (September 2001)

14. Gutknecht, O., Ferber, J., Michel, F.: Madkit: Une expérience d'architecture de plate-forme multi-agent générique. In: 8iémes Journées Francophones pour l'Intelligence Artificielle Distribuée et les Systémes Multi-Agents (JFI-ADSMA'2000), Saint Jean La Vêtre, France (2000)
15. Koestler, A.: The Ghost in the Machine. Hutchinson (1967)
16. Maturana, F., Shen, W., Norrie, D.: Metamorph: An adaptive agent-based architecture for intelligent manufacturing. International Journal of Production Research 37(10), 2159–2174 (1999)
17. Minor, N., Burkhart, R., Langton, C.: The swarm simulation system: A toolkit for building multi-agent simulations (1996)
18. Poslad, S., Buckle, P., Hadingham, R.: The fipa-os agent platform: Open source for open standards. In: Proc. of the 5th International Conference and Exhibition on the Practical Application of Intelligent Agents and Multi-Agents, pp. 355–368 (2000)
19. Riley, P.: SPADES A System for parallel-agent, discrete-event simulation. AI Magazine 24(2), 41–42 (2003)
20. Rodriguez, S., Hilaire, V., Koukam, A.: Fomal specification of holonic multi-agent system framework. In: Sunderam, V.S., van Albada, G.D., Sloot, P.M.A., Dongarra, J.J. (eds.) ICCS 2005. LNCS, vol. 3516, pp. 719–726. Springer, Heidelberg (2005)
21. Rodriguez, S., Hilaire, V., Koukam, A.: Holonic modelling of environments for situated multi-agent systems. In: Second International Workshop on Environments for Multiagent Systems @ AAMAS 2005, pp. 133–138 (2005)
22. Rodriguez, S., Hilaire, V., Koukam, A.: Towards a methodological framework for holonic multi-agent systems. In: Fourth International Workshop of Engineering Societies in the Agents World, pp. 179–185, Imperial College London, UK (EU) (2003)
23. Rodriguez, S.A.: From analysis to design of Holonic Multi-Agent Systems: a Framework, methodological guidelines and applications. PhD thesis, Université de Technologie de Belfort-Montbéliard (2005)
24. Simonin, O., Ferber, J.: Modélisation des satisfactions personnelle et interactive d'agents situés coopératifs. In: JFIADSMA'01: 9èmes Journées Francophones d'Intelligence Artificielle Distribuée et Systèmes Multi-Agents, pp. 215–226 (2001)
25. Wyns, J.: Reference architecture for Holonic Manufacturing Systems - the key to support evolution and reconfiguration. PhD thesis, Katholieke Universiteit Leuven (1999)

Concurrent Modeling of Alternative Worlds with Polyagents

H. Van Dyke Parunak and Sven Brueckner

NewVectors LLC, 3520 Green Court, Suite 250, Ann Arbor, MI 48105 USA
Tel.: +1 734 302 5660
{van.parunak,sven.brueckner}@newvectors.net

Abstract. Agent-based modeling is a powerful tool for systems modeling. Instantiating each domain entity with an agent captures many aspects of system dynamics and interactions that other modeling techniques do not. However, an entity's agent can execute only one trajectory per run, and does not sample the alternative trajectories accessible to the entity in the evolution of a realistic system. Averaging over multiple runs does not capture the range of individual interactions involved. We address these problems with a new modeling entity, the polyagent, which represents each entity with a single persistent avatar supported by a swarm of transient ghosts. Each ghost interacts with the ghosts of other avatars through digital pheromone fields, capturing a wide range of alternative trajectories in a single run that can proceed faster than real time.

1 Introduction

The fundamental entity in an agent-based model (ABM), the agent, corresponds to a discrete entity in the domain. The fundamental operator is interaction among agents. The fundamental entity in an equation-based model (EBM) [22] is a system observable, and the fundamental operator is its evolution (e.g., by a differential equation).

ABM's often map more naturally to a problem than do EBM's, are easier to construct and explore, and provide more realistic results [17, 21], but have a shortcoming. Observables in an EBM are often averages across agents, and implicitly capture the range of agent variation (at an aggregate level). By contrast, the agent representing an entity in an ABM can execute only one trajectory per run of the system, and does not capture the alternative trajectories that the entity might have experienced. Averaging over multiple runs still does not capture the range of individual interactions involved.

A new modeling construct, the *polyagent*, represents each entity with a single persistent *avatar* and multiple transient *ghosts*. Each ghost interacts with the ghosts of other avatars through digital pheromones, exploring many alternative trajectories in a single run that can proceed faster than real time for many reasonable domains. We have used this approach in several applications. This paper articulates the polyagent as an explicit modeling construct and provides some guidance concerning its use.

Section 2 reviews the sampling challenge sampling in ABM. Section 3 proposes the polyagent as an answer to this challenge, and Section 4 compares it with other technology. Section 5 reports on polyagent systems we have constructed. Section 6

L. Antunes and K. Takadama (Eds.): MABS 2006, LNAI 4442, pp. 128–141, 2007.

discusses what these examples teach us and considers directions for research on polyagents. Section 7 concludes.

2   The Challenge of Modeling Multi-agent Interactions

Imagine $n + 1$ entities in discrete time. At each step, each entity interacts with one of the other n. Thus at time t its interaction history $h(t)$ is a string in n^t. Its behavior is a function of $h(t)$. This toy model generalizes many domains, including predator-prey systems, combat, innovation, diffusion of ideas, and disease propagation.

It would be convenient if a few runs of such a system told us all we need to know, but this is not likely to be the case, for three reasons.

1. We may have imperfect knowledge of the agents' internal states or details of the environment (for example, in a predator-prey system, the carrying capacity of the environment). If we change our assumptions about these unknown details, we can expect the agents' behaviors to change.
2. The agents may behave non-deterministically, either because of noise in their perceptions, or because they use a stochastic decision algorithm.
3. Even if the agents' reasoning and interactions are deterministic and we have accurate knowledge of all state variables, nonlinearities in decision mechanisms or interactions can result in overall dynamics that are formally chaotic, so that tiny differences in individual state variables can lead to arbitrarily large divergences in agent behavior. A nonlinearity can be as simple as a predator's hunger threshold for eating a prey or a prey's energy threshold for mating.

An EBM typically deals with aggregate observables across the population. In the predator-prey example, such observables might be predator population, prey population, average predator energy level, or average prey energy level, all as functions of time. No attempt is made to model the trajectory of an individual entity.

An ABM must explicitly describe the trajectory of each agent. In a given run of a predator-prey model, depending on the random number generator, predator 23 and prey 14 may or may not meet at time 354. If they do meet and predator 23 eats prey 14, predator 52 cannot later encounter prey 14, but if they do not meet, predator 52 and prey 14 might meet later. If predator 23 happens to meet prey 21 immediately after eating prey 14, it will not be hungry, and so will not eat prey 21, but if it did not first encounter prey 14, it will consume prey 21. And so forth. A single run of the model can capture only one set of many possible interactions among the agents.

In our general model, during a run of length τ, each entity will experience one of n^τ possible histories. (This estimate is of course worst case, since domain constraints may make many of these histories inaccessible.) The population of $n + 1$ entities will sample $n + 1$ of these possible histories. It is often the case that the length of a run is orders of magnitude larger than the number of modeled entities ($\tau >> n$).

Multiple runs with different random seeds is only a partial solution. Each run only samples one set of possible interactions. For large populations and scenarios that permit multiple interactions on the part of each agent, the number of runs needed to sample the possible alternative interactions thoroughly can quickly become prohibitive. In the application described in Section 4.3, $n \sim 50$ and $\tau \sim 10,000$, so the sample of the space of possible entity histories actually sampled by a single run is vanishingly small. We would need on the order of τ runs to generate a meaningful sample, and executing that many runs is out of the question.

We need a way to capture the outcome of multiple possible interactions among agents in a few runs of a system. Polyagents are one solution to this problem.

3 The Polyagent Modeling Construct

A polyagent represents a single domain entity. It consists of a single *avatar* that manages the correspondence between the domain and the polyagent, and a swarm of *ghosts* that explore alternative behaviors of the domain entity.

The *avatar* corresponds to the agent representing an entity in a conventional multi-agent model of the domain. It persists as long as its entity is active, and maintains state information reflecting its entity's state. Its computational mechanisms may range from simple stigmergic coordination to sophisticated BDI reasoning.

Each avatar generates a stream of *ghost agents*, or simply *ghosts*. Ghosts typically have limited lifetime, dying off after a fixed period of time or after some defined event to make room for more ghosts. The avatar controls the rate of generation of its ghosts, and typically has several ghosts concurrently active.

Ghosts explore alternative possible behaviors for their avatar. They interact with one another stigmergically, through a digital pheromone field, a vector of scalar values ("pheromone flavors") that is a function of both location and time. That is, each ghost chooses its actions stochastically based on a weighted function of the strengths of the various pheromone flavors in its immediate vicinity, and deposits its own pheromone to record its presence. A ghost's "program" consists of the vector of weights defining its sensitivity to various pheromone flavors.

Having multiple ghosts multiplies the number of interactions that a single run of the system can explore. Instead of one trajectory for each avatar, we now have one trajectory for each ghost. If each avatar has k concurrent ghosts, we explore k trajectories concurrently. But the multiplication is in fact greater than this.

The digital pheromone field supports three functions [1, 10]:

1. It *aggregates* deposits from individual agents, fusing information across multiple agents and through time. In some of our implementations of polyagents, avatars deposit pheromone; in other, ghosts do. Aggregation of pheromones enables a single ghost to interact with multiple other ghosts at the same time. It does not interact with them directly, but only with the pheromone field that they generate, which is a summary of their individual behaviors.

2. It *evaporates* pheromones over time. This dynamic is an innovative alternative to traditional truth maintenance in artificial intelligence. Traditionally, knowledge bases remember everything they are told unless they have a reason to forget something, and expend large amounts of computation in the NP-complete problem of reviewing their holdings to detect inconsistencies that result from changes in the domain being modeled. Ants immediately begin to forget everything they learn, unless it is continually reinforced. Thus inconsistencies automatically remove themselves within a known period.

3. It *propagates* pheromones to nearby places, disseminating information.

This third dynamic (propagation) enables each ghost to sense multiple other agents. If n avatars deposit pheromones, each ghost's actions are influenced by up to n other agents (depending on the propagation radius), so that we are exploring in effect $n*k$ interactions for each entity, or n^2*k interactions overall. If individual ghosts deposit pheromones, the number of interactions being explored is even greater, on the order of k^n. Of course, the interactions are not played out in the detail they would be in a conventional multi-agent model. But our empirical experience is that they are reflected with a fidelity that is entirely adequate for the problems we have addressed.

Pheromone-based interaction not only multiplies the number of interactions that we are exploring, but also enables extremely efficient execution. In one application, we support 24,000 ghosts concurrently, faster than real time, on a 1 GHz Wintel laptop.

The avatar can do several things with its ghosts, depending on the application.

- It can activate its ghosts when it wants to explore alternative possible futures, modulating the rate at which it issues new ghosts to determine the number of alternatives it explores. It initializes the ghosts' weight vectors to define the breadth of alternatives it wishes to explore.
- It can evolve its ghosts to learn the best parameters for a given situation. It monitors the performance of past ghosts against some fitness parameter, and then breeds the most successful to determine the parameters of the next generation.
- It can review the behavior of its swarm of ghosts to produce a unified estimate of how its own behavior is likely to evolve and what the range of likely variability is.

4 Comparison with Other Paradigms

Our polyagent bears comparison with several previous multi-agent paradigms and two previous uses of the term (Table 1).

Polyagents are distinct from the common use of agents to model different functions of a single domain entity. For example, in ARCHON [23], the domain entity is an electrical power distribution system, and individual agents represent different functions or perspectives required to manage the system. In a polyagent, each ghost has the same function: to explore one possible behavior of the domain entity. The plurality of ghosts provides, not functional decomposition, but a range of estimates of alternative behaviors.

Many forms of evolutionary computation [4] allow multiple representatives of a single

Table 1. Comparing the Polyagent with Other Technologies

	Multiple agents per domain entity	Avatar/Ghost dualism	Parallel search of alternative behaviors	Parallel search of multiple possible interactions
Polyagent	X	X	X	X
Functional agents	X			
Evolutionary computation	X		X	
Fictitious play	X		X	
Ant colony optimization	X		X	X
Kijima's polyagents				
Polyagent therapies				

entity to execute concurrently, to compare their fitness. In these systems, each agent samples only one possible series of interactions with other entities. Pheromone-based coordination in the polyagent construct permits each ghost to adjust its behavior based on many possible alternative behaviors of other entities in the domain.

Similarly, the multiple behaviors contemplated in fictitious play [8] take place against a static model of the rest of the world.

Like the polyagent, ant-colony optimization [2] uses pheromones to integrate the experiences of parallel searchers. The polyagent's advance is the notion of the avatar as a single point of contact for the searchers representing a single domain entity.

The term "polyagent" is a neologism for several software agents that collectively represent a domain entity and its alternative behaviors. The term is used in two other contexts that should not lead to any confusion. In medicine, "polyagent therapy" uses multiple treatment agents (notably, multiple drugs combined in chemotherapy). Closer to our domain, but still distinct, is the use of the term by K. Kijima [6] to describe a game-theoretic approach to analyzing the social and organizational interactions of multiple decision-makers. For Kijima, the term "poly-agent" makes sense only as a description of a system, and does not describe a single agent. In our approach, it makes sense to talk about a single modeling construct as "a polyagent."

5 Examples of Polyagents

We discovered polyagents by reflecting on several applications that we have constructed and observing their common features.

5.1 Factory Scheduling

Our first application of polyagents was to real-time job-shop scheduling [1]. We prototyped a self-organizing multi-agent system with three species of agents: processing resources, work-pieces, and policy agents. Avatars of processing resources with different capabilities and capacities and avatars of work-pieces with dynamically changing processing needs (due to re-work) jointly optimize the flow of material through a complex, high-volume manufacturing transport system. In this application, only the avatars of the work-pieces actually deploy ghosts. The policy agents and avatars of the processing resources (machines) are single agents in the traditional sense.

In a job shop, work-pieces interact with one another by blocking access to the resources that they occupy, and thus delaying one another. Depending on the schedule, different work-pieces may interact, in different orders. Polyagents explore the space of alternative routings and interactions concurrently in a single model.

Work-piece avatars currently loaded into the manufacturing system continuously deploy ghosts that emulate their decision processes in moving through various decision points in the manufacturing process. Each of these decisions is stochastic, based on the relative concentration of attractive pheromones in the neighborhood of the next decision point. These pheromones are actually deposited by the policy agents that try to optimize the balance of the material flow across the transport network, but they are modulated by the ghosts. Thus, an avatar's ghosts modulate the pheromone field to which the avatar responds, establishing an adaptive feedback loop into the future.

The avatars continuously emit ghosts that emulate their current decision process. The ghosts travel into the future without the delay imposed by physical transport and processing of the work-pieces. These ghosts may find the next likely processing step and wait there until it is executed physically, or they may emulate the probabilistic outcome of the step and assume a new processing state for the work-piece they are representing. In either case, while they are active, the ghosts contribute to a phero-mone field that reports the currently predicted relative load along the material flow system. When ghosts for alternative work-pieces explore the same resource, they in-teract with one another through the pheromones that they deposit and sense.

By making stochastic decisions, each ghost explores an alternative possible routing for its avatar. The pheromone field to which it responds has been modulated by all of the ghosts of other work-pieces, and represents multiple alternative routings of those work-pieces. Thus the ghosts for each work-piece explore both alternative futures for that work-piece, and multiple alternative interactions with other work-pieces.

Policy agents that have been informed either by humans or by other agents of the desired relative load of work-pieces of specific states at a particular location in turn deposit attractive or repulsive pheromones. Thus, through a local adaptive process, multiple policy agents supported by the flow of ghost agents adapt the appropriate levels of pheromone deposits to shape the future flow of material as desired.

By the time the avatar makes its next routing choice, which is delayed by the physical constraints of the material flow through the system, the ghosts and the policy agents have adjusted the appropriate pheromones so that the avatar makes the "right" decision. In effect, the policy agents and the ghosts control the avatar as long as they can converge on a low-entropy pheromone concentration that the avatar can sample.

5.2 Path Planning for Robotic Vehicles

Two pressures require that path planning for robotic vehicles be an ongoing activity. 1) The agent typically has only partial knowledge of its environment, and must adapt its behavior as it learns by observation. 2) The environment is dynamic: even if an agent has complete knowledge at one moment, a plan based on that knowledge be-comes less useful as the conditions on which it was based change. These problems are particularly challenging in military applications, where both targets and threats are constantly appearing and disappearing.

In the DARPA JFACC program, we approached this problem by imitating the dy-namics that ants use in forming paths between their nests and food sources [9]. The ants search stochastically, but share their discoveries by depositing and sensing nest and food pheromone. Ants that are searching for food deposit nest pheromone while climbing the food pheromone gradient left by successful foragers. Ants carrying food deposit food pheromone while climbing the nest pheromone gradient. The initial pheromone trails form a random field, but quickly collapse into optimal path as the ants interact with one another's trails.

The challenge in applying this algorithm to a robotic vehicle is that the algorithm depends on interactions among many ants, while a vehicle is a single entity that only traverses its path once. We use a polyagent to represent the vehicle (in our case, an aircraft) whose route needs to be computed [13, 19]. As the avatar moves through the battlespace, it continuously emits a swarm of ghosts, whose interactions mimic the ant dynamics and continuously (re)form the path in front of the avatar. These ghosts seek targets and then return to the avatar. They respond to several digital pheromones:

- *RTarget* is emitted by a target.
- *GNest* is emitted by a ghost that has left the avatar and is seeking a target.
- *GTarget* is emitted by a ghost that has found a target and is returning to the avatar.
- *RThreat* is emitted by a threat (e.g., a missile battery).

Ideally, the digital pheromones are maintained in a distributed network of unattended ground sensors dispersed throughout the vehicle's environment, but they can also reside on a central processor, or even on multiple vehicles. In addition, we provide each ghost with *Dist*, an estimate of how far away the target is.

In general, ghosts are attracted to RTarget pheromone and repelled from RThreat pheromone. In addition, before they find a target, they are attracted to GTarget pheromone. Once they find a target, they are attracted to GNest pheromone. A ghost's movements are guided by the relative strengths of these quantities in its current cell and each neighboring cell in a hexagonal lattice. It computes a weighted combination of these factors for each adjacent cell and selects stochastically among the cells, with probability proportionate to the computed value.

Each ghost explores one possible route for the vehicle. The avatar performs two functions in overseeing its swarm of ghosts.

1. It *integrates* the information from the several ghosts in their explorations of alternative routes. It observes the GTarget pheromone strength in its immediate vicinity, and guides the robot up the GTarget gradient. GTarget pheromone is deposited only by ghosts that have found the target, and its strength in a given cell reflects the number of ghosts that traversed that cell on their way home from the target. So the aggregate pheromone strength estimates the likelihood that a given cell is on a reasonable path to the target.

2. It *modulates* its ghosts' behaviors by adjusting the weights that the ghosts use to combine the pheromones they sense. Initially, all ghosts used the same hand-tuned weights, and differences in their paths were due only to the stochastic choices they made in selecting successive steps. When the avatar randomly varied the weights around the hand-tuned values, system performance improved by more than 50%, because the ghosts explored a wider range of routes. We then allowed the avatar to evolve the weight vector as the system operates, yielding an improvement nearly an order of magnitude over hand-tuned ghosts [18].

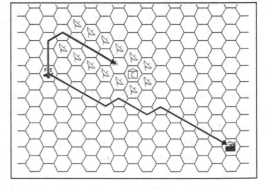

Fig. 1. Gauntlet Routing Problem

We tested this system's ability to route an aircraft in simulated combat [13]. In one example, it found a path to a target through a gauntlet of threats (Fig. 1). A centralized route planner seeking an optimal path by integrating a loss function and climbing the resulting gradient was unable to solve this problem without manually introducing a waypoint at the gauntlet's entrance. The polyagent succeeded because some of the ghosts, moving stochastically, wandered into the gauntlet, found their way to the target, and then returned, laying pheromones that other ghosts could reinforce.

Another experiment flew multiple missions through a changing landscape of threats and targets. The figure of merit was the total surviving strength of the Red and Blue forces. In two scenarios, the aircraft's avatar flew a static route planned on the basis of complete knowledge of the location

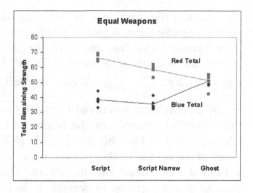

Fig. 2. Real-Time vs. Advance Planning.— "Script" is a conservative advance route based on complete knowledge. "Script narrow" is a more aggressive advance route. "Ghost" is the result when the route is planned in real time based on partial knowledge.

of threats and targets, without ghosts. The routes differed based on how closely the route was allowed to approach threats. A third case used ghosts, but some threats were invisible until they took action during the simulation. Fig. 2 compares these three cases. The polyagent's ability to deal with partial but up-to-date knowledge both inflicted more damage on the adversary and offered higher survivability than pre-planned scripts based on complete information.

Route planning shows how a polyagent's ghosts can explore alternative behaviors concurrently, and integrate that experience to form a single course of action. Since only one polyagent is active at a time, this work does not draw on the ability of polyagents to manage the space of possible interactions among multiple entities.

5.3 Characterizing and Predicting Agent Behavior

The DARPA RAID program [7] focuses on the problem of characterizing an adversary in real-time and predicting its future behavior. Our contribution to this effort [15] uses polyagents to evolve a model of each real-world entity (a group of soldiers known as a fire team) and extrapolate its behavior into the future. Thus we call the system "the BEE" (Behavior Evolution and Extrapolation).

The BEE process is inspired by prediction mechanism commonly used in physical systems. Nonlinearities in the dynamics of most realistic systems drive the exponential divergence of trajectories originating close to one another, a phenomenon popularly denominated as "chaos." As a result, while we can predict a short distance into the future, our vision becomes blurred as we look further. This is as true for intelligence operations as it is for physical systems.

In many applications, we can replace a single long-range prediction with a series of short-range ones. The difference is between driving a car in the daytime and at night. In the daytime, one may be able to see several miles down the road. At night, one can only see as far as the headlamps shine, but since the headlamps move with the car, at any moment the driver has the information needed to make the next round of decisions.

In physical systems, one typically describes the systems with vector differential equations, e.g., $\frac{d\vec{x}}{dt} = f(\vec{x})$. At each moment,

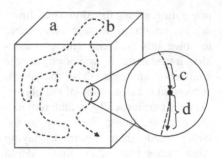

we fit a convenient functional form for f to the system's trajectory in the recent past, and then extrapolate this fit (Fig. 3, [5]). Constant repetition of this process provides a limited look-ahead into the future. The process can be applied in reverse as well, allowing us to project from a series of current observations into the past to recover likely historical antecedents of the current state. This program is straightforward with a system described numerically. Polyagents apply it to agent behavior.

Fig. 3. Tracking a Nonlinear Dynamical System. a = system state space; b = system trajectory over time; c = recent measurements of system state; d = short-range prediction

Fig. 4 is an overview of the BEE process. Ghosts live on a timeline indexed by τ that begins in the past at the insertion horizon and runs into the future to the prediction horizon. τ is offset with respect to the current time t. The timeline is divided into discrete "pages," each representing a successive value of τ. The avatar inserts the ghosts at the insertion horizon. In our current system, the insertion horizon is at

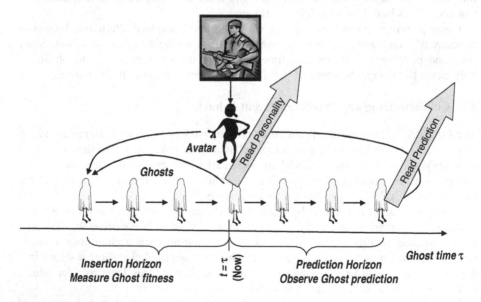

Fig. 4. Behavioral Emulation and Extrapolation. Each avatar generates a stream of ghosts that sample the personality space of its entity. They evolve against the entity's recent observed behavior, and the fittest ghosts run into the future to generate predictions.

$\tau - t = -30$, meaning that ghosts are inserted into a page representing the state of the world 30 minutes ago. At the insertion horizon, the avatar samples each ghost's rational and emotional parameters (desires and dispositions) from distributions to explore alternative personalities of the entity it represents. The avatar is also responsible for estimating its entity's goals (using a belief network) and instantiating them in the environment as pheromone sources that constrain and guide the ghosts' behavior. In estimating its entity's goals and deliberately modulating the distribution of ghosts, the avatar reasons at a higher cognitive level than do the pheromone-driven ghosts.

Each page between the insertion horizon and $\tau = t$ ("now") records the historical state of the world at its point in the past, represented as a pheromone field generated by the avatars (which at each page know the actual state of the entity they are modeling). As ghosts move from page to page, they interact with this past state, based on their behavioral parameters. These interactions mean that their fitness depends not just on their own actions, but also on the behaviors of the rest of the population, which is also evolving. Because τ advances faster than real time, eventually $\tau = t$ (actual time). At this point, the avatar evaluates each of its ghosts based on its location compared with the actual location of its corresponding real-world entity.

The fittest ghosts have three functions.

1. The avatar reports personality of the fittest ghost for each entity to the rest of the system as the likely personality of the corresponding entity. This information enables us to characterize individual warriors as unusually cowardly or brave.
2. The avatar breeds the fittest ghosts genetically and reintroduces their offspring at the insertion horizon to continue the fitting process.
3. The fittest ghosts for each entity run past the avatar's present into the future. Each ghost that runs into the future explores a different possible future of the battle, analogous to how some people plan ahead by mentally simulating different ways that a situation might unfold. The avatar analyzes the behaviors of these different possible futures to produce predictions of enemy behavior and recommendations for friendly behavior. In the future, the pheromone field with which the ghosts interact is generated not by the avatars, but by the ghosts themselves. Thus it integrates the various possible futures that the system is considering, and each ghost is interacting with this composite view of what other entities may be doing.

The first and third functions are analogous to the integrating function of the avatars in route planning, while the second is analogous to the modulation function.

This model has proven successful both in characterizing the internal state of entities that we can only observe externally, and in predicting their future behavior. [15] details the results of experiments based on multiple wargames with human participants. We can detect emotional state of entities as well as a human observer, but faster. Our prediction of the future of the battle is also comparable with that of a human, and much better than a "guessing" baseline based on a random walk.

6 Discussion

These projects reflect several common features that deserve recognition as a new and useful modeling construct, and that we now articulate as a "polyagent."

- Multiple agents (the ghosts) concurrently explore alternative possible behaviors of the domain entity being modeled.
- The ghosts interact through a digital pheromone field that permits simultaneous reasoning about the multiple possible interactions among the domain entities.
- A single, possibly more complex agent (the avatar), *modulates* the swarm of ghosts, controlling the number of ghosts, the rate at which they are introduced, and the settings and diversity of their behavior. In our most sophisticated cases (route planning and agent fitting), the avatar evolves the ghosts.
- The avatar also *integrates* the behaviors of its several ghosts (either directly or by observing the pheromones they deposit) to produce a single higher-level report on the domain entity's likely behavior.

Our use of polyagents involves a fair amount of art, and is motivated by their successful application in multiple applications. Theoretical work is needed to make the technique more rigorous. One challenging question is the legitimacy of merging pheromones of multiple ghosts representing alternative futures for agent A of one type into a single field that then guides the behavior of agent B of a different type. This process is qualitatively distinct from the merger of pheromone deposits from multiple agents living in the *same world* to form an optimized path guiding other agents of the *same type* (the heart of conventional ant optimization). The multiple-worlds version enables B to explore concurrently its possible interactions with multiple alternative realizations of A, but we need to justify this process more formally.

The strength of a pheromone field depends, *inter alia*, on the frequency with which agents visit various locations. Thus it may be viewed as a probability field describing the likelihood of finding an agent of a given type at a given location. If those agents are ghosts representing alternative futures of an entity's trajectory, the probability field may be interpreted in terms of the likelihood of different future states. Table 2 suggests several parallels between this perspective on polyagents and quantum physics [3]. In the spirit of our earlier work applying metaphors from theoretical physics to understanding multi-agent systems [12, 14, 16, 20], we will use concepts from quantum mechanics to provide an intellectual and formal model for engineering polyagent systems and interpreting their behavior.

Like quantum wave models, polyagents explore multiple possible behaviors and interactions. Unlike wave functions, they can do so predictively. We can

Table 2. Quantum Physics and Polyagents

Quantum Physics	Polyagents
Duality between (single, localized) particle and (distributed) wave function	Duality between (single, localized) avatar and (distributed) swarm of ghosts
Interactions among wave functions' amplitude fields model interactions among particles	Ghosts' pheromone fields can be interpreted as probability densities that model interactions of agents
Wave function captures a range of possible behaviors	Swarm of ghosts captures a range of possible behaviors
Observation collapses the wave function to a single behavior	Avatar interprets the aggregate behavior of the ghosts and yields a single prediction of behavior

configure polyagents to model what will happen in the future based on current policies, then use the avatars' summary of what will happen to guide changes to those policies.

The inspiration that we draw from nonlinear dynamics in using polyagents for prediction (Section 5.3) also poses a caution. The "headlamp" model of prediction is necessary because divergence of trajectories makes long-range predictions inaccurate. The further into the future one tries to look, the more noisy the picture becomes, and performance may actually be better using shorter-range predictions than longer-range ones. We call this phenomenon the "prediction horizon." Recently, we have demonstrated the existence of this horizon quantitatively in polyagent prediction using a simple predator-prey model [11].

7 Conclusion

One strength of ABM's over EBM's is that they capture the idiosyncracies of each entity's trajectory. In complex domains, this strength is also a weakness, because any single set of trajectories is only a sample from a large space of possible trajectories. Possible interactions among the agents explode combinatorially, making this space much too large to explore thoroughly by repeated experiments.

Polyagents can sample multiple interactions in a single run. An avatar mediates between the real-world entity being modeled and a swarm of ghosts that sample its alternative possible trajectories. The avatar may employ sophisticated cognitive reasoning, but the ghosts are tropistic, interacting through digital pheromone fields that they deposit and sense in their shared environment. The avatar modulates the generation of ghosts, and interprets their aggregate behavior to estimate its entity's likely behavior.

We have applied this system to scheduling and controlling manufacturing jobs, planning paths for unpiloted air vehicles through a complex adversarial environment, and characterizing the internal state of fighting units from observations of their outward behavior, and then projecting their likely behavior into the future to form predictions. Empirically, the polyagent functions well, but invites theoretical work on the interpretation of multiple ghosts interacting with a pheromone field that represents multiple alternative realizations of other entities. Several parallels with quantum physics suggest the latter discipline may be a guide in developing a more formal model.

Acknowledgements

This material is based on work supported by the Defense Advanced Research Projects Agency (DARPA) under Contract Nos. F3062-99-C-0202 and NBCHC040153. Any opinions, findings and conclusions or recommendations expressed in this material are those of the author(s) and do not necessarily reflect the views of the DARPA or the Department of Interior-National Business Center (DOI-NBC). Distribution Statement "A" (Approved for Public Release, Distribution Unlimited).

References

1. Brueckner, S.: Return from the Ant: Synthetic Ecosystems for Manufacturing Control. Dr.rer.nat. Thesis at Humboldt University Berlin, Department of Computer Science (2000), http://dochost.rz.hu-berlin.de/dissertationen/brueckner-sven-2000-06-21/PDF/Brueckner.pdf
2. Dorigo, M., Stuetzle, T.: Ant Colony Optimization. MIT Press, Cambridge, MA (2004)
3. Feynman, R., Hibbs, A.R.: Quantum Mechanics and Path Integrals. McGraw-Hill, New York (1965)
4. Jacob, C.: Illustrating Evolutionary Computation With Mathematica. Morgan Kaufmann, San Francisco (2001)
5. Kantz, H., Schreiber, T.: Nonlinear Time Series Analysis. Cambridge University Press, Cambridge, UK (1997)
6. Kijima, K.: Why Stratification of Networks Emerges in Innovative Society: Intelligent Poly-Agent Systems Approach. Computational and Mathematical Organization Theory 7(1), 45–62 (2001)
7. Kott, A.: Real-Time Adversarial Intelligence & Decision Making (RAID) (2004), http://dtsn.darpa.mil/ixo/programdetail.asp?progid=57
8. Lambert, T.J., Epelman III, M.A., Smith, R.L.: A Fictitious Play Approach to Large-Scale Optimization. Operations Research 53(3) (2005)
9. Parunak, H.V.D.: Go to the Ant: Engineering Principles from Natural Agent Systems. Annals of Operations Research 75, 69–101 (1997), http://www.newvectors.net/staff/parunakv/gotoant.pdf
10. Parunak, H.V.D.: Making Swarming Happen. In: Proceedings of Swarming and Network-Enabled C4ISR, Tysons Corner, VA, ASD C3I (2003), http://www.newvectors.net/staff/parunakv/MSH03.pdf
11. Parunak, H.V.D., Belding, T.C., Brueckner, S.: Prediction Horizons in Polyagent Models. In: Proceedings of Sixth International Joint Conference on Autonomous Agents and Multi-Agent Systems (AAMAS07), Honolulu, HI, pp. 930–932 (2007), http://www.newvectors.net/staff/parunakv/AAMAS07PH.pdf
12. Parunak, H.V.D., Brueckner, S.: Entropy and Self-Organization in Multi-Agent Systems. In: Proceedings of The Fifth International Conference on Autonomous Agents (Agents 2001), Montreal, Canada, pp. 124–130. ACM Press, New York (2001), http://www.newvectors.net/staff/parunakv/agents01ent.pdf
13. Parunak, H.V.D., Brueckner, S., Sauter, J.: Digital Pheromones for Coordination of Unmanned Vehicles. In: Weyns, D., Parunak, H.V.D., Michel, F. (eds.) E4MAS 2004. LNCS (LNAI), vol. 3374, pp. 246–263. Springer, Heidelberg (2005), http://www.newvectors.net/staff/parunakv/E4MAS04_UAVCoordination.pdf
14. Parunak, H.V.D., Brueckner, S., Savit, R.: Universality in Multi-Agent Systems. In: Kudenko, D., Kazakov, D., Alonso, E. (eds.) Adaptive Agents and Multi-Agent Systems II. LNCS (LNAI), vol. 3394, pp. 930–937. Springer, Heidelberg (2005), http://www.newvectors.net/staff/parunakv/AAMAS04Universality.pdf
15. Parunak, H.V.D., Brueckner, S.A.: Extrapolation of the Opponent's Past Behaviors. In: Kott, A., McEneany, W. (eds.) Adversarial Reasoning: Computational Approaches to Reading the Opponent's Mind, pp. 49–76. Chapman and Hall/CRC Press, Boca Raton, FL (2006)

16. Parunak, H.V.D., Brueckner, S.A., Sauter, J.A., Matthews, R.: Global Convergence of Local Agent Behaviors. In: Proceedings of Fourth International Joint Conference on Autonomous Agents and Multi-Agent Systems (AAMAS05), Utrecht, The Netherlands, pp. 305–312. ACM Press, New York (2005),
    http://www.newvectors.net/staff/parunakv/AAMAS05Converge.pdf
17. Parunak, H.V.D., Savit, R., Riolo, R.L.: Agent-Based Modeling vs. Equation-Based Modeling: A Case Study and Users' Guide. In: Sichman, J.S., Conte, R., Gilbert, N. (eds.) Multi-Agent Systems and Agent-Based Simulation. LNCS (LNAI), vol. 1534, pp. 10–25. Springer, Heidelberg (1998), http://www.newvectors.net/staff/parunakv/mabs98.pdf
18. Sauter, J.A., Matthews, R., Parunak, H.V.D., Brueckner, S.: Evolving Adaptive Pheromone Path Planning Mechanisms. In: Alonso, E., Kudenko, D., Kazakov, D. (eds.) Adaptive Agents and Multi-Agent Systems. LNCS (LNAI), vol. 2636, pp. 434–440. Springer, Heidelberg (2003), http://www.newvectors.net/staff/parunakv/AAMAS02Evolution.pdf
19. Sauter, J.A., Matthews, R., Parunak, H.V.D., Brueckner, S.A.: Performance of Digital Pheromones for Swarming Vehicle Control. In: Proceedings of Fourth International Joint Conference on Autonomous Agents and Multi-Agent Systems, Utrecht, Netherlands, pp. 903–910. ACM Press, New York (2005),
    http://www.newvectors.net/staff/parunakv/AAMAS05SwarmingDemo.pdf
20. Savit, R., Brueckner, S.A., Parunak, H.V.D., Sauter, J.: Phase Structure of Resource Allocation Games. Physics Letters A 311, 359–364 (2002),
    http://arxiv.org/pdf/nlin.AO/0302053
21. Shnerb, N.M., Louzoun, Y., Bettelheim, E., Solomon, S.: The importance of being discrete: Life always wins on the surface. In: Proc. Natl. Acad. Sci. USA 97(19), 10322–10324 (2000), http://www.pnas.org/cgi/reprint/97/19/10322
22. Sterman, J.: Business Dynamics. McGraw-Hill, New York (2000)
23. Wittig, T.: ARCHON: An Architecture for Multi-agent Systems. Ellis Horwood, New York (1992)

Integrating Learning and Inference in Multi-agent Systems Using Cognitive Context

Bruce Edmonds and Emma Norling

Centre for Policy Modelling
Manchester Metropolitan University
bruce@edmonds.name, norling@acm.org

Abstract. Both learning and reasoning are important aspects of intelligence. However they are rarely integrated within a single agent. Here it is suggested that imprecise learning and crisp reasoning may be coherently combined via the cognitive context. The identification of the current context is done using an imprecise learning mechanism, whilst the contents of a context are crisp models that may be usefully reasoned about. This also helps deal with situations of logical under- and over-determination because the scope of the context can be adjusted to include more or less knowledge into the reasoning process. An example model is exhibited where an agent learns and acts in an artificial stock market.

1   About Context

Both learning and reasoning are far more feasible when their scope is restricted to a particular context because this means that only the relevant knowledge needs to be dealt with. However if any significant degree of generality is to be obtained in this manner [1] then an intelligence must be able to appropriately change this focus as the external context (the context we inhabit in [2]) changes. In other words there needs to be some internal correlate of the external context that allows an intelligence to identify which set of beliefs apply. We will call this internal correlate the cognitive context (this is the "internal" approach identified in [3]). There are (at least) two tasks necessary for this:

– identifying the appropriate cognitive context from perceptions, and
– accessing the appropriate beliefs given the identified cognitive context.

The success of this strategy of assessing the relevance of knowledge via identifiable 'contexts' depends upon whether the environment is usefully divided up in such a manner. This is a contingent matter – one can imagine (or devise) environments where this is so and others where it is not. The "pragmatic roots" of context, i.e. why context works, depends upon the underlying pattern of commonalities that occur in an environment or problem domain [4]. A cognitive context indicates the boundaries of what might be relevant in any situation.

Context serves not only to make it feasible to deal with our knowledge at any one time but also, at a more fundamental level, to make our modeling of

L. Antunes and K. Takadama (Eds.): MABS 2006, LNAI 4442, pp. 142–155, 2007.
© Springer-Verlag Berlin Heidelberg 2007

the world at all feasible. The efficacy of our limited learning and inference in dealing with our complex world is dependent on the presumption that many of the possible causes or effects of important events remain relatively constant [5]. Otherwise we would need to include all possible causes and affects in our models and decision making processes, which is clearly infeasible. It is the existence of relative constancy of many factors in particular situations that makes our limited modeling ability useful: we can learn a simple model in one circumstance and successfully use it in another circumstance that is sufficiently similar to the first (i.e. in the same 'context').

It is the possibility of the transference of knowledge via fairly simple models from the circumstances where they are learnt to the circumstances in which they are applied that allows the emergence of context. The utility of 'context' comes from the possibility of such transference. If this were not feasible then 'context', as such, would not arise. For such a transference to be possible a number of conditions need to be met, namely that:

- some of the possible factors relevant to important events are separable in a practical way,
- a useful distinction can be made between those factors that can be categorized as foreground features and the others (the constant, background features),
- similar background factors are capable of being reliably recognized later on as the same 'context',
- the world is regular enough for such models to be learnable,
- the world is regular enough for such learnt models to be useful where such a context can be recognized.

While this transference of learnt models to applicable situations is the basic process, observers and analysts of this process might identify some of these combinations of features that allow recognition and abstract them as 'a context'. Note that it is not necessarily possible that such an observer will be able to do this as the underlying recognition mechanism may be obscure, too complex or difficult to analyze into definable cases.

Such a strategy answers those of the 'frame problem' [6]. Firstly, although the frame problem may be unsolvable in general it is learnable in particular contingent cases. Secondly, the identification of appropriate contexts are not completely accessible to reasoning or crisp definition – rather it is an unreliable, information-rich, and imprecise process. Thus knowing B in context A, is not translatable into statements like $A \rightarrow B$, because the A is not a reified entity that can be reasoned about.

The power of context seems to come from this combination of 'fuzzy,' fluid context identity and crisp, relatively simple context 'contents'. Thus context straddles the fields of machine learning (ML) and knowledge representation and reasoning (KRR). ML seems to have developed appropriate methods for complex and uncertain pattern recognition suitable for the identification of context. KRR has developed techniques for the manipulation of crisp formal expressions.

Context (as conceived here) allows both to be used for different functions in an coherent way.

2   The Research Context

In 1971, in his ACM Turing Award lecture, John McCarthy suggested that the explicit representation and manipulation of context might be a solution to the effective lack of generality in many AI systems (these ideas were later developed and written up in [1]). Since then context and context-like ideas have been investigated in both the KRR and ML communities, culminating in several workshops and a series of international conferences entirely devoted to the subject. Below work in these areas is briefly summarized in order to set the stage for the work that is reported here.

2.1   Context in Reasoning

McCarthy's idea was to reify the context to a set of terms, i, and introduce an operator, ist, which basically asserts that a statement, p, holds in a context labeled by i. Thus:

$$c : ist(i, p)$$

reads "p is true in context i" which is itself asserted in an outer context c. ist is similar to a modal operator but the context labels are terms of the language. Reasoning within a single context operates in a familiar way, thus we have:

$$\forall i(ist(i, p) \land ist(i, p \to q) \to ist(i, q))$$

In addition one needs a series of 'lifting' axioms, which specify the relation between truth in the different contexts. For example if $i \geq j$ means that "i is more general than context j", then we can lift a fact to a supercontext using:

$$\forall i \forall j(i \geq j) \land (ist(i, p) \land \neg ab(i, j, p) \to ist(j, p))$$

where ab is an abnormality predicate for lifting to supercontexts. This framework is developed in [7]. There are a whole series of formal systems which are closely related to the above structure, including, notably: the situations of Barwise and Perry [2], Gabbay's fibered semantics [8], and the local semantics of the Mechanized Reasoning Group at Trento [9].

One of the problems with this sort of approach is that it is likely that trying to apply generic reasoning methods to context-dependent propositions and models, will be either inefficient or inadequate [10]. The generic approach forces a choice of the appropriate level of detail to be included, so that it is likely that either much information that is irrelevant to the appropriate context will be included (making the deduction less efficient) or much useful information that is specific to the relevant context may be omitted (and hence some deductions will not be possible).

Another problem is that, in practice, this type of approach requires a huge amount of information to be explicitly specified: contexts, contents of each context and bridging rules.

2.2 Context in Learning

The use of context in machine learning can be broadly categorized by goal, namely: to maintain learning when there is a hidden/unexpected change in context; to apply learning gained in one context to different contexts; and to utilize already known information about contexts to improve learning. There are only a few papers that touch on the problem of learning the appropriate contexts themselves. Included in those that do, Widmer [11] applies a meta-learning process to a basic incremental learning neural net; the meta-algorithm adjusts the window over which the basic learning process works. Here it is an assumption that contexts are contiguous in time and so a time-window is a sufficient representation of context. Harries et al. [12] employ a batch learner as a meta-algorithm to identify stable contexts and their concepts; this makes the assumption that the contexts are contiguous in the 'environmental variables' and the technique can only be done off-line. Aha describes an incremental instance-based learning technique which uses a clustering algorithm to determine the weight of features and hence implicitly adjust context [13].

Contextual knowledge has been used to augment existing machine learning techniques in a number of instances. Turney [14] used explicit identification of what the contextual factors would be, but others have used implicit features (e.g. Aha [13]). Turney [15] discusses the problem of the effects of context on machine learning and surveys some heuristics used to mitigate these effects [16].

2.3 Context in Human Cognition

The use of context is a pervasive heuristic in human cognition. It appears that we use context in almost every area of our thinking and action, including: language understanding; memory; concepts and categorization; affect and social cognition and (probably) problem solving and reasoning [17]. In the past some researchers perceived the context-dependency of human thought purely as a disadvantage or side-effect, but now it is becoming increasingly clear that it is an essential tool for enabling effective learning, reasoning and communication in a complex world. We speculate that much of the power of human thought comes from an ability to rapidly switch between different cognitive contexts, whilst only doing relatively simple inference within these (with the exception of problem solving or fault-diagnosis, which use more sophisticated inference).

It has been recognized for a while that the external (and linguistic) context plays a role in the understanding of natural language. However it is only recently that the importance of context in communication has been appreciated. The external context is not merely a resource for understanding utterances that is accessed when all other mechanisms fail; a way of sorting out otherwise ambiguous sentences. Rather it is one of the primary mechanisms. We will not discuss the use of context in language more as it is a huge and controversial area in which we are not experts.

Although human cognition is not a necessary starting point for motivating the design of an intelligence, it is a fruitful one, especially when looking for solutions that will scale up to cope with problems of real world complexity. What the human case shows is that it does appear that context is a useful heuristic in at least some real-world cases.

3   Combining Context-Dependent Learning and Reasoning

Restricting both reasoning and learning to an appropriate context makes both more feasible. However, as with any other technique, there are a number of difficulties with applying a context-dependent approach to reasoning. Firstly:

- Explicitly specifying a set of knowledge appropriate for a whole set of potential contexts is both time-consuming and labor-intensive.

Thus with a few honorable exceptions (e.g. CYC [18]), most systems of context-dependent learning or reasoning are only tried out with a few contexts. A possible answer to this (and the one employed here) is to learn the contexts and the context-dependent knowledge. The second is easier than the first; for, as indicated above in Sect. 2.2, there are a number of techniques to learn the knowledge associated with contexts.

The learning of the contexts themselves (i.e. how to recognize when a set of beliefs learnt in a previous situation are again applicable) requires a sort of meta-learning. As documented above, there are such techniques in existence. However most of these require reasonably strong assumptions about the particular nature of the contexts concerned. For example [19] learns context for plans within a BDI framework, but this is limited to the strict definition of plan context, and is further constrained by the knowledge elicitation process. An exception is [20] which describes how contexts can be co-learnt along with the knowledge associated with those contexts. This applies an evolutionary learning algorithm where the knowledge is distributed across a space, where different positions in that space are associated with different sets of perceptions or different parts of a problem. This can be clearly understood via the following ecological analogy. If the space can be thought of as a landscape where different parts of the landscape have different properties, and different plants require different properties (some might thrive in marshy land, others sunny and dry, etc.). The set of solutions can be seen as varieties of a plant. The different varieties propagate and cross with others in each locality so that, eventually, each variety adapts and, at the same time, spreads across the areas that it is best adapted for. The patches where different sets of varieties thrive define the different ecological niches – corresponding to the different contexts via this analogy.

The ability to learn context allows us to progress beyond the 'loose' loop of:

```
repeat
   learn/update beliefs
   deduce intentions, plans and actions
until finished
```

to a more integrated loop of:

```
repeat
    repeat
        recognise/learn/choose context
        induce/adapt/update beliefs in that context
        deduce predictions/conclusions in that context
    until predictions are consistent
            and actions/plans can be determined
    plan & act
until finished.
```

Such a co-development of cognitive contexts alongside their 'contents' gives rise to a new problem when the knowledge in these contexts is used to infer predictions and decisions. Thus a second problem is this:

– When some of the contents turn out to be wrong, how can one tell when it is the context that is wrong and when it is the contents that are wrong?

There is no universal answer to such a question – it will, in general, depend upon the nature of the domain and hence the appropriate contexts in that domain. However there is a heuristic, as follows: if only a few of the elements of knowledge associated with a context are disconfirmed, it is likely that these are wrong (update the set); if many of the elements are disconfirmed then it is likely that the context is wrong (change it and learn from this).

Thus in the proposed architecture there are four modules: (1) the context identification system; (2) the context-dependent memory; (3) the local learning/induction algorithm; and (4) the inference system, as shown in Fig 1.

The context identification system (CIS) takes a rich range of inputs and learns in a flexible and imprecise way an indication of the context (which it outputs to the memory). The CIS learns as the result of negative feedback when too much of the knowledge in the cognitive context is simultaneously disconfirmed.

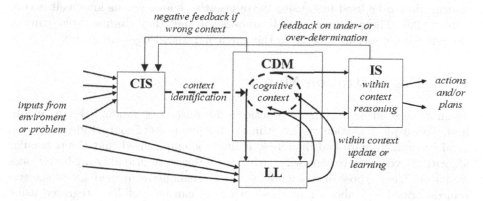

Fig. 1. How the context-identification system (CIS), the context-dependent memory (CDM), the local learning algorithm (LL), and inference system (IS) work together

The context-dependent memory (CDM) takes the indication given by the CIS and identifies all those memory items stored within that context. It evaluates the (current) truth of these and if too many are false it returns negative feedback to the CIS which will identify another context. If a sufficient number of indicated contents are true, then the local learning updates the items within that context. Those items that are (currently) true are passed to the inference system.

The local learning algorithm (LL) performs a local update of the knowledge in the memory. It may include the propagation of successful items towards the focus, but may also include the deletion/correction of items that were false and the possible insertion of new induced/learned.

Finally the planning/inference system (IS) tries to deduce some decisions as to the actions or plans to execute. It could do this in a number of ways, but this could include trying to predict the future states of the world given possible actions and comparing the predictions using its goals.

Two common problems with inference systems that attempt to deduce predictions or decisions from an arbitrary collection of knowledge are under- and over-determination. Under-determination is when there is not enough information to come to a conclusion or decision that needs to be reached. In other words there may be a key proposition, α, such that neither α nor $\neg\alpha$ can be inferred. Over-determination is when there is contradictory information in the knowledge, i.e. when there is an α such that both α and $\neg\alpha$ can be deduced.

This architecture allows a useful response in these two situations. In the case of under-determination the context can be expanded so that more knowledge can be made available to the IS so that it may make more inferences. In the case of over-determination the context can be reduced so that some of the knowledge can be excluded, the knowledge that is peripheral to the context.

Many non-monotonic logics can be seen as attempts to solve the above problems in a generic way, i.e. without reference to any contingent properties obtained from the particular contexts they are applied in. So, for example, some use 'entrenchment' to determine which extra information can be employed (e.g. oldest information is more reliable [21]), and others allow a variety of default information to be used (e.g. using extra negative knowledge as long as it is consistent [22]). These may work well on occasion, but they cannot exploit any of the relevance relations specific to the particular knowledge and context.

4   A Demonstration Model

To show these ideas working in practice a demonstration model is briefly exhibited. This deploys particular algorithms to the processes of context identification, local learning/update and inference. It must be emphasised that the particular algorithms we used are somewhat arbitrary – there are probably far better ones available. The purpose of this model is to be a demonstrator model, and the system described here shows how these processes can be usefully integrated using context dependency rather than representing an ideal.

4.1   The Environment

To support contextual learning, the chosen environment needs to be sufficiently rich (1) to be worth learning contextual information about, and (2) that an entity may predict and reason about many different aspects at once. The heuristic must be able to distinguish between an incorrect choice of context (when many beliefs/predictions are proven to be wrong) and incorrect beliefs/predictions (when only a few are wrong).

The environment selected to meet these requirements was a small artificial stock market [23], where the past actions of other traders, the prices, volumes, money etc. are observable. This is a constrained but dynamic setting, where any actions have significant effects on the environment because the other traders will then adapt their strategies. The prices follow a pattern typical of many markets – there are booms and busts; much apparent noise; only a weak, long-term correlation of prices with dividends; and a long-term exponential trend in prices.

All traders are initialised with a certain amount of cash and a small random level of each stock. There is a 'running-in' period where all actions are random, to provide for the initial conditions for learning. If the demand was greater than the supply then the price goes up by the set increment, otherwise it goes down by the same incremement.

GP Traders. The context trader competes within this environment with other traders having identical abilities in terms of perception and action but a much simpler (non-context-dependent) GP algorithm. For each of these traders, in each cycle its population of strategies is evolved once using a fairly standard GP algorithm with the fitness determined by an evaluation of the increase in total assets that would have resulted if that strategy was used over a certain number of time periods. The best is used to determine the current strategy which is then moderated for possibility (e.g. it may want to buy 2000 units of a certain stock but only have enough cash for 5 units!).

Each strategy is composed of a set of typed trees which, when evaluated, yields a number. There is one tree for each stock, plus one stats tree which can be used to learn a useful result that can be used in the other trees. Each GP trader agent has a small population of these strategies.

4.2   General Structure of Context Agent

The general structure is illustrated in Figure 1. Key signals into/out from/ between modules are as follows:

- A vector of 69 different perceptions are fed into both the CIS and LL;
- The (guess at the) current appropriate context is sent from CIS to CDM as a pair of a coordinate and a radius;
- If the context is wrong a 'bad context' signal is sent from CMD to CIS

- If the set of expressions passes basic tests, the set of expressions within the currently identified context is sent to the IS;
- If the set of expressions is inconsistent a signal of 'over-determination' is sent to the CIS, if there is insufficient information to deduce a decision then a signal of 'under-determination' is sent to the CIS;
- The IS outputs decisions in terms of buying and selling stocks;
- The LL acts upon the contents of the CDM using present and past information about the environment to do so.

4.3   The Context Identification System (CIS)

The CIS is implemented using a simple table with four entries: a vector of possible perceptions; a weight; a radius; and an output coordinate of the CDM. The distance between the vector of input perceptions and the first column entries multiplied by the weight are calculated and the row with the minimum value 'fired'. The radius and coordinate are output to the CDM, as is illustrated in figure 2. In the case of negative feedback, the fired weight is increased. Thus the table forms a simple self-organized critical system [24].

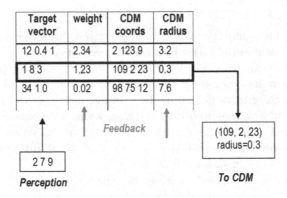

Fig. 2. The CIS implemented as a simple table using the closest match moderated by the weights. The corresponding CDM coordinate and radius is output.

The table was randomly initialised; the input vector in the first column is of size 69 initialised with random values in the [-10, 110] range; the CDM coordinates being in the [0,100] range; the initial weights were all 1; the initial radii were all 20.

Changes occur to the CIS table as follows. If the set of knowledge output from the CDM turns out to be inconsistent or inadequate, the IS signals this to the CIS and the radius in the fired row is reduced or increased respectively. If the context was wrongly identified then the corresponding weight is increased to reduce the times this is fired.

4.4   The Context-Dependent Memory (CDM)

The CDM is another table, associating items of knowledge expressed as strongly typed trees, with coordinates. When given a focus coordinate and radius from the CIS it identifies those items within the radius of the focus coordinate. This CDM thus has similarities to the way that SDM memory works [25]. It evaluates these knowledge items against the current state of the world and the proportion of correct items calculated. If this value is low, negative feedback is provided to the CIS and control is passed back to the CIS, otherwise the LL module acts on the identified knowledge set and (in parallel) the set is passed to the IS.

Knowledge items are represented as typed trees using a fairly rich language of nodes and terminals. These include nodes for logical operators (and, or, implies, not); arithmetic operators (plus, minus, times, divide); comparisons (greater than, less than); temporal operators (last, variable lag) and others (e.g. randomIntegerUpTo). Terminals include: Boolean constants (T, F); a selection of numeric constants; prices of stocks; actions of other traders in each stock; cash owned; stocks owned; trading volumes; stock index; whether the price of a stock has gone up or down; etc.

Thus an example expression is:

```
[IMPLIES
    [greaterThan
        [times
            [doneByLast ['gPTrader-4'] ['stock-3']]
            [presentStockOf ['stock-2']]
        ]
        [talkResult ['stock-2']]
    ]
    [lastBoolean
        [priceDownOf ['stock-1']]
    ]
]
```

4.5   The Local Learning Algorithm (LL)

The LL is based on Strongly-Typed Genetic Programming [26]. The LL algorithm samples the contents of the CDM and applies an evolutionary algorithm to it. Each cycle the LL does the following:

```
For each expression in the current context currently true
    If randomNumber < propogationProb
        Copy expression 25% towards the focus
            Mutating it with probability mutationProb
    If anotherRandomNumber < crossoverProb
        Randomly choose anotherExpression in context
        Cross expression and anotherExpression and store
            Store result shifted 25% towards the focus
```

```
            From the average position of parents
     Next expression
     For each expression in the current context currently false
         If randomNumber < cullProb
             Delete expression
     Next expression
```

If the total population is greater than a set maximum, then those expressions that have been accessed least recently in the whole memory are deleted to bring the population down to the maximum.

4.6   The Inference System (IS)

The IS does the following: it takes the set of expressions in the current context that are currently true; it simplifies the expressions using the current state of the perceptions (substituting the known values for sub-expressions and doing some arithmetic and logical simplification); then it applies a set of inference rules to the resulting set for a maximum of 10 sub-cycles (or until no new inferences can be made); the result of this (in terms of inferences about the next price movements) determines the actions or signals that result.

Inference rules used are the following: $A \wedge B \models A$; $A \wedge B \models B$; $A, A \rightarrow B \models B$; $\neg B, A \rightarrow B \models \neg A$; $\neg \neg A \Rightarrow A$; $\neg(priceUp) \Rightarrow priceDown$, $\neg(priceDown) \Rightarrow priceUp$.

The results are evaluated as follows: if neither priceUp nor priceDown are inferred for the next time period for any stock then no action is taken and a signal sent that this context is under-determined; if for a stock priceUp is inferred but not priceDown for that stock the agent buys; if for a stock priceDown is inferred but not priceUp for that stock the agent sells; and if both priceUp and priceDown are inferred the 'over-determined' signal is sent.

4.7   Preliminary Results

The agent that used the architecture did not initially do as well as the GP learners it was pitted against. The latter learn in a quick-and-dirty way evolving strategies that would have performed best over the last 5 time periods only. The context agent has a lot more learning to do than them before it becomes effective. As you can see from Fig. 3 the context trader does worse up to time 400 (as it learns) but then catches up by roughly 40 orders of magnitude (that is, the rate of increase in asset value is higher for the context trader beyond time 400).

However we can show that this agent does learn and reason in a context-dependent way. Figure 4 shows that the agent does make trades and hence infers enough to make predictions about the movements of prices.

The last graph (Fig. 5) shows the rate of bad context identification over time – this drops to zero over the time.

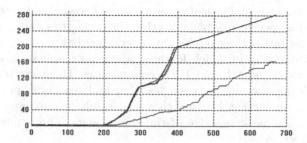

Fig. 3. The logarithm of the total assets of traders (context is lower line) against time

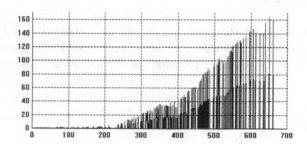

Fig. 4. The logarithm of the values of trades made by the context agent over time

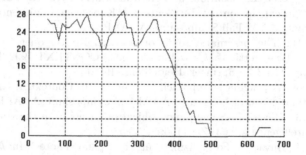

Fig. 5. The number of bad contexts identified over the last 50 time periods

Clearly these results are only from a single run and thus do not prove anything. However they are not to prove the technique but merely show its feasibility. In the future we hope to be able to greatly improve these results.

5   Conclusion

We have shown how context can be used to integrate learning and reasoning in a coherent manner, improving the tractability of both whilst retaining most of the advantages of both. As an additional benefit it provides sensible responses to the problems of under- and over-determination in knowledge. Knowledge update can be done in a specific manner reflecting the properties and relevance of the knowledge items rather than relying on generic heuristics.

This is but one way in which learning and reasoning can interact. Due to the divide between the ML and KRR communities, there are too few studies of the possible interactions between learning and reasoning processes. These interactions are important because they can result in outcomes that are not obvious from a simple knowledge of the components. This study goes a little way in this direction.

Acknowledgments

We would like to thank the participants of the conferences on Modelling and Using Context for their comments on these and related ideas, particularly Anita Fetzner. We would also like to thank the reviewers of this paper for their comments.

References

1. McCarthy, J.: Generality in artificial-intelligence – Turing award lecture. Communications of the ACM 30(12), 1030–1035 (1987)
2. Barwise, J., Perry, J.: Situations and Attitudes. MIT Press, Cambridge (1983)
3. Hayes, P.: Contexts in context. In: Context in Knowledge Representation and Natural Language, AAAI Fall Symposium, AAAI Press (1997)
4. Edmonds, B.: The pragmatic roots of context. In: Bouquet, P., Serafini, L., Brézillon, P., Benercetti, M., Castellani, F. (eds.) CONTEXT 1999. LNCS (LNAI), vol. 1688, pp. 119–134. Springer, Heidelberg (1999)
5. Zadrozny, W.: A pragmatic approach to context. In: Context in Knowledge Representation and Natural Language, AAAI Fall Symposium, AAAI Press (1997)
6. McCarthy, J., Hayes, P.: Some philosophical problems from the standpoint of AI. Machine Intelligence 4, 463–502 (1969)
7. McCarthy, J., Buvac, S.: Formalizing context (expanded notes). In: Aliseda, A., van Glabbeek, R., Westerstahl, D. (eds.) Computing Natural Language. CSLI Lecture Notes, vol. 81, pp. 13–50. CSLI Publications, Stanford, California (1998)
8. Gabbay, D.: Fibring logics. Clarendon, Oxford (1999)
9. Ghidini, C., Giunchiglia, F.: Local models semantics, or contextual reasoning = locality + compatibility. Artificial Intelligence 127(3), 221–259 (2001)
10. Greiner, R., Darken, C., Santoso, N.: Efficient reasoning. ACM Computing Surveys 33(1), 1–30 (2001)
11. Widmer, G.: Tracking context changes through meta-learning. Machine Learning 27, 259–286 (1997)
12. Harries, M., Sammut, C., Horn, K.: Extracting hidden contexts. Machine Learning 32, 101–112 (1998)
13. Aha, D.: Incremental, instance-based learning of independent and graded concept descriptions. In: Proceedings of the 6th International Workshop on Machine Learning, pp. 387–391. Morgan Kaufmann, San Francisco (1989)

14. Turney, P.: Robust classification with context-sensitive features. In: Industrial and Engineering Applications of Artificial Intelligence and Expert Systems, IEA/AIE-93, Edinburgh, Gordon and Breach, pp. 268–276 (1993)
15. Turney, P.: The identification of context-sensitive features: A formal definition of context for concept learning. In: ICML-96 Workshop on Learning in Context-Sensitive Domains, Bari, Italy, pp. 53–59 (1996)
16. Turney, P.: The management of context-sensitive features: A review of strategies. In: ICML-96 Workshop on Learning in Context-Sensitive Domains, Bari, Italy, pp. 60–66 (1996)
17. Kokinov, B., Grinberg, M.: Simulating context effects in problem solving with AMBR. In: Akman, V., Bouquet, P., Thomason, R.H., Young, R.A. (eds.) CONTEXT 2001. LNCS (LNAI), vol. 2116, pp. 221–234. Springer, Heidelberg (2001)
18. Lenat, D.: CYC – a large-scale investment in knowledge infrastructure. Communications of the ACM 38(11), 33–38 (1995)
19. Norling, E.: Folk psychology for human modelling: Extending the BDI paradigm. In: Proceedings of the Third International Joint Conference on Autonomous Agents and Multiagent Systems, New York (2004)
20. Edmonds, B.: Learning and exploiting context in agents. In: Proceedings of the 1st International Joint Conference on Autonomous Agents and Multiagent Systems (AAMAS), Bologna, Italy, pp. 1231–1238. ACM Press, New York (2002)
21. Gärdenfors, P.: Epistemic importance and minimal changes of belief. Australasian Journal of Philosophy 62(2), 136–157 (1984)
22. Reiter, R.: A logic for default reasoning. Artificial Intelligence 13(80) 81–132
23. Palmer, R., Arthur, W.B., Holland, J.H., LeBaron, B., Taylor, P.: Artificial economic life – a simple model of a stock market. Physica D 75, 264–274 (1994)
24. Bak, P.: How nature works: the science of self-organized criticality. Copernicus, New York (1996)
25. Kanerva, P.: Sparse Distributed Memory. MIT Press, Cambridge (1988)
26. Montana, D.J.: Strongly typed genetic programming. Evolutionary Computation 3(2), 199–230 (1995)

Can Agents Acquire Human-Like Behaviors in a Sequential Bargaining Game?
– Comparison of Roth's and Q-Learning Agents –

Keiki Takadama[1], Tetsuro Kawai[2], and Yuhsuke Koyama[3]

[1] The University of Electro-Communications
1-5-1, Chofugaoka, Chofu, Tokyo 182-8585 Japan
keiki@hc.uec.ac.jp
[2] Sony Corporation
6-7-35, Kita-Shinagawa, Shinagawa-ku, Tokyo 141-0001 Japan
tetsuro.kawai@gmail.com
[3] Tokyo Institute of Technology
4259 Nagatsuta-cho, Midori-ku, Yokohama 226-8503 Japan
koyama@dis.titech.ac.jp

Abstract. This paper addresses *agent modeling* in multiagent-based simulation (MABS) to explore agents who can reproduce human-like behaviors in the *sequential bargaining game*, which is more difficult to be reproduced than in the *ultimate game* (*i.e.,* one time bargaining game). For this purpose, we focus on the Roth's learning agents who can reproduce human-like behaviors in several simple examples including the ultimate game, and compare simulation results of Roth's learning agents and Q-learning agents in the sequential bargaining game. Intensive simulations have revealed the following implications: (1) Roth's basic and three parameter reinforcement learning agents with any type of three action selections (*i.e.,* ϵ-greed, roulette, and Boltzmann distribution selections) can neither learn consistent behaviors nor acquire sequential negotiation in sequential bargaining game; and (2) Q-learning agents with any type of three action selections, on the other hand, can learn consistent behaviors and acquire sequential negotiation in the same game. However, Q-learning agents cannot reproduce the decreasing trend found in subject experiments.

Keywords: agent-based simulation, agent modeling, sequential bargaining game, human-like behaviors, reinforcement learning.

1 Introduction

A *reproduction of human-like behaviors* by computer simulations is an important issue in multiagent-based simulation (MABS) [1,9] to validate computational models and simulation results. For this purpose, several researches attempt to reproduce simulation results that are close to subject experiment results. For example, Roth and Erev compared simulation results of simple reinforcement learning agents with results of subject experiments in several examples [4,16].

L. Antunes and K. Takadama (Eds.): MABS 2006, LNAI 4442, pp. 156–171, 2007.

Their intensive comparisons revealed that (1) computer simulation using simple reinforcement learning agents can more explain the result of subject experiments than economic theory; and (2) the former approach has more great potential of predicting results than the latter approach. In related work, Ogawa and their colleagues compared simulation results with subject experiment results in *monopolistic intermediary games* which has more complexity of the real world than examples addressed in Roth and Erev's works [6,13].[1] This research also revealed that simple reinforcement learning agents can reproduce the subject experiment results more precisely than the best response agents and random agents. These researches show that reinforcement learning agents have a high reproduction capability of human-like behaviors.

However, such capability was only investigated in a case where a payoff is determined and given to agents in *each negotiation* but not in a case where a payoff is determined after *a number of negotiations*. Considering the fact that *sequential negotiations* are naturally conducted in general human society instead of *one negotiation* (*i.e.*, it is a rare case where a negotiation process ends by only one negotiation), it is important to investigate the reproduction capability of reinforcement learning agents in sequential negotiations toward pursuing an acquisition of real human behaviors by computer simulations. For this purpose, we start by employing the *sequential bargaining game* as one of the typical negotiations and compare simulation results of reinforcement learning agents with results of subject experiments. We focus on the bargaining game because the bargaining is not only a fundamental negotiation but also appeared in several levels (*i.e.*, individual, company, and country levels) and therefore agents that can reproduce such human-like behaviors have a potential of providing new important aspects of negotiations. As a representative of such agents, we employ Roth's[2] reinforcement learning agents from social science and Q-learning agents [22] in the context of reinforcement learning [21] from computer science, and investigate their reproduction capability by applying either of three types of action selections (described in Section 3) to both Roth's and Q-learning agents.

This paper is organized as follows. Section 2 explains the bargaining game as an important example for sequential negotiations and an implementation of agents is described in Section 3. Section 4 presents computer simulations and Section 5 discusses the reproduction capability of human-like behaviors. Finally, our conclusions are given in Section 6.

2   Bargaining Game

As described in the previous section, we focus on *bargaining theory* [10,11] in *game theory* [14] and employ a *bargaining game* [17] where two or more players try to reach a mutually beneficial agreement through negotiations. This game has

---

[1] They conduced subject experiments in the framework of Spulber's model [20].

[2] Hereafter, we employ the name Roth as a representative of both Roth and Erev.

been proposed for investigating when and what kinds of offers of an individual player can be accepted by the other players.

To understand the bargaining game, let us give an example from Rubinstein's work [17] which illustrated a typical situation using the following scenario: two players, P_1 and P_2, have to reach an agreement on the partition of a "pie". For this purpose, they alternate offers describing possible divisions of the pie, such as "P_1 receives x and P_2 receives $1 - x$ at time t", where x is any value in the interval $[0, 1]$. When a player receives an offer, the player decides whether to accept it or not. If the player accepts the offer, the negotiation process ends, and each player receives the share of the pie determined by the concluded contract. If the player decides not to accept the offer, on the other hand, the player makes a counter-offer, and all of the above steps are repeated until a solution is reached or the process is aborted for some external reason (e.g., the number of negotiation processes is finite). If the negotiation process is aborted, neither player can receive any share of the pie.

Here, we consider the finite-horizon situation, where the maximum number of steps (MAX_STEP) in the game is fixed and all players know this information as common knowledge. In the case where MAX_STEP = 1 (also known as the *ultimatum game*), player P_1 makes the only offer and P_2 can accept or refuse it. If P_2 refuses the offer, both players receive nothing. Since a rational player is based on the notion of "anything is better than nothing", a rational P_1 tends to keep most of the pie to herself by offering only a minimum share to P_2. Since there are no further steps to be played in the game, a rational P_2 inevitably accepts the tiny offer.

By applying a backward induction reasoning to the situation above, it is possible to perform a simulation for MAX_STEP > 1. For the same reason seen in the ultimatum game, the player who can make the last offer is better positioned to receive the larger share by offering a minimum offer [19]. This is because both players know the maximum number of steps in the game as common knowledge, and therefore the player who can make the last offer can acquire a larger share with the same behavior of the ultimatum game at the last negotiation. From this feature of the game, the last offer is granted to the player who does not make the first offer if MAX_STEP is even, since each player is allowed to make at most MAX_STEP/2 offers. On the other hand, the last offer is granted to the same player who makes the first offer if MAX_STEP is odd. The main concern of the *sequential negotiations* is to investigate whether players continue the negotiation to maximize their share.

After this section, we use the terms "payoff" and "agent" instead of the terms "share" and "player" for their more general meanings in the bargaining game.

3   Modeling Agents

This section implements reinforcement learning agents in the framework of the sequential bargaining game as follows.

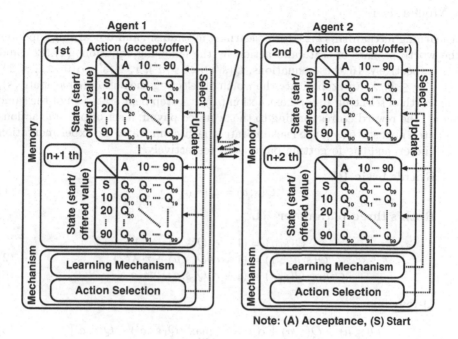

Fig. 1. Reinforcement learning agents

3.1 Agent Architecture

• Memory

As shown in Figure 1, memory stores a fixed number of matrices of *state* (which represents the start or the offered value from the opponent agent) and *action* (which represents the acceptance of the offered value or the counter-offer value). In particular, the MAX_STEP/2 + 1 number of matrices are prepared in each agent and used in turn at each negotiation to decide to accept an offer or make a counter-offer (see an example presented later in this section). In Figure 1, both agents have $n + 1$ number of matrices. In this model, agents independently learn and acquire different worths[3] of the state and action pair, called *Q-values*, in order to acquire a large payoff. Q-value, represented by $Q(s, a)$, indicates an expected reward (*i.e.*, the payoff in the bargaining game) that an agent will acquire when performing the action a in the situation s. Note that (1) both state and action in this model are represented by the discrete values in a 10 unit (*i.e.*, 10, 20, $\cdots$, 90); and (2) in addition to these 10–90 values, the matrix has a column labelled (S) and a row labelled (A), which are used to indicate the start, and accept an offer, respectively.

---

[3] In the context of reinforcement learning, worth is called "value". We select the term "worth" instead of "value" because the term "value" is used as a numerical number represented in the state and action.

• Mechanism

A learning mechanism (*i.e.*, Roth's learning mechanism and Q-learning) updates the worth of pairs of state and action by the following equations (1), (2), and (3) respectively. In these equations, $Q(s, a)$, $Q(s', a')$, r, $A(s')$, $\alpha(0 < \alpha \leq 1)$, $\gamma(0 \leq \gamma \leq 1)$, λ, and ϕ indicate the worth of selecting the action (a) at state (s), the worth of selecting 1 step next action (a') at 1 step next state (s') of the same agent, the reward corresponding to the acquired payoff, a set of possible actions at 1 step next state (s'), the learning rate, the discount rate, the experimentation parameter, and the forgetting parameter, respectively.

- **Roth's basic RL**[4]

$$Q(s, a) = Q(s, a) + r \tag{1}$$

- **Roth's three parameter RL**[5]

$$
\begin{aligned}
Q(s, a) &= (1 - \phi)Q(s, a) + r(1 - \lambda) \\
Q(s, a \pm 1) &= (1 - \phi)Q(s, a) + r(\lambda/2) \\
Other\ Q(s, a) &= (1 - \phi)Q(s, a),\ \forall s, a
\end{aligned}
\tag{2}
$$

- **Q-learning**

$$Q(s, a) = Q(s, a) + \alpha[r + \gamma \max_{a' \in A(s')} Q(s', a') - Q(s, a)] \tag{3}$$

For the above mechanisms, (1) Roth's basic RL (reinforcement learning) mechanism simply adds rewards to the Q-values, which strengthens Q-values when an agent acquires a reward; (2) Roth's three-parameter RE learning mechanism is extended from the basic one by adding both experimentation parameter λ and the forgetting parameter ϕ. This mechanism updates not only the Q-value of the actually selected action but also Q-values of two actions which are the most close to the actually selected action. For example, when an agent acquires r by offering 4, then the mechanism updates $Q(s, 3)$ and $Q(s, 5)$ in addition to $Q(s, 4)$. Furthermore, this mechanism decreases all Q-value except for $Q(s, a)$, $Q(s, a \pm 1)$ according to ϕ values; and (3) Q-learning mechanism estimates the expected rewards by using the one step next Q-values, which strengthens the sequential state and action pairs that contribute to acquiring the reward. This is done by updating $Q(s, a)$ to be close to $maxQ(s', a')$[6] and continues such updates until the bargaining game is completed. However, $Q(s, a)$ used at the final

---

[4] In Roth's original equation, $Q(s, a)$ is represented by $q_{nk}(t)$. For example, equation (1) is originally represented by $q_{nj}(t + 1) = \begin{cases} q_{nj}(t) + r & ,\ if\ j = k \\ q_{nj}(t), & otherwise \end{cases}$. Here, $q_{nj}(t)$ indicates Q-values of an action j of an agent n in time t. The k indicate an action that an agent takes.

[5] In Roth's original equation, λ is represented by ϵ. We use λ because ϵ is used in the action selection.

[6] Precisely, $Q(s, a)$ is updated to be $r + maxQ(s', a')$. But, r is only set when the reward is obtained in the sequential bargaining game, and thus $Q(s, a)$ is normally updated to be close to $maxQ(s', a')$.

negotiation is updated not to be close to $maxQ(s', a')$ but to r calculated by the payoff that an agent acquires. This is because there is no further negotiation when the bargaining game is completed, and thus $maxQ(s', a')$ is set to 0.

For the action selection (*the acceptance or counter-offer*), the following methods are employed.

- **ϵ-greedy selection**
  This method selects an action of the maximum worth (Q-value) at the 1-ϵ probability, while selecting an action randomly at the ϵ $(0 \le \epsilon \le 1)$ probability.
- **Roulette selection**
  This method probabilistically selects an action based on the ratio of Q-values over all actions, which is calculated by the following equation (4). The Roth's basic and three parameter RL agents [4,16] employ this selection mechanism.

$$P(a|s) = Q(s, a) / \sum_{a_i \in A(s)} Q(s, a_i) \qquad (4)$$

- **Boltzmann distribution selection**
  This method probabilistically selects an action based on the ratio of Q-values over all actions, which is calculated by the following equation (5). In this equation, T is the temperature parameter which adjusts randomness of action selection. Agents select their actions at random when T is high, while they select their greedy actions when T is low.

$$P(a|s) = e^{Q(s,a)/T} / \sum_{a_i \in A(s)} e^{Q(s,a_i)/T} \qquad (5)$$

3.2 An Example of a Negotiation Process

As a concrete negotiation process, agents proceed as follows. Defining {offer, offered}$_i^{A\{1,2\}}$ as the ith offer value (action) or offered value (state) of agent A_1 or A_2, A_1 starts by selecting one Q-value from the line $S(Start)$ (*i.e.*, one Q-value from {$Q_{01}, \cdots, Q_{09}$}[7] in the line S), and makes the first offer offer$_1^{A_1}$ according to the selected Q-value (for example, A_1 makes an offer 10% if it selects Q_{01}). Here, we count one *step* when either agent makes an offer. Then, A_2 selects one Q-value from the line offered$_1^{A_2}$(= offer$_1^{A_1}$) (*i.e.*, one Q-value from {$Q_{V0}, \cdots, Q_{V9}$}, where $V =$ offered$_1^{A_2}$(= offer$_1^{A_1}$)). A_2 accepts the offer if Q_{V0} (*i.e.*, the acceptance (A)) is selected; otherwise, it makes a counter-offer offer$_2^{A_2}$ according to the selected Q-value as the same way of A_1. This cycle is continued until either agent accepts the offer of the other agent or a negotiation is over (*i.e.*, the maximum number of steps (MAX_STEP) is exceeded by deciding

---

[7] At the first negotiation, one Q-value is selected from {$Q_{01}, \cdots, Q_{09}$} not from {Q_{00}, $Q_{09}, \cdots, Q_{90}$}. This is because the role of the first agent is to make the first offer and not to accpet any offer (by selecting Q_{00}) due to the fact that a negotiation has not started yet.

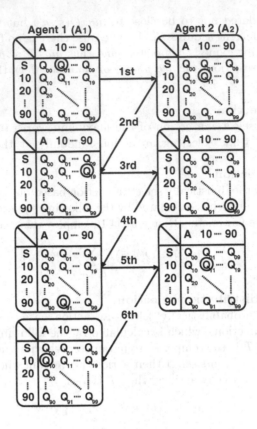

Fig. 2. An example of a negotiation process

to make a counter-offer instead of acceptance at the last negotiation step). Just after the cycle is over, all Q-values used in a sequential negotiation are updated according to either of equations (1) (2) or (3).

To understand this situation, let us consider the simple example where MAX_STEP = 6 as shown in Figure 2. Following this example, A_1 starts to make an offer 10%(= $\text{offer}_1^{A_1}$) to A_2 by selecting Q_{01} from the line $S(start)$. However, A_2 does not accept the first offer because it determines to make 10%(= $\text{offer}_2^{A_2}$) counter-offer by selecting Q_{11} from the line 10%(= $\text{offered}_1^{A_2}$, corresponding to A_1's offer). Then, in this exapmle, A_1 makes 90%(= $\text{offer}_3^{A_1}$) counter-offer by selecting Q_{19} from the line 10%(= $\text{offered}_2^{A_1}$), A_2 makes 90%(= $\text{offer}_4^{A_2}$) counter-offer by selecting Q_{99} from the line 90%(= $\text{offered}_3^{A_2}$), A_1 makes 10%(= $\text{offer}_5^{A_1}$) counter-offer by selecting Q_{91} from the line 90%(= $\text{offered}_4^{A_1}$), and A_2 makes 10%(= $\text{offer}_6^{A_2}$) counter-offer by selecting Q_{11} from the line 10%(= $\text{offered}_5^{A_2}$). Finally, A_1 accepts the 6th offer from A_2 by selecting Q_{10} from the line 10%, which results in A(acceptance). But, if A_1 makes a counter-offer instead of acceptance of the 6th offer from A_2 at the last negotiation step (which means to exceed the maximum number of steps), both agents can no longer receive any payoff, *i.e.*, they receive 0 payoff. Considering the case where Roth's basic RL A_1 accepts 10% offer from Roth's basic RL A_2 at the 6th negotiation step, A_1 and A_2 receive 10% and 90% payoffs, respectively, updating all Q-values used in a sequential negotiation as shown in Table 1.

Table 1. How is Q-table updated?

Agent 1	Agent 2
Q(S,10)=Q(S,10)+10	Q(10,10)=Q(10,10)+10
Q(10,90)=Q(10,90)+10	Q(90,90)=Q(90,90)+10
Q(90,10)=Q(90,10)+10	Q(10,10)=Q(10,10)+10
Q(10, A)=Q(10, A)+10	

Here, we count one *iteration* when the negotiation process ends or fails. In each iteration, Roth's learning and Q-learning agents update the worth pairs of state and action in order to acquire a large payoff.

4 Simulation

4.1 Simulation Cases

The following simulations were conducted in the sequential bargaining game as comparative simulations shown in Table 2.

- **Case 1: Roth's basic RL agents**
  Investigation of the results of Roth's basic RL agents, applying either of three action selections (*i.e.*, the ϵ-greed, roulette, and Boltzmann distribution selections).
- **Case 2: Roth's three parameter RL agents**
  Investigation of the results of Roth's three parameter RL agents, applying either of three action selections.
- **Case 3: Q-learning agents**
  Investigation of the results of Q-learning agents, applying either of three action selections.

4.2 Evaluation Criteria and Parameter Setting

In each simulation, (a) the payoff for both agents and (b) the negotiation process size are investigated. Here, the negotiation process size is the number of steps until an offer is accepted or MAX_STEP if no offer is accepted. All simulations are conducted for up to 10,000,000 iterations, which is enough for the agents to learn appropriate behaviors, and the results show the moving average of 10,000 iterations, which are all averaged over 10 runs.

As for the parameter setting, the variables are set as follows: (1) for the common parameters of the game, MAX_STEP (maximum number of steps in one

Table 2. Simulation cases

	ϵ-greedy selection	Roulette selection	Boltzmann distribution selection
Roth's basic RL	Case 1-a	Case 1-b	Case 1-c
Roth's three parameter RL	Case 2-a	Case 2-b	Case 2-c
Q-learning	Case 3-a	Case 3-b	Case 3-c

iteration) is 6; ϵ (ϵ-greedy selection) is 0.25, T (Boltzmann distribution selection) is 0.5; (2) for Roth's learning parameters, λ (experimentation parameter) is 0.05; ϕ (forgetting parameter) is 0.001; $S(1)$ (parameter related to initial Q-values) is 10; and (3) for Q-learning parameters, α (learning rate) is 0.1; γ (discount rate) is 1.0; initial Q-values is 0.1. Note that (1) preliminary examinations found that the tendency of the results does not drastically change according to the parameter setting; (2) all parameters of Roth's learning agents are based on Roth's original model [4,16]; and (3) initial Q-values in Roth's learning agents are set by the following equation (6) as the same as Roth's original works. In detail, $Q(s,a) = 1$ when $S(1) = 10$, because 10 actions (*i.e.*, one acceptance and nine counter offers) are possible actions in each state s (which means $|A(s)| = 10$).

$$Q(s,a) = S(1)/|A(s)|, \quad \forall s \tag{6}$$

We do not set the same initial Q-values of Roth's learning agents to Q-learning agents because it is too large for Q-learning that estimates expected payoffs (*i.e.*, nine is the biggest value) but not for Roth's learning that accumulates payoffs (*i.e.*, Q-values become large as the iteration increases).

Finally, all simulations were implemented by Java with standard libraries and conducted in Windows XP OS with Pentium 4 (2.60GHz) Processor.

4.3   Simulation Results

Figures 3 and 4 show the simulation results of Roth's three parameter RL agents and Q-learning agents, respectively. Note that the simulation results of Roth's basic RL agents are omitted because their results are fundamentally similar to those of Roth's three parameter ones. The upper, middle, and lower figures in Figures 3 correspond to the cases 2-a, 2-b, and 2-c, respectively, while those figures in Figure 4 correspond to the cases 3-a, 3-b, and 3-c, respectively. The left and right figures in all cases indicate the payoff and negotiation process size, respectively. The vertical axis in these figures indicates these two criteria, while the horizontal axis indicates the iterations. In the payoff figure, in particular, the solid and dotted lines indicate the payoff of agents 1 and 2, respectively.

These results suggest us that (1) simulation results of Roth's learning agents differ from those of Q-learning agents; but (2) simulation results among different action selections in both Roth's and Q-learning agents show a similar tendency.

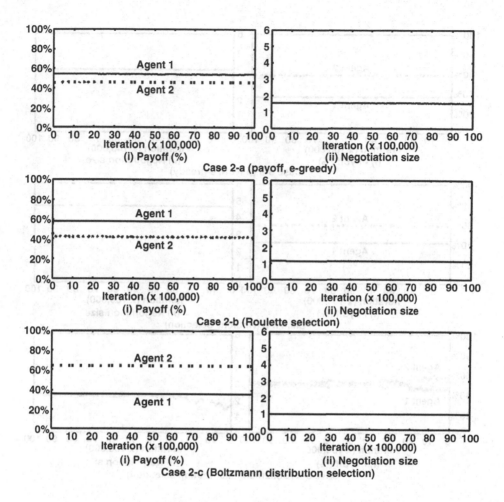

Fig. 3. Simulation results of Roth's three parameter RL agents

5 Discussion

5.1 Subject Experiment Result

Before discussing the simulation results of both Roth's and Q-learning agents, this section briefly describes the subject experiment result found in [8]. Figure 5 shows this result indicating the payoff of two human players in the left figures and negotiation process size in the right figures. The vertical and horizontal axes have the same meaning of Figures 3 and 4. In the payoff figure, in particular, the solid and dotted lines indicate the payoff of human players 1 and 2, respectively. Note that all values in this figure are averaged from 10 cases.

This result shows that (1) the payoff of two human players mostly converge around 50% and 50%, respectively; and (2) the negotiation process size increases

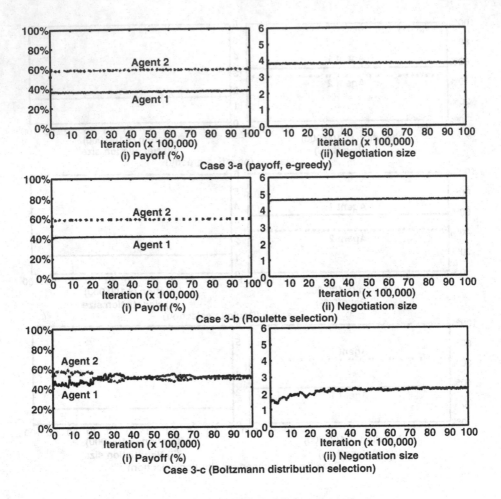

Fig. 4. Simulation results of Q-learning agents

a little bit in the first several iterations, decreases in the middle iterations, and finally converges around two. The result on the negotiation process size indicates that (2-i) human players acquire *sequential negotiations*; and (2-ii) the *decreasing trend* is occurred in the subject experiments.

5.2   Roth's Learning Agents

Regarding Roth's learning agents with any type of three action selections (*i.e.*, ϵ-greed, roulette, and Boltzmann distribution selections), Figure 3 shows that (1) the payoffs of two agents mostly converge around 40% and 60%; and (2) the negotiation process size is mostly one.

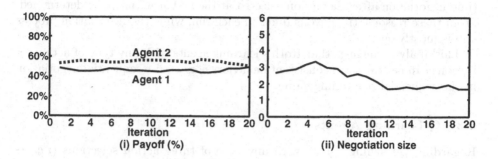

Fig. 5. Subject experiment results in [8]

From the payoff viewpoint, Roth's learning agents seem to acquire the similar results of subject experiments described in Section 5.1. However, this result is averaged values over 10 runs as described in Section 4.2 and the result in each run differs each other as shown in Table 3. This table indicates that the payoffs of both agents in the first run are 52% and 48%, those in the second run are 77.8% and 22.2%, and those in the fifth run are 20% and 80%, respectively. Note that (1) these values are completely different (no consistency) in each run; and (2) some of them show an opposite tendency (*i.e.*, the payoff of agent 1 is larger than that of agent 2 in some cases, while the payoff of agent 2 is larger than that of agent 1 in other cases). From the negotiation process size viewpoint, on the other hand, Roth's learning agents cannot acquire sequential negotiations because its size is mostly one which means the one time negotiation.

Table 3. The payoffs of Roth's three parameter RL agents in each run

		Run (Seed)					
		1	2	3	4	5	···
Payoff	Agent 1	52.0%	77.8%	77.4%	70.5%	20.0%	···
	Agent 2	48.0%	22.2%	22.6%	29.5%	80.0%	···

We obtain these results because of the early convergence on an acquisition of actions, which is caused when a big payoff is obtained by accidentally selecting a certain action. This convergence occurs due to an accumulation of Q-values of actions. As shown in equations (1) and (2) of Roth's learning agents, the reward obtained by the selected action is accumulated in Q-value (*i.e.*, the payoff or the $(1-\lambda)$ times of payoff is simply added in Q-value of the selected action), that increases the Q-value to the largest values among other Q-values. This makes agents continuously select the same action that has the largest Q-value. Furthermore, such an action can be determined at any negotiation time, which means that the actions selected at each negotiation time are determined one after another through several games and finally the game is completed by one time negotiation after the action selected at the first negotiation is determined. From these reasons, the payoffs differ in each run, while the negotiation process size is mostly one.

This analysis suggests that Roth's learning agents with any type of action selections can neither learn consistent behaviors nor acquire sequential negotiation in the sequential bargaining game.

5.3 Q-Learning Agents

Regarding Q-learning agents with any type of three action selections (*i.e.*, ε-greed, roulette, and Boltzmann distribution selections), Figure 4 shows that (1) the payoffs of two agents mostly converge around 40% and 60% (one of them is rather close to 50% and 50%); and (2) the negotiation process size is more than two.

This result suggests that Q-learning agents can acquire the similar results of subject experiments described in Section 5.1 from the payoff viewpoint and can acquire sequential negotiations from the negotiation process size viewpoint. We obtain these results because of no early convergence on an acquisition of actions. This is because Q-learning updates Q-values not by accumulating the reward but by estimating the expected reward. This makes agents complete the bargaining when they acquire the expected reward. However, since Q-values of actions are not so much different like in the Roth's learning agents, the negotiation may continue (*i.e.*, some games are completed by one time negotiation, while others are completed by the maximum time negotiation). This causes more than two time negotiations, which means that the negotiation process size is more than two. Finally, Q-learning agents cannot reproduce the decreasing trend found in subject experiments.

This analysis suggests that Q-learning agents with any type of action selections can learn consistent behaviors and acquire sequential negotiation in the sequential bargaining game.

5.4 Validity of Simulation Results and Design Guideline of Agents

The above analysis derives the following implications: (1) Roth's basic and three parameter reinforcement learning agents with any type of three action selections (*i.e.*, ε-greed, roulette, and Boltzmann distribution selections) can neither learn consistent behaviors nor acquire sequential negotiation in the sequential bargaining game; and (2) Q-learning agents with any type of three action selections, on the other hand, can learn consistent behaviors and acquire sequential negotiation in the same game. This indicates that Q-learning agents have a high reproduction capability of human-like behaviors. Here, we discuss the following aspects in terms of a validity of simulation results and a design guideline of agents.

– **Interaction**
  Comparing the iterations between subject experiment and computer simulation, humans require only 20 iterations to learn consistent behaviors and

acquire sequential negotiation, while Q-learning agents require 10,000,000 iterations. This seems that Q-learning agents cannot completely reproduce the human-like behaviors from the iteration viewpoint. However, the iteration aspect is not so much significant as the tendency and consistency aspect of the simulation results. This is because (1) a capability that humans have by nature is very higher than a capability that Q-learning agents have (*e.g.*, Q-learning agents do not have the capability of modeling of opponent players); and (2) the learning speed of agents can be varied by changing parameters (*e.g.*, Q-learning agents have the learning rate α), which means that an accuracy of simulation results does not make sense from the iteration viewpoint.

– **Fairness (Equity)**

Focusing on the fairness (or equity) of the payoff of both Q-learning agents, agents employing the Boltzmann distribution selections derive the roughly equal division of the payoff, which is most similar to the subject experiment result. In this sense, Q-learning employing the Boltzmann distribution selections have the great potential of being a candidate of the agent design element from the viewpoint of reproduction capability of human-behaviors. This implication can be supported by other research of the bargaining game in the context of experimental economics [5,7]. For example, Nydegger and Owen showed that there is a focal point[8] around 50% split in the payoff of two players [12]; Binmore suggested that fairness norms evolved to serve as an equilibrium selection criterion when members of a group are faced with a new source of surplus and have to divide it among its members without creating an internal conflict (p. 209) [2]; and the results done by Roth et al. showed the fairness even though the subjects playing the ultimatum game had distinct characteristics behaviors (precisely, four different countries: Israel, Japan, USA, and Slovenia) depending on their countries of origin [15].

6   Conclusions

This paper addressed *agent modeling* in multiagent-based simulation (MABS) to explore agents who can reproduce human-like behaviors in the *sequential bargaining game*, which is more difficult to be reproduced than in the *ultimate game*. For this purpose, we focused on the Roth's learning agents who can reproduce human-like behaviors in several simple examples including the ultimate game, and compared simulation results of Roth's learning agents and Q-learning agents in the sequential bargaining game. Intensive simulations have revealed the following implications: (1) Roth's basic and three parameter reinforcement learning agents with any type of three action selections (*i.e.*, ϵ-greed, roulette, and Boltzmann distribution selections) can neither learn consistent behaviors nor acquire sequential negotiation in the sequential bargaining game; and (2) Q-learning agents with any type of three action selections, on the other hand, can learn consistent behaviors and acquire sequential negotiation in the same

---

[8] The focal point is discussed in [18].

game. However, Q-learning agents cannot reproduce the decreasing trend found in subject experiments.

What should be noticed here is that these results have only been obtained from one example, $i.e.$, the sequential bargaining game. Therefore, further careful qualifications and justifications, such as analyses of results using other learning mechanisms and action selections or in other domains, are needed to generalize our results. Such important directions must be pursued in the near future in addition to the following future research: (1) an exploration of modeling agents who can reproduce the decreasing trend found in subject experiments; (2) simulation with more than two agents; and (3) an analysis of the case where human play the game with agents like in [3]; and (4) investigation of the influence of the discount factor [17] in the bargaining game.

Acknowledgements

The research reported here was supported in part by a Grant-in-Aid for Scientific Research (Young Scientists (B), 17700139) of Ministry of Education, Culture, Sports, Science and Technology (MEXT), Japan.

References

1. Axelrod, R.M.: The Complexity of Cooperation: Agent-Based Models of Competition and Collaboration. Princeton University Press, Princeton (1997)
2. Binmore, K.G.: Game Theory and the Social Contract: Just Playing, vol. 2. The MIT Press, Cambridge (1998)
3. Bosse, T., Jonker, C.M.: Human vs. Computer Behaviour in Multi-Issue Negotiation. In: First International Workshop on Rational, Robust, and Secure Negotiations in Multi-Agent Systems (RRS'05), pp. 11–24. IEEE Computer Society Press, Los Alamitos (2005)
4. Erev, I., Roth, A.E.: Predicting How People Play Games: Reinforcement Learning in Experimental Games with Unique, Mixed Strategy Equilibria. The American Economic Review 88(4), 848–881 (1998)
5. Friedman, D., Sunder, S.: Experimental Methods: A Primer for Economists. Cambridge University Press, Cambridge (1994)
6. Iwasaki, A., Ogawa, K., Yokoo, M., Oda, S.: Reinforcement Learning on Monopolistic Intermediary Games: Subject Experiments and Simulation. The fourth international workshop on Agent-based Approaches in Economic and Social Complex Systems (AESCS'05), pp. 117–128 (2005)
7. Kagel, J.H., Roth, A.E.: Handbook of Experimental Economics. Princeton University Press, Princeton (1995)
8. Kawai, T., Koyama, Y., Takadama, K.: Modeling Sequential Bargaining Game Agents Towards Human-like Behaviors: Comparing Experimental and Simulation Results. In: The First World Congress of the International Federation for Systems Research (IFSR'05), pp. 164–166 (2005)
9. Moss, S., Davidsson, P.: Multi-Agent-Based Simulation. In: Moss, S., Davidsson, P. (eds.) MABS 2000. LNCS (LNAI), vol. 1979, Springer, Heidelberg (2001)

10. Muthoo, A.: Bargaining Theory with Applications. Cambridge University Press, Cambridge (1999)
11. Muthoo, A.: A Non-Technical Introduction to Bargaining Theory. World Economics, 145–166 (2000)
12. Nydegger, R.V., Owen, G.: Two-Person Bargaining: An Experimental Test of the Nash Axioms. International Journal of Game Theory 3(4), 239–249 (1974)
13. Ogawa, K., Iwasaki, A., Oda, S., Yokoo, M.: Analysis on the Price-Formation-Process of Monopolistic Broker: Replication of Subject-Experiment by Computer-Experiment. The, JAFEE (Japan Association for Evolutionary Economics) Annual Meeting, 2005 (in Japanese) (2005)
14. Osborne, M.J., Rubinstein, A.: A Course in Game Theory. MIT Press, Cambridge (1994)
15. Roth, A.E., Prasnikar, V., Okuno-Fujiwara, M., Zamir, S.: Bargaining and Market Behavior in Jerusalem, Ljubljana, Pittsburgh, and Tokyo: An Experimental Study. American Economic Review 81(5), 1068–1094 (1991)
16. Roth, A.E., Erev, I.: Learning in Extensive-Form Games: Experimental Data and Simple Dynamic Models in the Intermediate Term. Games and Economic Behavior 8(1), 164–212 (1995)
17. Rubinstein, A.: Perfect Equilibrium in a Bargaining Model. Econometrica 50(1), 97–109 (1982)
18. Schelling, T.C.: The Strategy of Conflict. Harvard University Press (1960)
19. Ståhl, I.: Bargaining Theory, Economics Research Institute at the Stockholm School of Economics (1972)
20. Spulber, D.F.: Market Microstructure -Intermediaries and the theory of the firm. Cambridge University Press, Cambridge (1999)
21. Sutton, R.S., Bart, A.G.: Reinforcement Learning – An Introduction -. MIT Press, Cambridge (1998)
22. Watkins, C.J.C.H., Dayan, P.: Technical Note: Q-Learning. Machine Learning 8, 55–68 (1992)

Quantifying Degrees of Dependence in
Social Dependence Relations

Antônio Carlos da Rocha Costa[1,2] and Graçaliz Pereira Dimuro[1]

[1] Escola de Informática – Universidade Católica de Pelotas
Pelotas, RS, Brazil
[2] PPGC – Universidade Federal do Rio Grande do Sul
Porto Alegre, RS, Brazil
{rocha,liz}@atlas.ucpel.tche.br

Abstract. This paper refines a previously introduced procedure to quantify objective dependence relations between agents of a multiagent system. The quantification of the dependence relations is performed on a specially defined form of reduced dependence graphs, called *dependence situation graphs*. The paper also shows how the procedure can be used to determine a measure of the dependence that a society as a whole has on each agent that participates in it and, correlatively, a measure of the negotiation powers of the agents of such society. The procedure is also extended to allow for the refinement of the objective degrees of dependence into subjective ones, through the use of auxiliary coefficients that can represent some subjective aspects of the dependence relationships. A sample calculation of objective degrees of dependence and negotiation powers of agents of a simple multiagent system is presented, and a hint is given on how degrees of dependence could be used to support social reasoning processes.

1   Introduction

The problem of measuring the dependence relations that arise between agents when they operate in a social context has been put forward as an important problem since at least [1], where a quantitative notion of *strength* of a dependence relation is proposed.

The Conclusion of [9], for instance, indicated several features on which the quantification of the dependence relations could be based, such as the importance of a goal to an agent, the number of actions/resources needed to execute a plan, or the number of agents which are able to perform a needed action or to control a needed resource. In [6], dependence relations were given a quantitative evaluation on the basis of subjective notions, namely, the relative importance of goals to the agents and the cost of performing the necessary actions.

In [3] we proposed an approach to the solution of that the problem by appropriately separating the quantification process into two steps: the calculation of an *objective degree of dependence*, determined by an evaluation of the objective facts present in the

L. Antunes and K. Takadama (Eds.): MABS 2006, LNAI 4442, pp. 172–187, 2007.

dependence situations that arise from dependence relations, and the subsequent refinement of that objective degree of dependence, by making use of auxiliary coefficients to take into account the different factors that reflect the subjective evaluation of those dependence situations from the point of view of the agents present in them.

The main contribution of that paper is a procedure for the first step, the objective quantification of dependence situations. The procedure computes *degrees of dependence* between agents on the basis of a specially derived form of dependence graphs – the DS-graphs (*dependence situation graphs*) – so that a measure of the degree of dependence of each agent on the agents that can help it to achieve its goals may be given in an easy way. The resulting degrees of dependence are said to be *objective* because they take into account only information about the structure of the dependence situation, through the DS-graph, and do not involve subjective notions (e.g., the *importance* of goals).

Following one of the suggestions given in [9], concerning a basis for the quantification of degrees of dependence, the procedure takes into account essentially the number of agents that are able to perform each needed action, but it also takes into account the kind of dependence (AND-dependence, OR-dependence) that the structure of the dependence situation establishes between the involved agents. Thus the need for the DS-graphs, where those kinds of dependences are explicitly indicated.

Objective degrees of dependence may be subjectively refined in many ways, according to the needs of the application where they are to be used, by weighting them with subjective features that are relevant for the application. For instance, objective degrees of dependence may be refined by the quantification features suggested in [9], such as the importance of a goal to an agent or the cost of the necessary resources, or by the number of resources needed to achieve the goal, or else by probability that each agent has of really performing an action when the action is necessary.

Also, by summing up the objective degrees of dependence that the agents of a society have on each other, it is possible to define a measure of the dependence of the society, as a whole, on each of its agents. Correlatively, it is possible to define a measure of an agent's status and negotiation power [2] within the society.

Further more, objective degrees of dependence may be used to refine the social reasoning mechanisms that solve the problem of choosing partners for the formation of coalitions, such as the one introduced in [9,10].

In this paper, we revise the procedure introduced in [3] and introduce additional examples of its use. The paper is structured as follows. Section 2 summarizes the relevant ideas concerning social dependence relations and dependence situations. Section 3 reviews dependence-graphs and introduces the DS-graphs. Section 4 introduces a formal notation for DS-graphs. Section 5 defines the notion of *objective degree of dependence* and shows how they can be calculated on simple DS-graphs. Section 6 introduces additional concepts: objective degrees of dependence for DS-graphs containing transitive dependences and bilateral dependences; objective degrees of dependence of a society on each of its agents; a measure of an agent's negotiation power within a society; and a way to refine objective degrees of dependence with subjective estimates. Section 7 elaborates two example applications, and Section 8 brings the Conclusion and future work.

2   Dependence Relations and Dependence Situations

Social dependence relations are pointed out in [1] as one of the main objective reasons for the establishment of interactions between agents. Social dependence relations can be defined by:

Definition 1. *An agent α is said to socially depend on an agent β, with respect to an action a, for the purpose of achieving a goal g, denoted* (DEP α β a g), *if and only if:*

1. *g is a goal of α;*
2. *α cannot do a by itself;*
3. *β can do a by itself;*
4. *a being done by β implies g being (eventually) achieved.*

The definition characterizes social dependence relations as an objective feature of an agent's behavior, in the sense that it does not depend on the agent having it represented in his mental states (beliefs, plans, etc.). In the following, assume that $\alpha, \beta, \beta_1, \ldots$ are any agents.

Regarding the direction of the dependence, dependence relations between two agents can be classified either as unilateral or as bilateral:

Unilateral: $\exists a, g.(\text{DEP } \alpha \beta a g) \wedge \forall a', g'.\neg(\text{DEP } \beta \alpha a' g')$
    α depends on β with respect to some action a and some goal g, but there is no action and no goal with respect to which β depends on α
Bilateral: $\exists a, g.(\text{DEP } \alpha \beta a g) \wedge \exists a', g'.(\text{DEP } \beta \alpha a' g')$
    α depends on β with respect to some action a and some goal g, and β depends on α with respect to some action a' and some goal g'

Regarding the goals that set the stage for the dependence, bilateral dependence relations can be classified either as mutual or as reciprocal [1]:

Mutual: $\exists a, a', g.(\text{DEP } \alpha \beta a g) \wedge (\text{DEP } \beta \alpha a' g) \wedge a \neq a'$
    α depends on β, and β depends on α, with respect to the same common goal g
Reciprocal: $\exists a, a', g, g'.(\text{DEP } \alpha \beta a g') \wedge \text{DEP } \beta \alpha a' g) \wedge a \neq a' \wedge g \neq g'$
    α depends on β, and β depends on α, with respect to different private goals

Regarding the number of agents involved in a unilateral dependence, and the way their actions are combined to help achieve an agent's goal, social dependence relations can be classified either as OR-dependence or as AND-dependence, in many ways [10]. For instance:

OR-dependence, multiple partners, single goal, single action needed:
    $(\text{DEP } \alpha \beta_1 a_1 g) \vee (\text{DEP } \alpha \beta_2 a_2 g) \vee \ldots \vee (\text{DEP } \alpha \beta_n a_n g)$
    there are several alternative agents β_i, each being able to perform an action a_i that may lead an agent α to achieve the goal g

---

[1] In [1], a distinction is made between *cooperation* (social behavior induced by a relation of mutual dependence) and *social exchange* (social behavior induced by a relation of reciprocal dependence). We don't make such distinction and use preferably the term *social exchange* to denote both kinds of social behaviors.

AND-dependence, multiple partners, single goal, multiple actions needed:
  (DEP α β_1 a_1 g) $\wedge$ (DEP α β_2 a_2 g) $\wedge \ldots \wedge$ (DEP α β_n a_n g)
  there are multiple partners β_i, each having to perform a different action a_i to jointly lead agent α to achieve the goal g

As shown in the work on the DEPNET simulator [10], however, for the purpose of quantifying dependence relations it is not necessary to take actions and plans into account: it is enough to know that agent α is dependent on agent β to achieve goal g.

In case there are two or more agents that are able to help α to achieve g, it is further necessary to know just the general kind of dependence (either an AND-dependence or an OR-dependence) that arises between them and α.

Such simplified picture of a dependence relation, where only agents and goals are considered, along with the types of relations connecting them, is called a *dependence situation* [10].

Thus, the quantification procedure of dependence relations introduced below operates only on the information contained in such dependence situations, which motivates the definition of the *DS-graphs*, in the next section.

3   DS-Graphs: Graphs for Dependence Situations

Dependence graphs were introduced in [11] as a generalization of dependence networks [10], for the picturing of the various dependence relations that may exist within a multiagent system.

They are structures of the form $DG = (Ag, Gl, Pl, Ac, Ar, \Psi)$ where agents Ag, goals Gl, plans Pl and actions Ac are taken as nodes and are linked with each other by the arcs Ar as specified by function Ψ, thus construing the structure of the dependence relations to show how agents depend on other agents to achieve goals through plans involving actions performed by those other agents (see Fig. 1).

Since dependence graphs have usually quite complex structures, [11] also introduced the so-called *reduced dependence graphs*, where nodes representing plans are abstracted away and goals are used not as nodes, but as labels of arcs (see Fig. 2).

The procedure for the quantification of dependence relations that we will introduce below requires only the information contained in the so-called *dependence situations*,

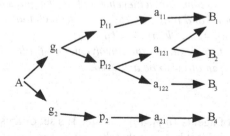

Fig. 1. An example dependence graph for a dependence relation between agent A and agents B_1, B_2, B_3, B_4: goals g_1, g_2; plans p_{11}, p_{12}, p_2; actions $a_{11}, a_{121}, a_{122}, a_{21}$

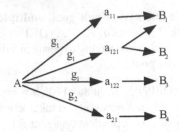

Fig. 2. The reduced dependence graph for the dependence graph of Fig. 1

which amounts to the immediate information content of the dependence relation expressed by the elements of the dependence graph, together with the types of dependences intervening between the agents (AND-dependences, OR-dependences).

This information about type is only indirectly represented in dependence graphs, through the way actions and goals are related to plans.

On the other hand, as mentioned before, the procedure abstracts away information about which plans (and actions) are involved, thus calculating degrees of dependence that are relative to an implicitly understood (e.g., currently used) set of plans.

To structure such minimal information contained in dependence situations, we define the notion of a *DS-graph* (dependence situation graph):

Definition 2. *Let Ag be a set of agents and Gl be the set of goals that those agents may have. A DS-graph over Ag and Gl is a structure $DS = (Ag, Gl, Ar, Lk, \Psi, \Delta)$ such that:*

1. *Ar is a set of arcs, connecting either an agent to a goal or a goal to an agent;*
2. *Lk is a set of links, connecting subsets of arcs;*
3. *$\Psi : Ar \rightarrow (Ag \times Gl) \cup (Gl \times Ag)$ is a function assigning either an agent and a goal or a goal and an agent to each arc, so that if $\Psi(ar) = (ag, g)$ then arc ar indicates that agent ag has the goal g, and if $\Psi(ar) = (g, ag)$ then arc ar indicates that goal g requires some action by agent ag in order to be achieved;*
4. *$\Delta : Lk \rightarrow \wp(Ar)$ is a function assigning links to sets of arcs, representing an AND-dependence between such arcs, so that $\Delta(l) = \{ar_1, \ldots, ar_n\}$ iff either:*
   (a) there are an agent ag and n goals $g_1, \ldots, g_n$ such that
       $\Psi(ar_1) = (ag, g_1), \ldots, \Psi(ar_n) = (ag, g_n)$
       indicating that ag aims the achievement of all the goals $g_1, \ldots, g_n$; or,
   (b) there are a goal g and n agents $ag_1, \ldots, ag_n$ such that
       $\Psi(ar_1) = (g, ag_1), \ldots, \Psi(ar_n) = (g, ag_n)$
       indicating that g requires the involvement of all the agents in the set $\{ag_1, \ldots, ag_n\}$ in order to be achieved.

Given a DS-graph:

1. if there are: a set of agents $\{ag_0, ag_1, \ldots, ag_n\}$; a set of arcs $\{ar_0, ar_1, \ldots, ar_n\}$; a goal g; a link l; and if it happens that $\Psi(ar_0) = (ag_0, g)$, and $\Psi(ar_i) = (g, ag_i)$ (for $1 \leq i \leq n$), and $\Delta(l) = \{ar_1, \ldots, ar_n\}$, then we say that agent ag_0 is AND-dependent on agents $ag_1, \ldots, ag_n$ with respect to goal g;

2. if there are: a set of agents $\{ag_0, ag_1, \ldots, ag_n\}$; a set of arcs $\{ar_1, \ldots, ar_n, ar_1', \ldots, ar_n'\}$; a set of goals $g_1, \ldots, g_n$; a link l; and if it happens that $\Psi(ar_1) = (ag_0, g_1), \ldots, \Psi(ar_n) = (ag_0, g_n)$, and $\Psi(ar_i') = (g_i, ag_1)$ (for $1 \leq i \leq n$), and $\Delta(l) = \{ar_1, \ldots, ar_n\}$, then we say that agent ag_0 is AND-dependent on agents $ag_1, \ldots, ag_n$ with respect to the goals $g_1, \ldots, g_n$;

3. if there are: a set of agents $\{ag_0, ag_1, \ldots, ag_n\}$; a set of arcs $\{ar_0, ar_1, \ldots, a_n\}$; a goal g; and if it happens that $\Psi(ar_0) = (ag_0, g)$, and $\Psi(ar_i) = (g, ag_i)$ (for $1 \leq i \leq n$), but there is no link l such that $\{ar_1, \ldots, ar_n\} \subseteq \Delta(l)$, then we say that agent ag_0 is OR-dependent on agents $ag_1, \ldots, ag_n$ with respect to goal g;

4. if there are: a set of agents $\{ag_0, ag_1, \ldots, ag_n\}$; a set of arcs $\{ar_1, \ldots, ar_n, ar_1', \ldots, ar_n'\}$; a set of goals $g_1, \ldots, g_n$; and if it happens that $\Psi(ar_1) = (ag_0, g_1), \ldots, \Psi(ar_n) = (ag_0, g_n)$, and $\Psi(ar_i') = (g_i, ag_i)$ (for $1 \leq i \leq n$), but there is no link l such that $\{ar_1, \ldots, ar_n\} \subseteq \Delta(l)$, then we say that agent ag_0 is OR-dependent on agents $ag_1, \ldots, ag_n$ with respect to the goals $g_1, \ldots, g_n$.

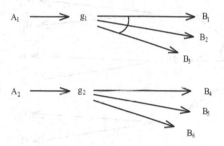

Fig. 3. Simple AND-dependence and OR-dependence relations for DS-graphs

Graphically, we use the convention that AND-dependence is represented by a curved link tying together the arcs involved in such dependence, while OR-dependence is represented by the absence of any such link. Figure 3 illustrates both AND-dependence (of agent A_1 on agents B_1, B_2, B_3 with respect to goal g_1) and OR-dependence (of agent A_2 on agents B_4, B_5, B_6 with respect to goal g_2).

4 A Notation for DS-Graphs

In this section we present formal definitions that support the calculation of *objective degrees of dependence* in DS-graphs. We develop a notation that allows for a succinct representation of the structure of dependence situations, and that is used as the basis for the definition of the calculation procedure.

A dependence situation is written using a *disjunctive dependence form*:

$$(\alpha \prec \wedge_{i_1}(\vee_{j_1}(\wedge_{k_1}\beta_{k_1})) \vee \ldots \vee \wedge_{i_n}(\vee_{j_n}(\wedge_{k_n}\delta_{k_n})) \mid \wedge_{i_1}g_{i_1} \vee \ldots \vee \wedge_{i_n}g_{i_n})$$

where the $\wedge_i g_i$ are alternative sets of conjunctive goals, only one of them having to be achieved in order to satisfy agent α. For any alternative set $\wedge_i g_i$ that is achieved, each goal g_i has to be achieved. However, each such g_i has to be achieved by just one of the alternative conjunctive sets $\wedge_k \beta_k$ of β agents.

We call *structured goals* the goals that appear in the goals part of dependence situations.

Note that in the dependence situations, the higher-level operators $\wedge$ and $\vee$ are assumed to be non-commutative, so that a correspondence can be kept between (sets of) agents and goals. This is also the reason why the number of sets of agents that are listed and the number of goals listed should be the same.

The set of dependence situations expressions is denoted by DS.

The mapping between the expressions defined above and the corresponding DS-graphs is immediate. Figure 4 illustrates the DS-graph corresponding to the dependence situation denoted by:

$$(A \prec ((B_{11} \wedge B_{12}) \wedge (B_{21} \vee B_{22})) \vee (B_{31} \wedge B_{32}) \mid (g_1 \wedge g_2) \vee g_3)$$

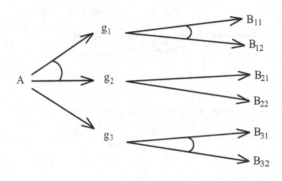

Fig. 4. Sample DS-graph

5   Calculating Objective Degrees of Dependence in DS-Graphs

To calculate objective degrees of dependence, a function dgr is defined, from the set of expressions of dependence situations to the positive reals in the interval from 0 to 1.

The calculation of the degree of dependence of an agent on other agents, with respect to a given goal, is informally defined as:

- if an agent is autonomous on another agent, with respect to the given goal, its degree of dependence on that agent is assigned the value 0;
- the total degree of dependence of an agent on all agents on which it is dependent, with respect to the given goal, is assigned the value 1;
- if the dependence expression that characterizes the dependence situation of an agent is of a conjunctive form with k terms, and its associated degree of dependence is d, then the degree of dependence of the agent with respect to each of the terms of the dependence expression is assigned the value d;

- if the dependence expression that characterizes the dependence situation of an agent is of a disjunctive form with k terms, and its associated degree of dependence is d, then the degree of dependence of the agent with respect to each of the terms of the dependence expression is assigned the value d/k.

The rationale behind such informal procedure extends the one in [2]:

- a conjunctive form indicates that each of its component is essential to the achievement of the involved goals, thus all such components should be valued at the same level of the involved goals;
- a disjunctive form indicates that its components are alternatives that are equally able to achieve the involved goals, thus they devaluate each other and should be uniformly valued by a fraction of the value of the involved goals.

This rationale gives rise to the formal definition of the function dgr:

Definition 3. *Let G be the structured goal of an agent α and let α be dependent on a set of other agents for the achievement of G. Then, the* objective degree of dependence *of α on each such agent is given by the function* dgr $:$ $DS \rightarrow [0\,;1]$, *defined by cases as follows. Let* $(\alpha \prec \bigvee_{1 \leq k \leq K} (\bigwedge_{1 \leq j_k \leq J_k} (\bigvee_{1 \leq j_{ki} \leq I_{j_k}} \beta_{j_{ki}})) \mid G)$ *where* $G = \bigvee_{1 \leq k \leq K} \bigwedge_{1 \leq j_k \leq J_k} g_{j_k}$ *is a structured goal, and the g_{j_k} are basic goals. Then:*

1. $\mathrm{dgr}[(\alpha \prec \bigvee_{1 \leq k \leq K} (\bigwedge_{1 \leq j_k \leq J_k} (\bigvee_{1 \leq j_{ki} \leq I_{j_k}} \beta_{j_{ki}})) \mid G)] = 1$
2. $\mathrm{dgr}[(\alpha \prec \bigwedge_{1 \leq j_k \leq J_k} (\bigvee_{1 \leq j_{ki} \leq I_{j_k}} \beta_{j_{ki}}) \mid G)] = 1/K$
3. *If* $\mathrm{dgr}[(\alpha \prec \bigwedge_{1 \leq j_k \leq J_k} (\bigvee_{1 \leq j_{ki} \leq I_{j_k}} \beta_{j_{ki}}) \mid G)] = n$
   then $\mathrm{dgr}[(\alpha \prec \bigvee_{1 \leq j_{ki} \leq I_{j_{ki}}} \beta_{j_{ki}} \mid G)] = n;$
4. *If* $\mathrm{dgr}[(\alpha \prec \bigvee_{1 \leq j_{ki} \leq I_{j_{ki}}} \beta_{j_{ki}} \mid G)] = n$
   then $\mathrm{dgr}[(\alpha \prec \beta_k) \mid G)] = n/I_{j_k}.$

The following is true about Definition 3:

a) the definition provides a computable notion of degree of dependence that correspond to the two basic kinds of social dependence relations (OR-dependence, AND-dependence);
b) as the notion of social dependence relation that supports them, the definition states an objective notion of degree of dependence, which is function of no subjective evaluation by the agents.

Whenever the goal G is clear from the context, $\mathrm{dgr}[(\alpha \prec \beta \mid G)]$ may be denoted by $\mathrm{dgr}[(\alpha \prec \beta)]$.

6 Additional Concepts

6.1 Degrees of Transitive Dependences

When analyzing the dependence situations between agents, it is often necessary to take into account dependence relations that go beyond the *direct dependence* between the agents. One form of such *indirect dependence* is the transitive social dependence.

Transitive social dependence arises because social dependence may happen in a transitive mode:

– if α depends on β with respect to some goal g, and β depends on γ w.r.t. some goal g', and g' is instrumental to g, then α depends on γ with respect to the combined goal $g \bullet g'$, which is implicitly adopted by α.

To define degrees of dependence for transitive dependence relations, a choice has to be made regarding the operation on degrees of dependence that is induced by the transitivity of the relations of social dependence. The choice of multiplication is an adequate one, since it suitably combines successive degrees of dependence:

Definition 4. *Let α be dependent on β with respect to goal g, and β be dependent on γ with respect to g', and g' be instrumental do g. Then, α is said to transitively depend on γ with respect to the combined goal $g \bullet g'$, denoted $(\alpha \prec \gamma, g \bullet g')$. Such transitive degree of dependence is calculated by*

$$\mathrm{dgr}[(\alpha \prec_\beta \gamma \mid g \bullet g')] = \mathrm{dgr}[(\alpha \prec \beta, g)] \cdot \mathrm{dgr}[(\beta \prec \gamma, g')]$$

Definition 4 enables the calculation of degrees of dependence that takes into account dependences on agents that are far away in the overall network of social relations, and not only degrees of dependence for direct dependence relations.

6.2   Degrees of Bilateral Dependence

The social dependence relations examined so far are said to be unilateral. When considering bilateral social dependence, a notion of *degree of bilateral dependence* has to be defined. The natural choice for the operation on the degrees of dependence that arise from bilateral dependences is addition:

Definition 5. *Let α and β be two agents such that α is dependent on β with respect to a goal g_1, and β is dependent on α with respect to a goal g_2. Then α and β are said to be bilaterally dependent on the combined goal $g_1 \otimes g_2$, denoted $(\alpha \prec\succ \beta \mid g_1 \otimes g_2)$. Such degree of bilateral dependence is calculated by*

$$\mathrm{dgr}[(\alpha \prec\succ \beta \mid g1 \otimes g2)] = \mathrm{dgr}[(\alpha \prec \beta \mid g_1)] + \mathrm{dgr}[(\beta \prec \alpha \mid g_2)]$$

The following is true about Definition 5:

1. $\mathrm{dgr}[(\alpha \prec\succ \beta \mid g_1 \otimes g_2)] = \mathrm{dgr}[(\beta \prec\succ \alpha \mid g_1 \otimes g_2)] = \mathrm{dgr}[(\alpha \prec\succ \beta \mid g_2 \otimes g_1)]$
2. the definition applies both to the cases of *reciprocal dependence* ($g_1 \neq g_2$) and to the cases of *mutual dependence* ($g_1 = g_2$).

6.3   Negotiation Power of Agents in Societies

Let M be a set of agents, and α a member of M. Let the subset of agents of M on which α depends be given by $dep(\alpha, M) = \{\beta \mid (\alpha \prec \beta \mid g)$ *for some* $g \in Goals(\alpha)\}$. Let $codep(M, \alpha) = \{\beta \in dep(S, \alpha) \mid (\beta \prec \alpha \mid g)$ *for some* $g \in Goals(\beta)\}$ be the subset of agents of M that *co-depend* on α, that is, the subset of agents of $dep(M, \alpha)$ which are themselves dependent on α.

We let $(\alpha \prec M)$ denote the fact that α belongs to M and that it depends on some subset of agents of M. We let $(M \prec \alpha)$ denote the fact that some subset of agents of M are co-dependent on α. The degree with which α depends on M, and the degree with which M co-depends on α, can both be calculated.

We define the *degree of dependence* of α on M as:

$$\mathrm{dgr}[(\alpha \prec M)] = \sum_{\beta \in dep(\alpha, M), g \in Goals(\alpha)} \mathrm{dgr}[(\alpha \prec \beta \mid g)]$$

We define the *degree of co-dependence* of M on α as:

$$\mathrm{dgr}[(M \prec \alpha)] = \sum_{\beta \in codep(M, \alpha), g \in Goals(\beta)} \mathrm{dgr}[(\beta \prec \alpha \mid g)]$$

In [2], the degree of co-dependence of M on α is called α's *social value* to M. The relation between α's social appeal to M, and the degree of dependence that α has on M determines α's capacity of establishing exchanges, cooperation, coalitions, etc., in M. In [2] this relation is called α's power of negotiation in M.

Formally, we may establish that the *negotiation power* of an agent α in a set of agent M is given by:

$$\mathrm{NgtPow}(\alpha, M) = \frac{\mathrm{dgr}[(M \prec \alpha)]}{\mathrm{dgr}[(\alpha \prec M)]}$$

6.4   Refining Objective Degrees of Dependence with Subjective Estimates

Many subjective estimates of goals, actions, resources and plans can influence the way agents perceive their dependences on other agents: importance, cost, preferences, emotional reactions, cultural biases, etc., all make the degrees of dependence depart in many ways from the values that can be objectively calculated by the procedure defined above.

Thus, we must define a means to allow the objective degrees of dependence to be refined by the subjective estimates of those various aspects of a dependence situation.

In a dependence situation, the *object agent* is the agent whose dependence is being analyzed, while a *third part agent* is an agent on which the object agent depends [10]. The *subjective factors* that may influence the determination of a degree of dependence are due either to the object agent (importance of goals, preferences among goals, etc.) or to the third part agents (costs of actions, probability of action execution, etc.).

In a DS-graph, the subjective factors due to the object agents should label the arcs connecting the object agents to the goals in concern, while the third part agent factors should label the arcs connecting the goals with the third part agents.

We thus extend definition 3:

Definition 6. *Let every* $w_i \in [0\,;1]$, *and* $G = \bigvee_{1 \leq k \leq K} \bigwedge_{1 \leq j_k \leq J_k} (w_{j_k} \cdot g_{j_k})$. *Then, the weighted objective degree of dependence* $\mathrm{wdgr} : DS \rightarrow [0\,;1]$ *is defined by cases as follows:*

1. $\mathrm{wdgr}[(\alpha \prec \bigvee_{1 \leq k \leq K}(\bigwedge_{1 \leq j_k \leq J_k}(\bigvee_{1 \leq j_{ki} \leq I_{j_{ki}}}(w_{j_{ki}} \cdot \beta_{j_{ki}}))) \mid G)] = 1$
2. $\mathrm{wdgr}[(\alpha \prec \bigwedge_{1 \leq j_k \leq J_k}(\bigvee_{1 \leq j_{ki} \leq I_{j_{ki}}}(w_{j_{ki}} \cdot \beta_{j_{ki}})) \mid \bigwedge_{1 \leq j_k \leq J_k}(w_{j_k} \cdot g_{j_k}))] = 1/K$

3. *If* $\mathrm{wdgr}[(\alpha \prec \wedge_{1 \leq j_k \leq J_k}(\vee_{1 \leq j_{ki} \leq I_{j_{ki}}}(w_{j_{ki}} \cdot \beta_{j_{ki}})) \mid \wedge_{1 \leq j_k \leq J_k}(w_{j_k} \cdot g_{j_k}))] = n$
   then $\mathrm{wdgr}[(\alpha \prec \vee_{1 \leq j_{ki} \leq I_{j_{ki}}}(w_{j_{ki}} \cdot \beta_{j_{ki}}) \mid g_{j_k}))] = w_{j_k} \cdot n;$
4. *If* $\mathrm{wdgr}[(\alpha \prec \vee_{1 \leq j_{ki} \leq I_{j_{ki}}}(w_{j_{ki}} \cdot \beta_{j_{ki}}) \mid g_{j_k})] = n$
   then $\mathrm{wdgr}[(\alpha \prec \beta_k \mid g_{j_k})] = w_{j_{ki}} \cdot (n/I_{j_k}).$

In this way, the objective degrees of dependence that we defined above clearly show their roles as *reference values*, upon which subjective factors may operate to modulate the objective evaluations with subjective factors. Negotiation powers calculated using weighted degrees of dependence are denoted with the form: $\mathrm{wNgtPow}(\alpha, M)$.

In Section 7 we give an example calculation of subjective degrees of dependence and its application to social reasoning.

7   Sample Calculations of Degrees of Dependence

7.1   Degrees of Dependence and Negotiation Powers

Let there be a situation with one *child* agent, 3 *nanny* agents that can buy *ice-creams*, and let *ice-creams* be bought only with the intervention of 2 agents, a *clerk* and a *cashier*. Let the dependence situation be:

$(child \prec nanny1 \vee nany2 \vee nanny3 \mid (GET\ ice\text{-}cream))$

$(nanny1 \prec clerk \wedge cashier \mid (BUY\ ice\text{-}cream))$

$(nanny2 \prec clerk \wedge cashier \mid (BUY\ ice\text{-}cream))$

$(nanny3 \prec clerk \wedge cashier \mid (BUY\ ice\text{-}cream))$

$(clerk \prec (nanny1 \vee nanny2 \vee nanny3) \wedge cashier \mid (SELL\ ice\text{-}cream))$

$(cashier \prec (nanny1 \vee nanny2 \vee nanny3) \wedge clerk \mid (SELL\ ice\text{-}cream))$

Fig. 5 illustrates this dependence situation, with the relation between agents and goals shown by dashed arrows, and black dots used as a way to represent OR-dependences. It is immediate that, for instance:

$$\mathrm{dgr}[(child \prec nanny1 \mid (GET\ ice\text{-}cream))] = 1/3$$
$$\mathrm{dgr}[(nanny1 \prec clerk \mid (BUY\ ice\text{-}cream))] = 1$$
$$\mathrm{dgr}[(clerk \prec nanny1 \vee nanny2 \mid (SELL\ ice\text{-}cream))] = 2/3$$

where the last calculation uses a derived calculation rule:

If $(\alpha \prec \beta_1 \vee \beta_2 \mid G)$ and $\mathrm{dgr}[(\alpha \prec \beta_1 \mid G)] = n_1$ and $\mathrm{dgr}[(\alpha \prec \beta_2 \mid G)] = n_2$
then $\mathrm{dgr}[(\alpha \prec \beta_1 \vee \beta_2) \mid G)] = n_1 + n_2$.

It is also easy to see that, if M is the given dependence situation, then $\mathrm{NgtPow}(nanny1, M) < \mathrm{NgtPow}(clerk, M)$, because $\mathrm{NgtPow}(nanny1, M) = 1/2$ and $\mathrm{NgtPow}(clerk, M) = 4/2$.

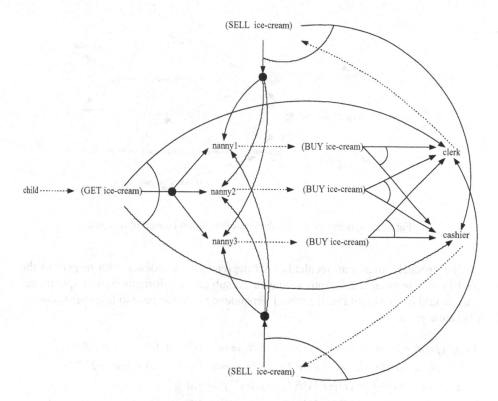

Fig. 5. DS-graphs for the ice-cream situation

7.2   Subjective Degrees of Dependence and Social Reasoning

We now present a very simple example calculation of subjective degrees of dependence. Let there be a system M with five agents: one *producer*, two *distributors* and two *consumers*. Let the dependence situation be as shown in Fig. 6.

The calculation determines:

$$\mathrm{dgr}[(prod \prec dist1 \mid (DELIVER \ product))] = 0.5$$
$$\mathrm{dgr}[(prod \prec dist2 \mid (DELIVER \ product))] = 0.5$$
$$\mathrm{dgr}[(dist1 \prec cons1 \mid (DELIVER \ product)] = 1.0$$
$$\mathrm{dgr}[(dist1 \prec cons2 \mid (DELIVER \ product)] = 1.0$$
$$\mathrm{dgr}[(prod \prec_{dist1} cons1 \mid (DELIVER \ product) \bullet (DELIVER \ product)] = 0.5$$
$$\mathrm{dgr}[(prod \prec_{dist1} cons2 \mid (DELIVER \ product) \bullet (DELIVER \ product)] = 0.5$$

so that the *producer* objectively depends equally on *consumer1* and on *consumer2*.

Let's now add some subjective information owned by the producer. Namely, let's add to the situation that the *producer* observed failures in the activities of the distributors, so that *distributor2* succeeds to acquire products to deliver only 30% of the time, while *distributor1* succeeds 90% of the time.

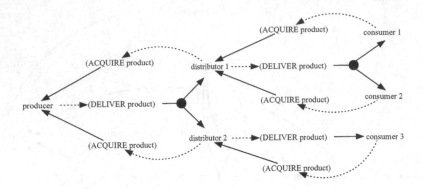

Fig. 6. DS-graphs for the production-distribution-consumption cycle

The producer, then, can recalculate its degrees of dependence with respect to the distributors, in order to take into account such subjective information. A simple procedure would be to weight the degrees of dependence with the probabilities of success to distribute products:

$$\text{wdgr}[(prod \prec (0.90 \cdot dist1) \mid (DELIVER\ \ product))] = 0.90 \times 0.5 = 0.45$$
$$\text{wdgr}[(prod \prec (0.30 \cdot dist2) \mid (DELIVER\ \ product))] = 0.30 \times 0.5 = 0.15$$
$$\text{wdgr}[(dist1 \prec cons1 \mid (DELIVER\ \ product))] = 1.0$$
$$\text{wdgr}[(dist2 \prec cons2 \mid (DELIVER\ \ product))] = 1.0$$
$$\text{wdgr}[(prod \prec_{dist1} cons1 \mid (DELIVER\ \ product) \bullet (DELIVER\ \ product))] = 0.45$$
$$\text{wdgr}[(prod \prec_{dist2} cons2 \mid (DELIVER\ \ product) \bullet (DELIVER\ \ product))] = 0.15$$

This reasoning could lead *producer* to feel subjectively that, taking into account the possible failures in the distribution process, and contrary to the purely structural calculation, it seems to be more dependent on *consumer1* than on *consumer2*.

This is also in accordance with the *producer*'s subjective point of view about the subjective negotiation powers of the *consumers*, which should be calculated thus:

$$\begin{aligned}
\text{wdgr}[(M \prec cons1)] &= \text{wdgr}[(prod \wedge dist1 \prec cons1)] \\
&= \text{wdgr}[(prod \prec_{dist1} cons1)] + \text{wdgr}[(dist1 \prec cons1)] \\
&= 0.45 + 1.0 = 1.45 \\
\text{wdgr}[(cons1 \prec M)] &= \text{wdgr}[(cons1 \prec prod \wedge dist1)] \\
&= \text{wdgr}[(cons1 \prec prod)] + \text{wdgr}[(cons1 \prec dist1)] \\
&= 1.0 + 1.0 = 2.0 \\
\text{wNgtPow}(cons1, M) &= \text{wdgr}[(M \prec cons1)]/\text{wdgr}[(cons1 \prec M)] \\
&= 1.45/2.0 = 0.725
\end{aligned}$$

and

$$\mathrm{wdgr}[(M \prec cons2)] = \mathrm{wdgr}[(prod \wedge dist2 \prec cons2)]$$
$$= \mathrm{wdgr}[(prod \prec_{dist2} cons2)] + \mathrm{wdgr}[(dist2 \prec cons2)]$$
$$= 0.15 + 1.0 = 1.15$$
$$\mathrm{wdgr}[(cons2 \prec M)] = \mathrm{wdgr}[(cons2 \prec prod \wedge dist2)]$$
$$= \mathrm{wdgr}[(cons2 \prec prod)] + \mathrm{wdgr}[(cons1 \prec dist2)]$$
$$= 1.0 + 1.0 = 2.0$$
$$\mathrm{wNgtPow}(cons2, M) = \mathrm{wdgr}[(M \prec cons2)]/\mathrm{wdgr}[(cons2 \prec M)]$$
$$= 1.15/2.0 = 0.575$$

so that, from the *producer*'s subjective point of view, and contrary to the purely structural point of view, *consumer1* has a stronger negotiation power in M than *consumer2*, which is in agreement with the interpretation of the notion of negotiation power, meaning power to promote better (more profitable) interactions.

Accordingly, if the *producer* were required to deliver its products to just one of the distributors, and to choose to which distributor it would continue to deliver its products, the calculation of the subjective degrees of dependence could be used as a preference criteria, supporting the choice to deliver only to *distributor1*.

This also may be stated clearly in another way by defining the notion of *relative negotiation power* of the producer with respect to each consumer and then calculating them.

Definition 7. *The relative negotiation power of agent α with respect to agent β in a system M is given by*

$$\mathrm{RelNgtPow}(\alpha, \beta)_M = \mathrm{NgtPow}(\alpha, M)/\mathrm{NgtPow}(\beta, M)$$

Applied to the *producer, consumer1* and *consumer2* agents we get:

$$\mathrm{wRelNgtPow}(prod, cons1)_M = \mathrm{wNgtPow}(prod, M)/\mathrm{wNgtPow}(cons1, M)$$
$$= 2.0/0.725 = 2.76$$
$$\mathrm{wRelNgtPow}(prod, cons2)_M = \mathrm{wNgtPow}(prod, M)/\mathrm{wNgtPow}(cons2, M)$$
$$= 2.0/0.575 = 3.48$$

Since the relative power of *producer* with respect to *consumer2* is greater then the power it has with respect to *consumer1*, the inconveniences that may arise from dismissing *consumer2* should be less then those coming from dismissing *consumer1*.

8   Conclusion

This paper refined the notion of objective degrees of dependence in dependence relations, previously introduced in other works, by consolidating a sound way to calculate them.

Many lines of work may derive from the results presented here. It is necessary to better explore the possible ways objective degrees of dependence may be combined with estimates of subjective factors, so that the dynamic evolution of the exchanges among agents, and the effective behaviors of the agents, can be considered in the moment of calculating the degrees of dependence.

It is necessary to improve the ways degrees of dependence can be used as criteria in social reasoning mechanisms, such as the ones concerned with the formation of coalitions ([6] proposed one such way, for utility-based subjective degrees of dependence).

For this to be profitable, however, it is also necessary to develop a theoretical account of the deep relations that seem to exist between the theory of dependence relations [1] and the theory of social exchange values [7,8,4,5]. That account could show how exchange values may be captured by auxiliary coefficients in subjective dependence relations, enriching the explanations of the higher level social notions that can be derived from social dependence, like influence, power, trust, etc.

In particular, such combination of the quantitative analysis of dependence situations and the qualitative analysis of the state of social exchanges suggests the possibility of new explorations in the assessment of the various ways agents may be included in social groups.

It is possible, for instance, that such combination of tools for the analysis of social relations can help an agent to compare alternative social environments, when looking for an environment where it would be better positioned with respect to the other agents with respect to issues such as, e.g., social power.

That is the case, too, of migrating agents, for whom different destination places may impose quite different social dependence situations, and thus empower the agent with different negotiation powers.

Also, one sees that already in the example of the producer-distributor-consumer system, the demand on the *producer* could be interpreted as a self imposed demand to improve its position in the system, since it can be calculated that its expectation of negotiation power (or, illusion of social power – as mentioned by one of the referees of the paper) with respect to the *consumers* is greater if the *producer* makes the option for producing with exclusivity for the consumer1 than if it chooses to produce exclusively for consumer2.

Acknowledgements. The authors thank Cristiano Castelfranchi and Jaime Sichman for critical remarks on previous versions of this paper. They also thank two anonymous referees that made the suggestions that agents may profit from the quantification procedure of dependence situations when looking for better a position in a social environment, and that expectations of negotiation power could be interpreted as illusions of power.

References

1. Castelfranchi, C., Miceli, M., Cesta, A.: Dependence Relations among Autonomous Agents. In: Werner, E., Demazeau, Y. (eds.) Decentralized A.I.-3., pp. 215–227. Elsevier, Amsterdam (1992)
2. Castelfranchi, C., Conte, R.: The Dynamics of Dependence Networks and Power Relations in Open Multiagent Systems. In: Proc. 2nd. Int'l Conf. on the Design of Cooperative Systems, Juan-les-Pins, France, June 12-14. Sophia-Antipolis, pp.125–137 (1996)

3. Costa, A.C.R., Dimuro, G.P.: Objective Degrees of Dependence in Social Dependence Relations. MASTA'05 - 3rd. Workshop on Multiagent Systems: Techniques and Applications. In: IEEE Proceedings of EPIA'05: Portuguese Conference on Artificial Intelligence. Covilhã, Portugal, p. 313–316 (December 5-8, 2005)
4. Costa, A.C.R., Dimuro, G.P.: Systems of Exchange Values as Tools for Multiagent Organizations. Journal of the Brazilian Computer Society, 11(1), 31–50 (2005) In: Special Edition on Multiagent Organizations (J. Sichman, O. Boissier, C. Castelfranchi, V. Dignum, eds.)
5. Costa, A.C.R., Dimuro, G.P.: Centralized Regulation of Social Exchanges between Personality-based Agents. In: Proc. COIN@ECAI 2006 - Coordination, Organization, Institutions and Norms in Agent Systems. Workshop at ECAI 2006 - European Conference on Artificial Intelligence. Riva del Garda (August 28, 2006)
6. David, N., Sichman, J.S., Coelho, H.: Agent-Based Social Simulation with Coalitions in Social Reasoning. In: Moss, S., Davidsson, P. (eds.) MABS 2000. LNCS (LNAI), vol. 1979, Springer, Heidelberg (2001)
7. Piaget, J.: Sociological Studies. Routlege, London (1995)
8. Rodrigues, M.R., Costa, A.C.R., Bordini, R.: A System of Exchange Values to Support Social Interactions in Artificial Societes. In: Proc. 2nd. Int'l Conf. on Autonomous Agnets and Multiagents Systems, AAMAS 2003, Melbourne, pp. 81–88 (2003)
9. Sichman, J.S., Demazeau, Y.: On Social Reasoning in Multi-Agent Systems. Revista Iberoamericana de Inteligencia Artificial 13, 68–84 (2001)
10. Sichman, J.S., Conte, R., Castelfranchi, C., Demazeau, Y., Social, A.: Reasoning Mechanism Based on Dependence Networks. In: Cohn, A.G. (ed.) Proc. 11th. European Conference on Artificial Intelligence, John Wiley & Sons, Baffins Lane, England (1994)
11. Sichman, J.S., Conte, R.: Multi-agent Dependence by Dependence Graphs. In: Falcone, R., Barber, S., Korba, L., Singh, M.P. (eds.) AAMAS 2002. LNCS (LNAI), vol. 2631, pp. 483–492. Springer, Heidelberg (2003)

Author Index

Lecture Notes in Artificial Intelligence (LNAI)

Vol. 4603: F. Pfenning (Ed.), Automated Deduction – CADE-21. XII, 522 pages. 2007.

Vol. 4597: P. Perner (Ed.), Advances in Data Mining. XI, 353 pages. 2007.

Vol. 4594: R. Bellazzi, A. Abu-Hanna, J. Hunter (Eds.), Artificial Intelligence in Medicine. XVI, 509 pages. 2007.

Vol. 4585: M. Kryszkiewicz, J.F. Peters, H. Rybinski, A. Skowron (Eds.), Rough Sets and Intelligent Systems Paradigms. XIX, 836 pages. 2007.

Vol. 4578: F. Masulli, S. Mitra, G. Pasi (Eds.), Applications of Fuzzy Sets Theory. XVIII, 693 pages. 2007.

Vol. 4573: M. Kauers, M. Kerber, R. Miner, W. Windsteiger (Eds.), Towards Mechanized Mathematical Assistants. XIII, 407 pages. 2007.

Vol. 4571: P. Perner (Ed.), Machine Learning and Data Mining in Pattern Recognition. XIV, 913 pages. 2007.

Vol. 4570: H.G. Okuno, M. Ali (Eds.), New Trends in Applied Artificial Intelligence. XXI, 1194 pages. 2007.

Vol. 4565: D.D. Schmorrow, L.M. Reeves (Eds.), Foundations of Augmented Cognition. XIX, 450 pages. 2007.

Vol. 4562: D. Harris (Ed.), Engineering Psychology and Cognitive Ergonomics. XXIII, 879 pages. 2007.

Vol. 4548: N. Olivetti (Ed.), Automated Reasoning with Analytic Tableaux and Related Methods. X, 245 pages. 2007.

Vol. 4539: N.H. Bshouty, C. Gentile (Eds.), Learning Theory. XII, 634 pages. 2007.

Vol. 4529: P. Melin, O. Castillo, L.T. Aguilar, J. Kacprzyk, W. Pedrycz (Eds.), Foundations of Fuzzy Logic and Soft Computing. XIX, 830 pages. 2007.

Vol. 4520: M.V. Butz, O. Sigaud, G. Pezzulo, G. Baldassarre (Eds.), Anticipatory Behavior in Adaptive Learning Systems. X, 379 pages. 2007.

Vol. 4511: C. Conati, K. McCoy, G. Paliouras (Eds.), User Modeling 2007. XVI, 487 pages. 2007.

Vol. 4509: Z. Kobti, D. Wu (Eds.), Advances in Artificial Intelligence. XII, 552 pages. 2007.

Vol. 4496: N.T. Nguyen, A. Grzech, R.J. Howlett, L.C. Jain (Eds.), Agent and Multi-Agent Systems: Technologies and Applications. XXI, 1046 pages. 2007.

Vol. 4483: C. Baral, G. Brewka, J. Schlipf (Eds.), Logic Programming and Nonmonotonic Reasoning. IX, 327 pages. 2007.

Vol. 4482: A. An, J. Stefanowski, S. Ramanna, C.J. Butz, W. Pedrycz, G. Wang (Eds.), Rough Sets, Fuzzy Sets, Data Mining and Granular Computing. XIV, 585 pages. 2007.

Vol. 4481: J. Yao, P. Lingras, W.-Z. Wu, M. Szczuka, N.J. Cercone, D. Ślęzak (Eds.), Rough Sets and Knowledge Technology. XIV, 576 pages. 2007.

Vol. 4476: V. Gorodetsky, C. Zhang, V.A. Skormin, L. Cao (Eds.), Autonomous Intelligent Systems: Multi-Agents and Data Mining. XIII, 323 pages. 2007.

Vol. 4460: S. Aguzzoli, A. Ciabattoni, B. Gerla, C. Manara, V. Marra (Eds.), Algebraic and Proof-theoretic Aspects of Non-classical Logics. VIII, 309 pages. 2007.

Vol. 4457: G.M.P. O'Hare, A. Ricci, M.J. O'Grady, O. Dikenelli (Eds.), Engineering Societies in the Agents World VII. XI, 401 pages. 2007.

Vol. 4456: Y. Wang, Y.-m. Cheung, H. Liu (Eds.), Computational Intelligence and Security. XXIII, 1118 pages. 2007.

Vol. 4455: S. Muggleton, R. Otero, A. Tamaddoni-Nezhad (Eds.), Inductive Logic Programming. XII, 456 pages. 2007.

Vol. 4452: M. Fasli, O. Shehory (Eds.), Agent-Mediated Electronic Commerce. VIII, 249 pages. 2007.

Vol. 4451: T.S. Huang, A. Nijholt, M. Pantic, A. Pentland (Eds.), Artifical Intelligence for Human Computing. XVI, 359 pages. 2007.

Vol. 4442: L. Antunes, K. Takadama (Eds.), Multi-Agent-Based Simulation VII. X, 189 pages. 2007.

Vol. 4441: C. Müller (Ed.), Speaker Classification II. X, 309 pages. 2007.

Vol. 4438: L. Maicher, A. Sigel, L.M. Garshol (Eds.), Leveraging the Semantics of Topic Maps. X, 257 pages. 2007.

Vol. 4434: G. Lakemeyer, E. Sklar, D.G. Sorrenti, T. Takahashi (Eds.), RoboCup 2006: Robot Soccer World Cup X. XIII, 566 pages. 2007.

Vol. 4429: R. Lu, J.H. Siekmann, C. Ullrich (Eds.), Cognitive Systems. X, 161 pages. 2007.

Vol. 4428: S. Edelkamp, A. Lomuscio (Eds.), Model Checking and Artificial Intelligence. IX, 185 pages. 2007.

Vol. 4426: Z.-H. Zhou, H. Li, Q. Yang (Eds.), Advances in Knowledge Discovery and Data Mining. XXV, 1161 pages. 2007.

Vol. 4411: R.H. Bordini, M. Dastani, J. Dix, A.E.F. Seghrouchni (Eds.), Programming Multi-Agent Systems. XIV, 249 pages. 2007.

Vol. 4410: A. Branco (Ed.), Anaphora: Analysis, Algorithms and Applications. X, 191 pages. 2007.

Vol. 4399: T. Kovacs, X. Llorà, K. Takadama, P.L. Lanzi, W. Stolzmann, S.W. Wilson (Eds.), Learning Classifier Systems. XII, 345 pages. 2007.

Vol. 4390: S.O. Kuznetsov, S. Schmidt (Eds.), Formal Concept Analysis. X, 329 pages. 2007.

Vol. 4389: D. Weyns, H. Van Dyke Parunak, F. Michel (Eds.), Environments for Multi-Agent Systems III. X, 273 pages. 2007.

Vol. 4386: P. Noriega, J. Vázquez-Salceda, G. Boella, O. Boissier, V. Dignum, N. Fornara, E. Matson (Eds.), Coordination, Organizations, Institutions, and Norms in Agent Systems II. XI, 373 pages. 2007.

Vol. 4384: T. Washio, K. Satoh, H. Takeda, A. Inokuchi (Eds.), New Frontiers in Artificial Intelligence. IX, 401 pages. 2007.

Vol. 4371: K. Inoue, K. Satoh, F. Toni (Eds.), Computational Logic in Multi-Agent Systems. X, 315 pages. 2007.

Vol. 4369: M. Umeda, A. Wolf, O. Bartenstein, U. Geske, D. Seipel, O. Takata (Eds.), Declarative Programming for Knowledge Management. X, 229 pages. 2006.